Saving the World's Wildlife

WWF – the first 50 years

For Tante Gabs
St Louis, 24 July 1916–Erlenbach, 16 June 2002

Alexis Schwarzenbach

Saving the World's Wildlife

WWF – the first 50 years

PROFILE BOOKS

Contents

Preceding page: Giant pandas (*Ailuropoda melanoleuca*),
Chengdu Breeding Centre, Sichuan Province, China

Overleaf: Harbour seals (*Phoca vitulina*), Wadden Sea,
Netherlands

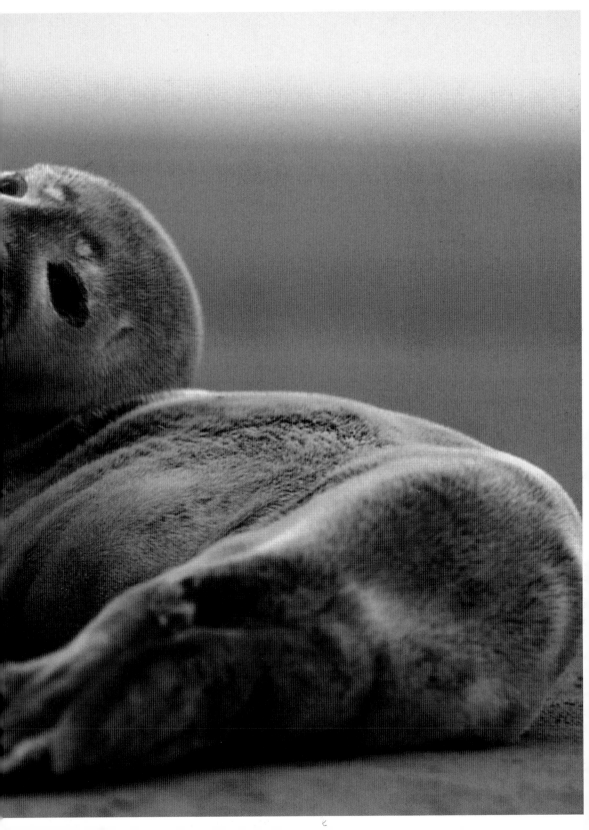

The Nicholson plan

'No 1, Löwenstrasse could hardly be a more apt address
... unless we could change it to Pandastrasse!'

The lion is the heraldic beast of Zurich, and Löwenstrasse, one of the main streets in the city's commercial centre, is named after it. On 11 September 1961 Hans Hüssy, a young Swiss lawyer who worked at a law firm with offices at 1 Löwenstrasse, officially registered the World Wildlife Fund as a charity under Swiss law.[1] In a letter to the trustees of the organisation he had founded on their behalf, Hüssy had the 'particular pleasure' of announcing the first donation to WWF at their Löwenstrasse office, 'a cheque on one Guinea by Mr. Antony E. Judd, London'.[2] While the choice of an address referring to one of the most well-known species of the animal kingdom was purely coincidental, it did seem like a good omen to the secretary general of the International Union for the Conservation of Nature and Natural Resources, Gerald Watterson. He

The *Sihlporte* office building at 1 Löwenstrasse, Zurich, WWF's first official address

had done the original sketches of the logo with which WWF was to become world-famous: 'No 1, Löwenstrasse could hardly be a more apt address … unless we could change it to Pandastrasse!'[3]

The addressee of this letter was Max Nicholson, director general of The Nature Conservancy, the British government's environmental agency, not to be confused with the homonymous American charity. For the best part of 1961 Nicholson had been working relentlessly for the creation of an international fund-raising organisation for wildlife conservation. His ornithologist friend Frank Fraser Darling once observed: 'When Max gets really excited about a subject you think he must have two sets of teeth!'[4] Nicholson's estate, lovingly preserved at the Linnean Society of London, illustrates what this meant in the case of WWF. In order to set up the organisation Nicholson arranged meetings, wrote strategy papers and sent them out to just about any naturalist he had ever come across both in Britain and abroad. He also travelled to America, Europe and Africa lobbying for what others quickly called 'the Nicholson plan'.[5] Clearly the driving force behind the creation of WWF, Max Nicholson, who read history at Oxford and had been a keen ornithologist ever since his early youth, had the rare gift of combining a passionate interest in the natural world with eloquence, organisational skills and a broad international outlook.[6]

Of particular relevance for the foundation of WWF was the fact that Nicholson, a British civil servant since 1940, had been directly involved in the creation of the International Union for the Protection of Nature, subsequently renamed International Union for the Conservation of Nature and Natural Resources (IUCN). Despite being 'the world's first global environmental organization', IUCN has never become a household name.[7] Founded at a UNESCO-sponsored conference in Fontainebleau near Paris in 1948, IUCN had a membership that mainly consisted of governments and their agencies. Rather than individual members, the organisation could count on the scientific expertise of environmental specialists around the world. As a network of scientists and governmental bodies the union was, in the words of one of its former directors general, 'conceived as a meeting ground, a facilitator and a supporter for its members, not an operational agency in its own right'.[8] Since key government members made sure that they did not incur any financial obligations when founding IUCN, the organisation 'had virtually no resources'.[9]

Max Nicholson at the British Ornithologists' Union, Bath, March 1962

Initially based in Brussels, IUCN decided to move to the Swiss town of Morges in 1960. By then the organisation had an accumulated deficit of $20,000 and was unable to pay either the rent or its staff of four.[10]

The serious financial difficulties of IUCN were one of the reasons for the foundation of WWF. Barton Worthington, one of Max Nicholson's senior staff at The Nature Conservancy, remembered: 'One day [Max] came in and poured out something like "Look Barton, IUCN is broke, world opinion is beginning to move our way, there are lots of good conservation projects sprouting all over the place, including the tropics, but there is absolutely no money to carry them out. Let's start a World Wildlife Fund."'[11] At the beginning of the 1960s, a decade marked by social change both in Europe and North America, environmental

Saving the World's Wildlife

issues were indeed beginning to interest far more people than ever before.[12] On both sides of the Atlantic, agrochemicals were one of the most hotly debated topics. In America, the biologist Rachel Carson argued in her 1962 landmark best-seller *Silent Spring* that the widespread use of toxic chemicals in agriculture was causing massive wildlife deaths, especially among birds prone to picking up seeds coated in pesticides – hence her book's title.[13] In some parts of Europe, for instance in Britain, the debate had started even before the publication of Carson's book. Based on a 1960 report by Max Nicholson's Nature Conservancy, Lord Shackleton, son of the Antarctic explorer, gave his maiden speech in the House of Lords in April 1961 on 'Toxic chemicals and wild life'. Shackleton blamed the 'massacre in the countryside' on toxic seed dressings and deplored the fact that 'chemical manufacturers are doing practically nothing in the way of long-term ecological research'.[14]

The deepening concern with the state of nature was not confined to the industrialised world. Because of population growth and other socio-economic phenomena such as migration and urbanisation, habitats came under increasing pressure all over the world, a fact studied and documented by increasing numbers of scientists working in the field and, since 1948, linked through IUCN.[15] Yet while the negative ecological impact of modernity was as visible in many parts of Asia and Latin America as it was in the West, what really struck a chord with the general public in Europe and North America was the fate of wildlife in Africa. The focus lay on East Africa and its prime landscape, the Serengeti, which to generations of Europeans and Americans had been represented, among others by politicians-cum-game hunters such as Theodore Roosevelt or Winston Churchill, as a prehistoric Garden of Eden largely untouched by human beings but inhabited by a great variety of fascinating mammals ranging from antelopes to zebras.[16] That Africa was in fact composed of dynamic landscapes lived in and shaped by human beings for centuries was recognised only much later.[17]

In the UK, the strength of the idea of East Africa as a unique animal paradise was underlined, in November 1960, by the success of a series of newspaper articles written by Julian Huxley, evolutionary biologist and former director general of UNESCO. After an extensive field trip to national parks and game reserves in Africa, undertaken on behalf of UNESCO in order to document the state of wildlife conservation and to make policy recommendations, Huxley published three articles in the *Observer*, Britain's leading Sunday newspaper.[18] Apart from emphasising that population growth was a major threat to African wildlife, Huxley also argued that a possible remedy lay in harvesting surplus wild animals for food, which promised better yields than the transformation of wilderness into farmland. The innovative game-cropping theory appealed to Huxley, an expert ecologist as well as an eminent eugenicist who managed to avoid the pitfall of racism: 'The bulk of inter-tropical Africa [...] is meat-hungry, badly short of animal protein, and therefore below par in mental and physical energy. [...] Game cropping, it seems, could become a major means for overcoming this dietary deficiency and putting the Africans on a proper plane of nutritional health.'[19] Coming from a family with a strong literary tradition, Huxley also argued his point as a humanist by underlining the moral obligation for nature conservation.[20] Comparing the cultural value of African landscapes to architectural and musical masterpieces of Western civilisation, Huxley defined Africa's national parks, which only a handful of his British audience would have had the means of visiting themselves, as a 'world asset' offering any visitor 'a priceless enrichment of experience and a unique glimpse of the world of nature as it was before the coming of man. They must be at all costs preserved.'[21]

A strong sense of urgency permeated Huxley's articles. While population growth was the core reason invoked by most naturalists trying to highlight the endangered state of nature in the post-war period, it was the geopolitical context of 1960 which alarmed Huxley's readers. Until the end of the 1950s, most of East Africa from Kenya down to present-day Botswana was under British rule, and the resolute way in which the Mau Mau insurgency in Kenya was dealt with by London seemed to indicate that it had no intention of abandoning its African empire.[22] Yet in February 1960 Prime Minister Harold Macmillan announced a radical change of policy. In a speech in Cape Town, Macmillan remarked that 'the wind of change' was blowing through Africa. He thereby openly committed Britain to decolonisation and the integration of its African possessions into the multiracial Commonwealth.[23] This process, which policy experts predicted to last at least until the 1970s, gained an unexpected momentum when most of

French-speaking Africa from Mauritania down to the Congo became independent in the course of 1960.[24]

Among naturalists fears began to develop that rapid decolonisation might undo the positive achievements of colonial rule, above all national parks established in Africa ever since the 1920s. In 1961 the eminent American ornithologist Roger Tory Peterson, whose pet project was the protection of Lake Nakuru in Kenya and who later served on the board of WWF-US, nervously told Max Nicholson: 'I very much fear that when the blacks take over in Kenya, as they almost surely will when they build up their strength in the new government, all of the gains of the past generation in wildlife preservation will be wiped out. [...] We are facing a crisis.'[25] Julian Huxley did not share such pessimistic views, and as a liberal anti-racist was personally committed to African independence. In order to mobilise public opinion, he nevertheless made direct reference to widespread metropolitan fears linked to decolonisation. In his *Observer* articles he wrote: '[T]here are many who believe that with the inevitable advent of African governments in most of the territories, game will be regarded as so much meat conveniently provided on the hoof [...], that National Parks will be looked on as unwanted relics of "colonialism" or as a silly European invention of no value to the up-and-coming African States, and that no large animals will be allowed to survive in African nature.'[26] Huxley's solution for post-colonial times was to educate Africans into appreciating wildlife as part of their natural heritage and to improve and expand national parks so that African governments could earn money through tourism. The only problem was 'that this will cost money – quite a lot of money', which neither governments, the UN nor any other organisation, least of all the hard-pressed IUCN, was either prepared or able to spend.[27]

Julian Huxley, portrait by Pamela Chandler, July 1961

One attentive reader of Huxley's articles, alarmed by the scenarios of doom sketched out in them, had an idea as to how the problem could be solved. In December 1960 Victor Stolan, a Czech-born naturalist who had come to Britain as a refugee and, after unsuccessfully trying to run a country hotel, lived

das Tier

INTERNATIONALE TIERILLUSTRIERTE

Herausgeber: Prof. Dr. Bernhard Grzimek ● Prof. Dr. Heini Hediger ● Prof. Dr. Konrad Lorenz
Konrad Lorenz: Uns treibt die Sehnsucht nach dem Paradies ● Herbert Wendt: Meister
des Bluffs ● Bernhard Grzimek: Nachgemachtes Zebra fliegt nach Afrika ● Heini Hediger:
Die weisse Giraffe ● Minister schoss Nashorn aus Hubschrauber ● Stierkampf als
Betrug entlarvt ● Sind Löwen grausam? ● Grosses Preisrätsel: 1. Preis Fotosafari in Ostafrika

Nr. 1 1. Oktober 1960
Erscheint monatlich
Verlag Hallwag, Stuttgart/Bern
Einzelnummer DM/Fr.
öS. 12.- **2.—**

Saving the World's Wildlife

'modestly in South Kensington',[28] wrote to Huxley that in view of 'the danger threatening African wild life [...] there must be a way to the conscience and the heart and pride and vanity of the very rich people to persuade them to sink their hands deeply into their pockets and thus serve a cause which is greater and nobler than any other one – absolutely'. As Stolan lacked the necessary contacts to realise his plan, he asked Huxley 'to put me in touch with somebody with whom ideas can be developed and speedily directed towards accumulating some millions of pounds without mobilising commissions, committees, etc. as there is no time for Victorian procedure'.[29] The ideal person for such a job was Max Nicholson, whom Huxley knew both as a friend and as one of the architects of IUCN. As Nicholson had also been playing, in the summer of 1960, with the idea of a fund-raising scheme to improve the finances of Britain's naturalist organisations, he replied to Stolan on Huxley's behalf: '[I]t has long seemed to me that it would not be difficult to raise, as you say, a substantial fund in aid of wild life conservation.'[30] The meeting with Stolan was, however, a disappointment. Nicholson afterwards told Huxley: 'Mr. Stolan is rather too much the naive enthusiast and rather too little the practical man of affairs to be very much help.'[31] In the following weeks Victor Stolan was quickly sidelined by Nicholson and other naturalists who ended up creating WWF.

While Victor Stolan was clearly not the super-rich 'émigré Czech business tycoon' which one author has turned him into, he did provide WWF with more than just a kick-off letter.[32] Apart from naive 'daydreams' about a charismatic leader and his 'charming' wife throwing cocktail parties for world leaders such as Charles de Gaulle, Konrad Adenauer or the Pope,[33] Stolan's plan for WWF also included collaborating with Bernhard Grzimek. The German veterinary was director of the Frankfurt Zoo and, ever since his Oscar-winning documentary *Serengeti Must Not Die* (1959), a key figure among Western naturalists with an interest in Africa.[34] In an important act of cross-cultural dialogue, Stolan, whose central European background enabled him to read German, pointed Nicholson

Das Tier, first edition, October 1960. The innovative wildlife magazine, edited by Bernhard Grzimek, Konrad Lorenz and Heini Hediger, impressed the founders of WWF

at Grzimek's innovative wildlife magazine *Das Tier*. Grzimek co-edited it with the Austrian animal psychologist Konrad Lorenz and the director of the Zurich Zoo, Heini Hediger.[35] The illustrated monthly, which first appeared in October 1960, combined attractive wildlife photographs with educational texts in an effort to promote the protection of nature. Nicholson was impressed with the 'most attractive and well-edited' magazine and took the global success of Grzimek's documentary on the Serengeti as 'further evidence of the timeliness and necessity' of the creation of an international environmental fund-raising organisation.[36] The founders of WWF tried to obtain the English and the French language rights to *Das Tier*, and the first WWF publication, a brochure which appeared in September 1961, was directly inspired by the layout and the tone of Grzimek's magazine.

Once the initiative had passed from Stolan to Nicholson, the first thing the latter did was to visit the richest country in the world, the USA, for the over-riding aim of the WWF project was to raise as much money as possible. Looking back on the 'earliest planning of the World Wildlife Fund', Nicholson remembered about his trip to New York: '[T]alks were held with leading American conservationists [...] but with no tangible result. Concluded that WWF must be started without the Americans.'[37] While Nicholson failed to note whom he discussed his fund-raising idea with, he appears to have heard of Russell Train, a young Washington lawyer, who in view of Africa's impending decolonisation was busy setting up the African Wildlife Leadership Foundation.[38] In 1991 Nicholson recalled that Russell Train's rival initiative – incidentally by a man who was later to play a key role in WWF – 'made us realize the full horror that within two years there might be a dozen competing wildlife funds, all going for the same source'.[39] Summing up his unsuccessful trip to the USA, Nicholson wrote: 'I was so depressed by the reaction I got in America that I thought I would have to report back to Julian Huxley that we couldn't get the support to do anything internationally.'[40]

Back in England, a chance encounter at the Royal Station Hotel in York lifted Nicholson's spirits. He met a friend and fellow ornithologist, the advertising executive Guy Mountfort, who like Nicholson had come to York for the annual meeting of the British Ornithologists' Union. Nicholson asked his friend 'whether something on the lines of a WWF would have a fair chance of winning support in the business world'.[41] Thirty years later Nicholson recalled: 'I put this to him in about a ninety-second conversation on the stairs. [...] And he thought for about ten seconds, and said, "I think it is [possible]". And I said, "Right, we're in business."'[42] Over Easter, which he spent at Larkhill House in Gloucestershire, Max Nicholson wrote what he subsequently identified as 'the first WWF document'[43] – a ten-page, single-spaced, typewritten 'draft of a scheme for bringing to an end the extraordinary, unnecessary and humiliating insolvency of the vitally important movement for the conservation of nature'.[44]

Nicholson's core argument was that existing nature conservation agencies the world over had worked out sound environmental projects but lacked the money to carry them out. Paraphrasing Victor Stolan's first letter to Julian Huxley, Nicholson described the existence of a 'still untapped readiness to help of millions of people (including many of wealth and influence)' and declared that 'what is needed is not a new organisation to duplicate and compete with the work of existing bodies but a new co-operative international project to make their efforts effective by providing them with adequate resources'. Nicholson compared the current state of environmentalism with 'a car with a half-pint fuel tank replenished only by an occasional cupful' and called for 'a new fuel tank with a petrol pump to fill and refill it'.[45] This passage neatly illustrates the early 1960s context within which WWF was created, for today the use of automobile symbolism in the context of founding an environmental organisation would probably be quite counterproductive.

Nicholson's scheme comprised five elements: 1) the registration of a foundation based in Switzerland with a permanent secretariat responsible for coordination and fund-raising; 2) the establishment of a scientifically advised 'operations group' allocating money to the most important conservation projects; 3) the creation of a 'Wildlife Crusaders' Club [...] composed of men of substance able and willing to give really worthwhile support both financially and in other ways to the cause of saving the world's wildlife'; 4) a series of 'National Appeals, to be launched simultaneously in the U.S.A., U.K., Germany and if possible in other countries' to raise money from the general public; 5) a multi-language publicity tool modelled on Grzimek's *Das Tier* in order 'to develop a long-needed international channel for large-scale communication of news and views about conservation of wild life'.[46] Together with a timetable and targets to be achieved in the following months, the paper was sent to twenty eminent naturalists in Britain, the United States, France, Sweden, Belgium, Switzerland, Germany, Thailand, South Africa and the Sudan, inviting those living in the UK for a meeting and asking those living abroad for written comments.[47]

Statements in covering letters to two American naturalists explain why Nicholson believed that his ambitious plan could become reality. To Fairfield Osborn, president of the New York Zoological Society, he apologised for 'a horribly long memorandum' but added: 'I still have this dream that some how some time it must be possible to get this money flowing in so that we can give our minds and energies to things that really matter.'[48] To Ira Gabrielson, president of the Wildlife Management Institute in Washington, Nicholson wrote: 'Animals and their welfare are probably just about the biggest potential money-raising cause in the world and professional treatment through a streamlined set-up on a world basis should bring in very much larger sums before too long and really make a conservation force that can talk on equal terms with all others.'[49] When writing about the appeal of animal welfare Nicholson certainly had one of Britain's most successful charities in mind, the Royal Society for the Prevention of Cruelty to Animals (RSPCA), founded in 1824.[50] It is thus more than likely that Nicholson, in emulation of the RSPCA, decided that while the WWF project was about raising money for all sorts of conservation projects, it was via the emotional appeal of animals that his ambitious plan had a chance of working out – and not by way of less universally attractive features of nature such as plants, soils or ecosystems.

In June 1961 Nicholson put his ideas to the test. In an article in *The Times*, the secretary of London's oldest dog refuge, Battersea Dogs Home, complained that his annual budget was only £19,000.[51] In a letter to the editor Nicholson pointed out that IUCN's annual budget was actually lower than that and that 'nearly all over the world to-day wild animals are being rendered homeless, drowned, starved, poisoned, oiled, poached, electrocuted, maimed or simply killed by man (otherwise than for food or sport) on a scale alarming not only to humanitarians but to scientists. The survival of entire species is threatened.' Anyone 'prepared personally to do something effective' about the deplorable state of wildlife was invited to get in touch – Nicholson received so many replies that he had to duplicate his answer, in which he sketched out the plan for WWF.[52]

At an IUCN board meeting held in Morges in April 1961 the financially straitened union, poised to become a major beneficiary of WWF, welcomed Max Nicholson's plan and issued an official endorsement. The meeting was held at the Musée Alexis Forel as IUCN did not yet have adequate facilities at its new Swiss headquarters.[53] Subsequently labelled the 'Morges Manifesto',[54] the endorsement was originally called 'An International Declaration' and bore the headline 'WE MUST SAVE THE WORLD'S WILD LIFE'. Signed by thirteen

821 Morges (Lac Léman) et le Mont Blanc

View of Morges, Lake Geneva, and the Mont Blanc, postcard, c. 1960

leading conservationists from Europe, Africa and America, most of whom were IUCN executive board members, the text was a summary of Nicholson's plan for WWF.[55] The signatories deplored the 'orgy of thoughtless and needless destruction' of wild animals and their habitats and stated that 'the nineteen-sixties promise to beat all past records for wiping out the world's wild life. Doubtless feelings of guilt and shame will follow, and will haunt our children, deprived of nature's rich inheritance by ignorance, greed and folly.' The solution offered by the Morges Manifesto was 'an international Trust, registered as a charity in Switzerland under a distinguished group of trustees'. This trust was to raise enough money for international conservation projects worked out by IUCN and other environmental organisations in order to prevent the irreversible loss of species: 'The emergency must be tackled with vigour and efficiency on the much enlarged scale which it demands.'[56]

In the course of this research no document could be located which explains the choice of Switzerland as the base for an organisation which was essentially worked out by Britons and in the UK. While Switzerland's economic and political stability as well as its traditional neutrality certainly were arguments that spoke in favour of it, the fact that the landlocked Alpine republic has never been a colonial power was probably decisive. Max Nicholson was well aware of the fact that IUCN, originally located in Belgium, had moved its headquarters to Switzerland because by 1960 there were 'doubts [...] about the appropriateness of Brussels as a base because of Belgium's colonial past'.[57] As a London-based WWF would undoubtedly have been associated with Britain's leading role in the history of imperialism, Nicholson most probably chose Switzerland for the same reason which had led to the relocation of IUCN. Mainly concerned with conservation in post-colonial Africa – the only concrete example of a wildlife 'emergency' mentioned in the Morges Manifesto was the critical situation of 'the world famous Congo national parks'[58] – WWF was established in a European country more likely than others to win the sympathies of Africans emerging from colonial rule.

Saving the World's Wildlife

Signatures on the Morges Manifesto, 29 April 1961, with
subsequently added pencil notes. Jean Baer (Switzerland),
François Bourlière (France), Charles Bernard (Switzerland),
Edward H. Graham (USA), Walery Goetel (Poland), Rocco
Knobel (South Africa), Wolfgang Burhenne (Germany),
Charles Vander Elst (Belgium), M. K. Shawki (Sudan),
Kai Curry-Lindahl (Sweden), Peter Scott (UK), Barton
Worthington (UK), E. C. Nicola (Netherlands-Switzerland)

Overleaf: Fritz Vollmar, African lion (*Panthera leo*), Kruger
National Park, South Africa, September 1971

The London
Preparatory Group

'One of the most valuable trademarks ever devised,
and it took about twenty minutes.'

In response to Max Nicholson's circular letter a total of nine meetings were held at The Nature Conservancy in London from April to September 1961. The meetings of what subsequently became known as WWF's 'London Preparatory Group' were attended by almost two dozen naturalists, most of whom were both British and male.[1] The only founding mother of WWF was the ornithologist Phyllis Barclay-Smith, in 1958 the first woman to become a Member of the Order of the British Empire for her work in conservation.[2] Barclay-Smith was present at five meetings, a relatively high attendance rate compared with most of her colleagues – Julian Huxley, for instance, came only twice.[3] Apart from Max Nicholson as host and chairman, the most influential member of the group was Guy Mountfort, a passionate ornithologist who had revolutionised the genre of bird guides by publishing, together with Roger Tory Peterson, a best-seller focusing on practical field marks.[4] Mountfort's main contribution to the meetings was his professional experience as director at the London advertising agency Mather & Crowther. This helped ensure that from the very beginning the WWF project was run like a state-of-the-art public relations campaign.

Guy Mountfort watching wildlife

At the first meeting of the group Guy Mountfort suggested inviting the 'public relations expert' Ian MacPhail to join them and afterwards made sure that the staunch Scotsman from Aberdeen became the first person to be employed by WWF.[5] MacPhail worked from his London home and accepted the job, although he knew that no money was around yet to pay for his salary. He wrote all press releases for the early WWF, was responsible for its printed matter and also advised the nascent charity on fund-raising and organisational issues. In a first memorandum MacPhail noted, among other things, that American tax regulations made it difficult to spend money raised in the USA outside of it – a first hint for the founders of WWF that the country they placed their highest financial hopes in was perhaps not easily integrated into an organisation with legal headquarters in Switzerland.[6] MacPhail also insisted on building up a strong corporate identity. He suggested a uniform 'house style' to be adopted by all national branches of the organisation and the creation of 'a symbol which overcomes the language barrier'.[7]

The first and most important element of the new charity's corporate identity was its name. At its third meeting the London Preparatory Group decided '[t]hat the title of the body should be "World Wild Life Fund" and the slogan "Save the World's Wild Life"'.[8] While the first and the last words of the title clearly stated that the new organisation had a global scope and was setting money apart for a particular purpose, the term 'wild life' chosen to identify its objectives was more ambiguous.[9] Guy Mountfort, who was not present when the name was chosen, warned the group of 'the undesirable journalistic use of the two words to denote social activities in night clubs'.[10] The spelling was changed, and from the sixth meeting onwards the name of the organisation was 'World Wildlife Fund'.[11] Yet this orthographic change failed to solve a more fundamental problem of terminology.

The various spellings of the term 'wildlife' – to this day the joint form coexists with 'wild life' and 'wild-life' – are a relatively new way of describing 'the native fauna and flora of a particular region'.[12] Prior to the 1879 publication of *Wild Life in a Southern County* by the British nature writer Richard Jeffries, who used the term for a collection of newspaper articles about rural Wiltshire, 'wild life' was used only with reference to human beings, either by English-speakers bragging about their adventures or in order to describe foreign civilisations.[13] The novelty and Anglo-Saxon specificity of the term is underlined by the fact that 'wildlife' has never found an equivalent in any other major European language. This was a problem the founders of WWF were quickly to be faced with and which the organisation only partially solved in a name change carried out in 1986 (see below, Chapter 7). The practical solution lay in using the acronym WWF, in internal documents ever since the beginning and in the fund's official communications from 1979 onwards.[14] This occurred despite the fact that Ian MacPhail had urged the London Preparatory Group not to refer to its creation by 'initials which can be turned into a word – such as UNESCO, RoSPA, UNO, NATO etc. as the international scene has already been bedevilled with such meaningless words'.[15]

At their sixth meeting WWF's founding parents decided that 'the symbol for the World Wildlife Fund should be a Panda'.[16] The minutes are silent on how this decision was reached, but Max Nicholson later remembered: 'We decided on three criteria: (a) it must be an attractive animal – one might say cuddly. (b) black and white, because of reproduction limits. (c) an endangered, or nearly endangered, species. The panda fitted all three.'[17] In addition, the fact that the panda was an Asian and not an African animal was also an advantage. Although the critical situation of African wildlife as described by Julian Huxley was a principal cause for the creation of WWF, the London Preparatory Group were adamant that their task was not restricted to one continent. For the first WWF press conference they anticipated the following situation: 'A larger version of the Panda symbol will be displayed behind the platform. This should pose the question "Why a Panda at a meeting about African Wildlife?" At the right time this will enable the Chairman to make the appropriate remark about the problem under discussion being a world wide one.'[18]

A hundred years before WWF chose the giant panda (*Ailuropoda melanoleuca*) as its symbol, the species was all but unknown, not only in the West but also in China. While panda coats had occasionally been among the luxury goods consumed by the Chinese imperial household in medieval and early modern times, unlike other animals pandas were not part of China's artistic tradition. Until well into the twentieth century only local, usually non-Han-Chinese farmers living within the panda's mountainous habitat in and around the province of Sichuan occasionally had a chance of seeing one of the shy animals alive. The scientific exploration of the panda began in 1869 when the French missionary Armand David sent coats and skulls to the Muséum national d'histoire naturelle in Paris. While David believed he had found a new bear species which he called *Ursus melanoleucos* (black and white bear), the director of the Muséum, Alphonse Milne-Edwards, realised that the remains belonged to a completely new genus which he labelled Ailuropodae, the cat-footed ones.[19] As no Westerner managed to see let alone capture a panda alive for another generation, the fame of the newly discovered animal constantly increased. This explains the excitement of the German anthropologist Walther Stötzner, who, on a research mission to China and Tibet, was 'the first European to see the bamboo bear alive'.[20]

In April 1914 the Stötzner expedition, funded by the King of Saxony and consisting of half a dozen German scientists, installed its base camp in the

Sichuan village of Lianghoku, 100 kilometres north-west of the provincial capital Chengdu. Stötzner asked villagers to go out hunting for pandas and within a few days a 'savage-looking' hunter of the Wassu tribe brought three dead animals. Their recipient exclaimed: 'Three bamboo bears at the same time! My joy is endless for no other mammal is as rare as this one.' Like the great mammals of East Africa marvelled at as wonderful relics of the Pleistocene, the panda living in a cartographically unexplored part of China had captured the imagination of *fin-de-siècle* scientific explorers such as Walther Stötzner: 'There is no other area of the entire world where the mysterious, intriguing animal can still be found. It only lives in these faraway, inaccessible, lonely High Alps as a relic of prehistoric times.' The anthropologist proudly took 'the first ever photograph of a freshly shot Ailuropus [*sic*]' before carefully removing all flesh from its skin so that the 'zoological treasure' could reach Europe

Anthropologist Walther Stötzner (back row, centre) and the other members of a German scientific expedition to China in 1914. They were the first Westerners to set eyes on a living panda.

intact.[21] When Stötzner published the tale of his journey in 1924 the illustrations of his book included a photograph not only of the prepared panda skin but also of an 'Ailuropus turned inside out' – for the benefit of Stötzner a Wassu youth held up a skinned panda in the midday sun.[22]

After another hunting trip by the locals Stötzner received one more dead panda, this time a 'very old' male, and a living cub. Seeing a panda alive had an extraordinary effect on the German explorer, who wrote in his travel diary: 'A small human being cannot be looked after with greater care than I have done in the case of this cute little bear. He looks like a ball of wool but has the same markings as the adults. Clumsily this little sweetie is stumbling about on his short little legs on a soft and warm blanket in the house.' However, the rapidly domesticated cub refused to drink either the lukewarm milk or the thin flour

Saving the World's Wildlife

soup with which Stötzner tried to feed it. When the animal died a few days later there was 'general grief' among the entire expedition team. The extent to which Stötzner identified with the baby panda as a 'Menschenkind', a fellow human being, is underlined by his desperate efforts to find it a human wet nurse.[23] The intense emotions the panda triggered in the 32-year-old German anthropologist shortly before the outbreak of the First World War foreshadowed the reaction of millions once the species began to appear in zoos, in the West from the late 1930s onwards and China ever since the 1950s.[24]

Walther Stötzner, 'The *Ailuropus* [sic] turned inside out', Lianghoku, April 1914

Although the stuffed remains of Stötzner's baby panda and those of an adult male were bought by the Zoological Museum of Zurich in 1923, the WWF logo was not inspired by a model available in the city in which the World Wildlife Fund was legally founded.[25] Instead the design was influenced by Chi Chi, a female panda born and captured in 1957. Exported from China by the Austrian game trader Heini Demmer, Chi Chi caused a sensation wherever she went – the last panda in a Western zoo had died in Chicago in 1953.[26] Demmer sent Chi Chi, originally destined for the United States, on a tour through Europe because Washington's trade embargo against communist China prevented her from travelling to the USA. In the end the panda was sold to London Zoo in 1958, where she quickly became one of Britain's most beloved animals. She entertained millions until her death in 1972 and received obituaries like a film star.[27]

Given the star status of Chi Chi, it is not surprising that the London Preparatory Group had her in mind when they decided to opt for the panda as their logo. Gerald Watterson, IUCN director general present at the meeting which took the decision in favour of the panda, appears to have combined his trip to England with a visit to London Zoo in order to make a first round of sketches.[28] Although Watterson's original drawings could not be located in the course of this research, he made copies of his Chi Chi sketches at the second board meeting of WWF in May 1962, scans of which were eventually included in WWF's digital photo library.[29] Watterson drew Chi Chi in various poses, lying flat on the floor, sitting

Giant Panda (*Ailuropoda melanoleuca*), Zoological
Museum of the University of Zurich.
In 1923 the museum acquired the remains of the panda
cub brought to Europe by Walther Stötzner

Fritz Vollmar, Chi Chi, London Zoo, 1968

down, standing up or simply wandering about. In the end the image selected for the logo was a frontal view of the panda approaching the beholders and looking them straight in the eyes.

The British painter and naturalist Peter Scott, another member of the London Preparatory Group whom Watterson visited at his Gloucestershire home in July 1961, turned the sketch into a proper logo. Scott simplified the design by replacing hatched spaces with plain black and by rounding off the overall figure so that it could easily fit within both a square and a circle. Compared with Watterson's version Scott's adopted a slightly elevated point of view so that instead of seeing the panda at eye level the beholder was looking down on it. This created a perspective more reminiscent of a zoo than of meeting an animal in the wild. Nevertheless, the Scott logo retained and emphasised the most important element endearing pandas to people – the colour scheme and the shape of the face. The animals' round, big-eyed features provide even an adult panda with a lot of extra cuteness, an emotional capital which in other mammal species usually only the very young are endowed with.

According to Max Nicholson, creating the logo proceeded very quickly. In 1991 he recalled: 'One of the most valuable trademarks that has ever been devised,

and it took about twenty minutes.'[30] It was largely due to the efforts of Peter Scott, who effectively ran WWF in the first decade of its existence, that the logo he designed became associated with one of the most successful environmental organisations of the twentieth century. The multi-talented son of the Antarctic explorer Robert, Scott earned his living as a painter of wildfowl and had founded the Severn Wildfowl Trust in the Gloucestershire village of Slimbridge in 1946. Apart from being an Olympic yachtsman with excellent social connections, he was also a well-known radio and TV presenter. By the time Scott joined the London Preparatory Group the 51-year-old was not only an executive board member of IUCN but had also just completed an autobiography. *The Eye of the Wind* began to climb the British best-seller lists in July 1961.[31] What made the famous naturalist, who in 1973 was the first person to receive a knighthood for 'services to conservation', an invaluable asset for the early WWF was Scott's efficiency as a committee man.[32] The long-term director general of WWF-Netherlands, Niels Halbertsma, recalls: 'Sir Peter was a wonderful and committed man. I can still see him during meetings. He would sit there and make little watercolours of birds, licking his paintbrush with his tongue to mix colours. One would think that he was totally absorbed by his work. But then suddenly when there was a specific

Gerald Watterson, sketches for the first WWF logo, copy executed in 1962

Prince Philip and Peter Scott at WWF's International Secretariat, Morges, 1967

decision to be taken he would say "Mr. Chairman, I think that ...' and you would realise that he had been listening very carefully and could place his finger on exactly what was to be said.'[33]

Apart from the logo a deed of foundation was another pressing item on the agenda of the London Preparatory Group. As this required 'an expert in Swiss company and taxation law', Guy Mountfort remembered Hans Hüssy, the 31-year-old Zurich lawyer who had recently helped to set up Mather & Crowther's office in Switzerland.[34] Hüssy was responsible for making sure that the new charity was tax exempt but also had to translate the English deed of foundation into German, the only language the new charity was going to be registered under. While it was not difficult to make literal translations of the technical passages dealing with the structure and the organisation of WWF, Hüssy realised that the key term 'wildlife' was 'impossible to translate'.[35] He thus left the name of the fund in English and translated 'wildlife specialists' with '*Spezialisten auf dem Gebiete der Erhaltung der Natur*' – 'experts in questions of nature preservation'.[36]

Because of a recent terminology debate within IUCN, other aspects of the deed were also difficult to translate. At the 1956 general assembly in Edinburgh IUCN had changed its name from 'International Union for the Protection of Nature' to 'International Union for Conservation of Nature and Natural Resources'. An important voice in the name-change debate was the American ecologist Lee Talbot, two decades later WWF's first conservation director. He argued that '"Protection of nature" in English often carries the connotation of a sentimental, impractical, negative objective [...] and that an organization bearing this name cannot be taken seriously.' Talbot and other anglophone members of the union recommended the replacement of the terms 'protection' and 'nature' with 'conservation' and 'natural resources'.[37] While the word 'nature', dear to many European members of IUPN, was not entirely dropped, the name change to International Union for Conservation of Nature and Natural Resources 'marked the adoption of the US–UK view of conservation [...] in place of the more

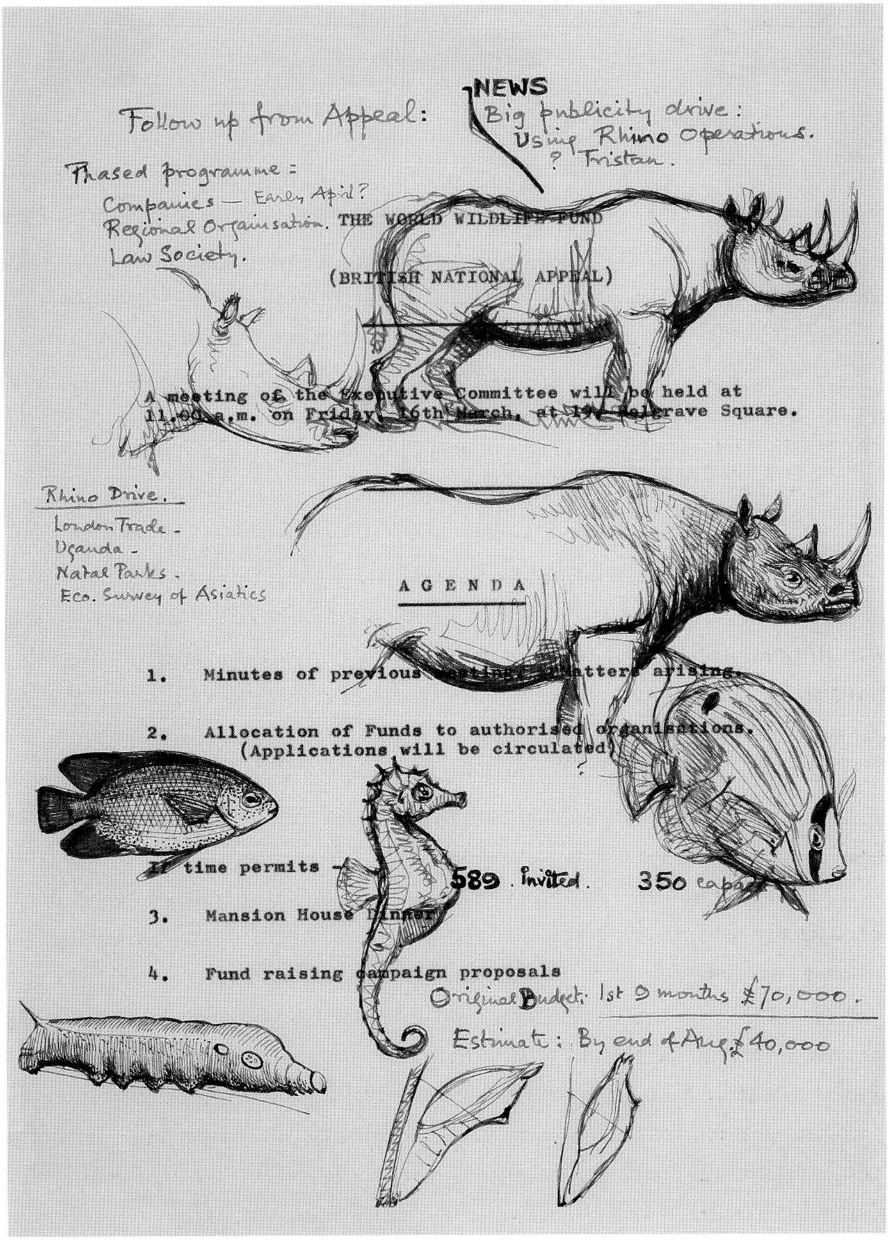

Follow up from Appeal:

Phased programme =
Companies — Early April?
Regional Organisation.
Law Society.

NEWS
Big publicity drive:
Using Rhino operations.
? Tristan.

THE WORLD WILDLIFE FUND

(BRITISH NATIONAL APPEAL)

A meeting of the Executive Committee will be held at
11.00 a.m. on Friday, 16th March, at 19 Belgrave Square.

Rhino Drive.
London Trade -
Uganda -
Natal Parks -
Eco. Survey of Asiatics

A G E N D A

1. Minutes of previous meeting & matters arising.

2. Allocation of Funds to authorised organisations.
    (Applications will be circulated)

If time permits —

589 invited.   350 capac.

3. Mansion House Dinner

4. Fund raising campaign proposals
    Original Budget: 1st 9 months £70,000.
    Estimate: By end of Aug £40,000

Peter Scott, animal drawings on a WWF-UK agenda,
March 1962

Fairfield Osborn, president of the New York Zoological Society and founder of The Conservation Foundation

sentimental protectionism that survived in some parts of Europe'.[38] Max Nicholson, for one, believed that the change adopted in Edinburgh had the additional advantage of bringing the Americans 'properly on board', especially their most eminent figure, Fairfield Osborn.[39] In 1948 the president of the New York Zoological Society had written *Our Plundered Planet*, an ecological best-seller translated into thirteen languages.[40] While the book had essentially been about the conservation of natural resources, especially soils, its success prompted Osborn to create The Conservation Foundation, a conservation policy institute which in the 1980s was to merge with WWF-US (see below, Chapter 8).

WWF's English deed of foundation reflected the Anglo-American environmentalist discourse which had led to IUCN's name change: it avoided the term 'nature' and used 'natural resources' instead. The first passage defining WWF's objectives stated, for instance, that WWF shall 'collect, manage and disburse funds […] for the conservation of world fauna, flora, forests, landscape, water, soils and other natural resources'.[41] Yet when Hans Hüssy, unaware of the terminology debate and, apart from nature experiences as a boy scout in his home canton of Aargau, a complete novice to conservation matters, had to translate this passage into German, instead of a literal translation he opted for an analogous one.[42] Hüssy not only dropped the reference to soils so dear to the Americans around Fairfield Osborn but also (re-)introduced the seemingly sentimental European nature terminology: the '*Stiftungszweck*' of WWF was to be '*die weltweite Erhaltung der Fauna und Flora, der Wälder, Landschaften und anderer Erscheinungsformen der Natur*'.[43] As Hüssy provided the London Preparatory Group with an English translation of the legally binding German version of the deed, Max Nicholson and the other founding parents of WWF ought to have realised that they were setting up a

Deed of foundation, World Wildlife Fund, Zurich, 11 September 1961

Saving the World's Wildlife

Oeffentliche Urkunde

über die Errichtung der

Stiftung

"WORLD WILDLIFE FUND"

mit Sitz in Zürich

———

Vor dem unterzeichneten öffentlichen Urkundsbeamten
des Notariates Zürich (Altstadt) ist heute im Amtslokal
an der Talstrasse 25 in Zürich 1 erschienen:

Herr Dr. Hans A. H ü s s y , geb. 1930, von Safenwil AG,
Rechtsanwalt, wohnhaft Hadlaubstrasse 41, Zürich 6,

und erklärt zu Protokoll mit dem Ersuchen um öffentliche
Beurkundung:

Ich, Dr. Hans A. Hüssy, errichte hiermit unter dem
Namen

"WORLD WILDLIFE FUND"

eine Stiftung mit Sitz in Zürich, gemäss nachstehenden
Bestimmungen:

charity 'for the purpose of the world-wide preservation of fauna and flora, woods, landscapes, waters, and other phenomena of nature'.[44] But in fact, until the first general revision of the deed in 1973, when a very clumsy German rendering of 'natural resources', *'natürliche Hilfsquellen'*, was inserted, nobody noticed.[45]

WWF was to be governed by a board of trustees reflecting the international scope of the fund. Apart from British members of the London Preparatory Group such as Peter Scott and Guy Mountfort, the first board consisted of naturalists from the USA, Sweden, Belgium and Switzerland.[46] Most trustees were recruited via the IUCN network, among them the union's president, the Swiss biology professor Jean Baer, and its director general, Gerald Watterson. For the presidency, the founders of WWF were looking for an 'outstanding public figure' and initially pinned their hopes on Prince Philip, the consort of Queen Elizabeth II.[47] Approached by Peter Scott, the Duke of Edinburgh turned down the invitation because he was heavily engaged as president of the International Equestrian Federation, but agreed to become a trustee of WWF and the president of its British branch. As Prince Bernhard, the consort of Queen Juliana of the Netherlands, happened to be in London on the same day, Prince Philip suggested that Peter Scott should offer him the job. He knew that Prince Bernhard was staying at Claridge's Hotel.[48] The reply was positive and Peter Scott later recalled with great pride that he had managed to enlist 'Two princes in one day!'[49] What he failed to remember, however, was the panic caused by Bernhard's interim refusal to take the job. 'I am a little concerned that we may have crossed some wires about the Presidency of the World Wildlife Fund,' Scott told Bernhard in August 1961.[50] Max Nicholson realised that Prince Bernhard had to be convinced 'that his Presidency need not involve him in any executive work'.[51] This was achieved by Peter Scott becoming WWF's First Vice-President, responsible for most of the presidential workload. As Bernhard agreed to this deal only in early 1962, IUCN's president Jean Baer briefly also served as the first president of WWF.[52]

The first appearance together of Prince Bernhard and Prince Philip was at the

Prince Philip and Prince Bernhard at the launch of WWF-US, New York, 7 June 1962. In the background is Ian MacPhail sporting a kilt. Prince Bernhard was president of WWF International from 1962 to 1976

Saving the World's Wildlife

launch of WWF-US in June 1962 by means of a fund-raising dinner held at the Waldorf Astoria Hotel in New York. Introduced by Prince Bernhard, the Duke of Edinburgh explained the need for conservation in a speech peppered with wildlife emergencies. The example of rhinos poached for their horns caused greatest interest. Several newspapers picked up on the passage in which Prince Philip declared that in China 'for some incomprehensible reason, they seem to think that [rhino horn] acts as an aphrodisiac. In China – I ask you. I should

Luc Hoffmann, founder of the ornithological research station La Tour du Valat, Camargue, France

have thought that the population statistics alone would have convinced any one that those things were quite obviously unnecessary!'[53] Most articles about the event, attended by large sections of New York's social elite, were illustrated with photographs of the two dashing princes smiling away in black tie. The *New York Times* even published two articles. One gave a summary of Prince Philip's speech and the other reviewed the pastel-dominated 'late spring fashion' worn by women guests.[54]

While both Prince Bernhard and Prince Philip were in turn to become much more actively involved in the management of the fund, another early recruit who was to have a lasting influence on WWF was the Swiss ornithologist Luc Hoffmann. Heir to one of Switzerland's largest fortunes because of his family's ownership of the Basle-based Hoffmann-La Roche chemical enterprises, Hoffmann held a doctorate in biology and in 1947 had begun an ornithological research station, La Tour du Valat, in the Rhône estuary in the south of France.[55] In touch with IUCN ever since its foundation in Fontainebleau in 1948, when a delegation of the union had visited his research site in the Camargue, the 38-year-old Swiss ornithologist hoped that WWF would help him establish a nature reserve in the Guadalquivir estuary in Spain, a project he had been deeply involved in ever since the late 1950s.[56] In August 1961 Luc Hoffmann wrote to his closest scientific ally in Spain, the ornithologist Antonio Valverde, that there was new hope for saving the Marismas of the Guadalquivir because of the invention of a 'truly magical key for the protection of Nature

Saving the World's Wildlife

which is called "World Wildlife Fund".[57] Once Hoffmann had been brought on board WWF the London Preparatory Group, who had chosen an Asian animal as their logo but had been motivated by fears about the future of Africa's national parks, also had an attractive European conservation project at hand which underlined the global scope of their project.

Africa, however, remained what most preoccupied the founders of WWF. While meetings were held at Max Nicholson's London office events in the former Belgian colony of the Congo became truly alarming. After the hasty retreat of the Belgians in June 1960 the secession of the mineral-rich eastern province of Katanga, overtly supported by Brussels, had dragged the vast country in the heart of Africa into political chaos and civil war.[58] Lasting until 1965, when General Mobutu seized power, and costing approximately 100,000 lives, the Congo crisis drastically illustrated the catastrophic potential of decolonisation. The conflict's most prominent victim was the country's first prime minister, Patrice Lumumba, who was killed in Katanga in January 1961 with the approval of Belgian officials.[59] What the founders of WWF and other naturalists worried about most was the fate of the Parc National Albert. Home to rare and underexplored species such as the mountain gorilla and the okapi, which Europeans had discovered only at the beginning of the twentieth century, the nature reserve in the eastern Congo had been the first national park to be established in Africa in 1925.[60] While the 'alarming happenings in the Congo […] so detrimental to wild life' were already invoked in Victor Stolan's initial correspondence with Max Nicholson, by April 1961 'the critical situation which threatens the Congo National Parks' was the top priority of IUCN and the parks were the only specific wildlife emergency mentioned in the Morges Manifesto.[61]

Two months later Max Nicholson received more bad news from the Congo by way of Charles Leofric Boyle, president of the Fauna Preservation Society and a member of WWF's London Preparatory Group. A British pathologist in Uganda, K. R. S. Morris, sent a letter to Boyle in June 1961. The doctor deplored the 'indiscriminate slaughter' of elephants going on in the Congo and bitterly complained about London's decolonisation plans for East Africa – 'the shoddy work of the U.K. government and especially of [Colonial Secretary Iain] MacLeod'.

Morris reported that 'abnormally large' amounts of Congolese ivory, smuggled into Uganda and Kenya, had seriously upset the ivory market and that in the Sudan a white hunter had recently told him of 'enormous amounts of elephants and other game to be met now in the Southern Sudan just across from the Congo from where they had been driven by the terrific amount of shooting'. In Uganda, missionaries and refugees had told Morris 'the same story [...] of uninhibited shooting going on in Congo with the richest ground being provided by the Semliki valley, Parc National Albert. Anyone with a gun takes part, or without by arrows, spears, traps, but of course the soldiers, having more guns and cartridges, get biggest whack, usually in hunting parties, far more effective, and sharing the meat or cash. [...] The finest elephants I've ever seen have been in the Semliki and I feel bitterly that they should be disappearing at this sort of rate and by these sorts of people.'[62]

In view of these developments IUCN's Africa Special Project acquired an ever greater importance for WWF's London Preparatory Group. The IUCN project had been adopted in 1960 as a direct result of Julian Huxley's UNESCO report and was to culminate in an international conference on the future of African wildlife and national parks to be held in September 1961 in Arusha, the city closest to the Serengeti in the British Territory of Tanganyika.[63] As this event was likely to attract international media interest, Max Nicholson and his collaborators decided to use the Arusha conference as the 'launching pad' for WWF.[64] In July 1961 they began to formulate a 'Declaration of a State of Emergency' eventually signed by 43 internationally renowned naturalists, including two professors from behind the Iron Curtain, G. P. Dementiev from the USSR and W. Szafer from Poland.[65] As in the Morges Manifesto written in April, the emphasis of the declaration lay on wildlife emergencies. Yet this time the African case – 'on current trends several of the largest land mammals in Africa [...] may no longer be surviving by about 1970' – was combined with examples from other regions. The need for habitat protection was illustrated with Luc Hoffmann's wetlands project in Spain and the negative effects of population growth 'threatening shortly to leave no room for wild animals [...] in many densely populated countries' by the example of Ceylon.[66] While the reference to population growth was eventually dropped from the declaration, the reference to 'toxic chemicals distributed as seed dressings [...]

Saving the World's Wildlife

massacring animal life on an alarming scale in many countries' was retained and eventually complemented by a reference to 'oil pollution in the sea'.[67]

The London Preparatory Group tried to persuade Julius Nyerere, prime minister of Tanganyika and host of the Arusha conference, to sign the 'Declaration of a State of Emergency'.[68] In view of the many other problems his country was facing, above all the challenge of bringing about a peaceful transition of power, the politician destined to become Tanganyika's first president upon independence in December 1961 refused to sign a paper which put 'the cause [of wildlife preservation] out of proportion'.[69] Peter Scott wrote to Max Nicholson: 'Nyerere's reaction to the State of Emergency is a bore, though I have had some doubts about it for a while. A full official Declaration of a State of Emergency does seem in danger of being thought inappropriate in the present political state of the world.'[70] As Nyerere agreed, however, to issue a personal statement declaring his government's commitment to wildlife conservation, the London Preparatory Group prepared a text for him.[71]

Sir Richard Turnbull, governor of Tanganyika, addressing the Arusha conference, September 1961

During the conference Julius Nyerere and two of his key ministers announced that 'the survival of our wildlife is a matter of grave concern to us all in Africa. [...] In accepting the trusteeship of our wildlife we solemnly declare that we will do everything in our power to make sure that our children's grandchildren will be able to enjoy this rich and precious inheritance.'[72] Calling for outside financial help to fulfil the task, Nyerere's 'Arusha Manifesto' was nothing else than a summary of Julian Huxley's post-colonial conservation strategy which aimed at turning national parks into revenue earners for African governments. This plan had meanwhile received British government support. Not only did the Colonial Office provide the Nyerere government with the funds necessary to host the Arusha conference, Huxley's *Observer* articles were also reprinted by the Fauna

Preservation Society as little booklets containing forewords by Julius Nyerere and the architect of British decolonisation, Colonial Secretary Iain MacLeod. The reprints were 'distributed in large numbers by H.M.G!', as their author was pleased to note in March 1961.[73]

It thus looked as though, with the help of the World Wildlife Fund, decolonisation in British East Africa and its Serengeti treasure trove had a fair chance of taking a course less detrimental to wildlife than in the Congo. Success, however, depended on raising enough money to assist African governments in their conservation efforts. In order to convince the general public of the need to give generously, the London Preparatory Group decided to communicate wildlife stories of particular drama and intensity. In May 1961 Max Nicholson told Fairfield Osborn in New York that WWF would use 'world (at present African) wild life emergencies, with the most news value and pulling power that can be found as an extra means of bringing in new contributors among both wealthy men not hitherto tapped and also millions of ordinary people who would be quite glad to give something if they were approached through national bodies in the leading countries'.[74] In June Ian MacPhail was told to look for 'horror pictures'[75] and Peter Scott wrote to Max Nicholson: 'Somehow we must try to produce an item of wildlife bad news – shock tactics – to coincide with Arusha.'[76]

The intense search for dramatic wildlife stories led to the first WWF publication, a carefully worded and lavishly illustrated brochure in a wide, eye-catching format, entitled *Save the World's Wildlife*. Prepared by Ian MacPhail and produced by Mather & Crowther, its principal aim was to seize the attention of individual members of the general public – 'How you can help to save the world's wildlife' was one of the key slogans. The core argument of the brochure, namely that a 'state of emergency' was 'facing the wildlife of the world',[77] was illustrated with the best 'horror pictures' MacPhail had been able to find. They included a drought-suffering 'mother elephant' and her calf in Kenya's Tsavo East National Park, an oil-covered 'guillemot [...] patiently waiting for death' on an unidentified beach, an African rhino poached because of an 'absurd belief' harboured in the 'Far East' that the animal's horn 'has magical properties' and a 'heap of [bird] corpses found during one day on a British farm' blamed on the widespread use of 'poisonous chemicals' in agriculture.[78]

SAVE THE
WORLD'S
WILDLIFE

WWF's first publication was the brochure *Save the World's Wildlife*, released on 28 September 1961. The cover photograph of a mouse lemur was donated by Bernhard Grzimek

47

SOME OF THE CAUSES FOR ALARM

POLLUTION OF THE SEA

THIS GUILLEMOT is patiently waiting for death. It is covered with thick oil which has been discharged on the sea by a ship. It cannot swim or fly and has swallowed a large amount of oil. Oil-pollution is a world-wide problem and through the efforts of the International Council for Bird Preservation (C.I.P.O.) the governments of the leading maritime countries have agreed to co-operate in taking steps to keep the seas clean. However, much must be done before this cruel and wanton destruction of sea birds is ended. *This means money.*

DROUGHT

A MOTHER ELEPHANT digs in a dried-up river bed in a pathetic attempt to find water for her calf. All over the world thousands of wild animals suffer a slow and painful death from thirst caused by drought. In the Tsavo East National Park in Kenya 10,000 animals perished in the first half of 1961 in spite of the valiant efforts of the gamewardens to save them. The alleviation of suffering of this kind can be achieved by building small dams or drilling water-holes, but in other instances it can entail the costly laying of pipelines to rivers miles away. *This means money.*

POACHING

THIS RHINOCEROS has been killed by poachers, its horns slashed off and its body left to rot. All over the tropical world Rhinos of all species are being poached out of existence – for their horns.

The horn of the Rhinoceros has no use in itself – unlike ivory it cannot be carved and polished. There is, however, in the Far East an absurd belief that when ground to powder and drunk in water, it has magical properties. There is a ready black market and as the Far Eastern species are being methodically wiped out the demand is being met in Africa. Elephants too, are victims of the poachers in spite of the severe penalties if caught. The only really effective solution is to get as many of these great creatures as possible to places of safety. *This means money.*

POISON ON THE LAND

A HEAP OF CORPSES found during one day on a British farm. In many parts of the world this is a familiar daily sight. In the attempt to control harmful insects and other pests by poisonous chemicals thousands of birds, which in fact help to control pests, die a slow death. Many of the victims are song-birds. Reports from field observers are distressing – many dying birds fall out of trees, out of the sky or flutter helplessly on the ground. Animals which eat the dead birds – even domestic pets, dogs, cats and kittens have died in evident suffering. Toxic chemicals not only kill the native birds of a particular country but also birds passing through on migration. Farming must advance, but not on heaps of corpses. Short-sighted and selfish practices must be vigilantly studied and vigorously restrained. *This means money.*

HYDRO-ELECTRIC POWER

HYDRO-ELECTRIC SCHEMES are intended to increase a country's prosperity and raise the standard of living of its people, but could destroy tens of thousands of wild creatures.

Often lack of forethought results in needless destruction. Conservationists have always striven to be tolerant and understanding of problems of this nature. Much of the damage to wildlife, as a result of dam-building and other large engineering projects, could be avoided if the advice of conservationists were sought in the early planning stages. This is why all construction engineers, regional planners, foresters etc, should, as part of their student training, acquire an understanding of conservation. *This means money.*

7

Extracts from *Save the World's Wildlife*, September 1961.
In a deliberate attempt to shock viewers, 'horror pictures'
were used to illustrate wildlife emergencies

Instead of a panda, of which by 1961 there were probably no pictures taken in the wild, the cover of WWF's first publication displayed a portrait of a mouse lemur, one of the wide range of diminutive primates whose habitat is confined to Madagascar.[79] This animal portrait, whose main feature was a pair of big black eyes looking intensely into the camera, was donated by Okapia, the Frankfurt-based picture agency of Bernhard Grzimek. The fact that the name of the famous German zoo director appeared nowhere in the brochure was probably no coincidence, for Grzimek had strong reservations towards WWF as yet another fund-raising organisation trying to capitalise on his successful renderings of African wildlife. When Ian MacPhail asked him for 'some of your own spectacular pictures from "Serengeti shall not die"', Grzimek was irritated rather than flattered.[80] He wrote to Gerald Watterson: 'Do you know something about Mr. MacPhail? If his brochure would be published by IUCN or some similar organization I would consider to help him, but I cannot give pictures etc. to everybody who wants to write about Africa or animals.'[81] Other photographers reacted more positively to the overtures of the London Preparatory Group, among them the Swiss photographer Emil Schulthess, who had won international acclaim with a trip across late-colonial Africa in 1956. He gave WWF three of his most accomplished wildlife photographs: a giraffe bending down to eat from a thorn bush in the Nairobi National Park in Kenya, an impressive frontal view of an elephant bull taken in the Parc National Albert in the Congo, and a portrait of a black rhino with a 'fantastically large horn' accompanied by her young, which Schulthess managed to photograph in Kenya's Amboseli Park.[82]

Launch of WWF at the Royal Society of Arts, London, 28 September 1961. From left to right: Peter Scott, Lord Hurcomb holding a panda, Julian Huxley and Jean Baer

While African themes clearly dominated the brochure's imagery, the text put WWF's case in an explicitly global context, despite quoting Nyerere's Arusha Manifesto in a passage dealing with the need for environmental education.

Saving the World's Wildlife

Specific wildlife emergencies discussed came from all over the world and direct appeals to the readers were gender and race neutral. The global approach was most conspicuous in the 'World Wildlife Charter', which appeared on the last pages of the brochure. This text was an environmentalist code of ethics drawn up by Max Nicholson and signed by 22 international conservationists. Apart from a plethora of IUCN notables, the supporters included key American naturalists, among them Fairfield Osborn. In very general terms the charter spelt out the moral reasons for conservation. The signatories 'solemnly' pledged, among other things, 'to make sure that room shall be left for wildlife', 'to protect all wildlife from unintentional or wanton cruelty' and 'to encourage children to develop a love and understanding of wildlife'. The London Preparatory Group hoped to get the text, approved by IUCN, officially endorsed by the United Nations.[83]

The World Wildlife Fund was officially launched at a press conference held at the Royal Society of Arts in London on 28 September 1961. Meticulous planning went into the preparation of the event. Already in July Ian MacPhail had provided the press with a first confidential 'World Wildlife Newsletter' and made IUCN communicate the 'Declaration of a State of Emergency' a week before the launch.[84] With a strict embargo until the press conference, the *Save the World's Wildlife* brochure was sent out in advance to major London newspapers together with reprints of Huxley's *Observer* articles. Also the content and the time allocated to each speaker during the actual launch were planned down to the most minute detail. For instance, in the fifteen-minute block allocated to Lord Hurcomb, the chairman of The Nature Conservancy was to stress that the problem under discussion 'is not one of man versus nature or of animals and birds rather than men – it is an absolutely fundamental basic human interest and the time has come to recognise it as such'.[85] The presentation, which also included speeches by Julian Huxley, Peter Scott and Jean Baer, was rounded off by the projection of the film *SOS Rhino*, produced by a personal friend of Prince Philip, Aubrey Buxton of Anglia TV. The film showed 'one of the many problems' the new organisation set out to address.[86]

The press conference was an enormous success. Thanks to a great wave of reports in all media, including radio and television, money began flowing in at the sensational rate 'of more than £1000 a day', as a jubilant Max Nicholson

Daily Mirror, shock issue, 9 October 1961. Drawing on the text and images of WWF's first brochure, Britain's largest tabloid urged its readers to support the new charity.

noted two weeks after the launch.[87] The biggest coup was a 'shock issue' of Britain's largest tabloid, the *Daily Mirror*. Based entirely on texts and images of the WWF brochure, it ran a six-page, front-to-back-cover wildlife emergency story on 9 October 1961. Displaying the Emil Schulthess portrait of the rhino with its young and the panda logo on the cover, the *Mirror* warned its 4.6 million readers that countless species were 'DOOMED to disappear from the face of the earth due to Man's FOLLY, GREED, NEGLECT'. Generous support of WWF was of paramount importance because 'unless something is done swiftly animals like this rhino and its baby will soon be as dead as the dodo'.[88] As a result of this article alone WWF received '20,000 letters and gifts in four days'.[89] One month after the legal foundation of the fund in Zurich Max Nicholson was proud to inform WWF supporters abroad: 'We have, therefore, good confirmation of our diagnosis of the publicity value of the World Wildlife emergency and the possibilities of converting it into effective money-raising.'[90]

Saving the World's Wildlife

Despite a preoccupation with African wildlife, the founders
of WWF aimed at conservation on a global scale. Here a
scarlet macaw (*Ara macao*) is seen along the Rio Negro
riverbank, Amazonas, Brazil

Endangered paradises

African photographs by Emil Schulthess

Emil Schulthess, lion cubs (*Panthera leo*),
Royal Nairobi Park, Kenya, 1956

Key wildlife photographs used in WWF's first brochure were donated by the Swiss photographer Emil Schulthess. Like Max Nicholson and his colleagues, Schulthess worried about the future of Africa's wildlife as a result of decolonisation. In a ten-month car trip undertaken in 1956, he had crossed late-colonial Africa from Tunisia to the Cape. Consciously avoiding large cities and industrial areas, the photographer was interested in 'primordial Africa [...] which hour by hour, day by day is being pushed back by "development"'. Focusing on villages, landscapes and wildlife, Schulthess wanted to show contemporaries back home 'the extraordinary powers of this wonderland, the mystery and traditions of its black peoples living in close touch with nature, and its impressive animal kingdom'. He found Africa's fauna preserved in national parks and game reserves established by the colonial authorities. The first 'animal paradises' Emil Schulthess visited were those of the Belgian Congo. In the Parc National Albert, he took some of his best wildlife pictures, among them the hippos resting on the bank of the Rutshuru river. The parks established by the British in East Africa were also full of great photo opportunities. In Kenya's Amboseli Park, Schulthess not only took the photograph of the rhino and its young which the *Daily Mirror* ended up putting on the front page of its shock issue in favour of WWF, but also managed to capture the impressive beauty of an elephant herd progressing through a forest. En route to the Cape, Schulthess visited more parks in Tanganyika and Northern and Southern Rhodesia, as well as in South Africa. Arriving in the most developed country of the continent, however, the photographer could no longer avert his gaze from the negative effects of modernity. He went up a skyscraper in the country's commercial capital and noted: 'In the megalopolis Johannesburg we saw the face of the "other", the present-day Africa.'

Preceding page: Emil Schulthess, hippos (*Hippopotamus amphibius*) at the Rutshuru river, Parc National Albert, Belgian Congo, 1956

Overleaf: Emil Schulthess, black rhinoceros (*Diceros bicornis*) with young, Amboseli Park, Kenya, 1956

Emil Schulthess, zebras (*Equus zebra*),
Royal Nairobi Park, Kenya, 1956

Emil Schulthess, equator sign on the Nakuru–Eldoret road,
Kenya, 1956

Overleaf: Emil Schulthess, elephant herd (*Loxodonta
africana*), Amboseli Park, Kenya, 1956

Emil Schulthess, giraffe (*Giraffa camelopardalis*),
Royal Nairobi Park, Kenya, 1956

Emil Schulthess, impala antelopes (*Aepyceros melampus*),
Royal Nairobi Park, Kenya 1956

Overleaf: Emil Schulthess, Tanganyika, 1956

Emil Schulthess, magpie shrike (*Urolestes melanoleucus*),
Kruger National Park, South Africa, 1956

Emil Schulthess, Johannesburg, South Africa, 1956

Launching of a new ark

'My preoccupation is to see that every press report
which can possibly carry a reference to the WWF should
do so.'

WWF's first report, written by Peter Scott and covering the first four years of the fund's existence, was entitled *Launching of a New Ark*. Although the report claimed that WWF 'seeks to avoid coming into competition with any other conservation organisation', this was bound to happen even though the fund was believed to operate in an 'expanding market'.[1] In the UK conflict quickly broke out with the Fauna Preservation Society, which was headed by a member of the London Preparatory Group, Charles Leofric Boyle. While WWF first had to resist Boyle's attempts to integrate the fund into the society,[2] once the two organisations began cooperating in an effort to save the severely endangered Arabian oryx in 1962 – remnants of a last herd were captured in Yemen and flown to Arizona, where they were successfully bred in captivity[3] – WWF's honorary treasurer, Guy Mountfort, bitterly complained about the older organisation taking all the credit: 'My preoccupation is to see that every press report which can possibly carry a reference to the WWF should do so.'[4]

In similar fashion WWF had to stand up to other pre-existing environmental organisations wherever the fund tried to establish itself. In Switzerland, for instance, there was the Schweizerischer Bund für Naturschutz, created in 1909 under the leadership of the conservation pioneer Paul Sarasin, and the more recent but very successful Rheinaubund founded in 1960 in opposition to a hydroelectric power plant.[5] In the USA, the first country to create national parks with the foundation of Yosemite (1864) and Yellowstone (1872), there was a particularly high density of conservation organisations, such as the Sierra Club, founded in 1892, the National Audubon Society, founded in 1905, or the Wildlife Management Institution, founded in 1911.[6]

Fairfield Osborn, who in addition to heading the New York Zoological Society dating back to 1895 had created The Conservation Foundation in 1948, declined to become a trustee of WWF. He questioned 'the desirability of still another medium in the United States designed to collect funds for wildlife protection in view of the fact that in our country, far beyond all others, there already exist a number of vital organizations dedicated to the same purpose'.[7] Owing largely to the persuasive powers of Max Nicholson, Osborn temporarily gave up his opposition to WWF but within a year resigned again from the board of WWF-US.[8]

Also, the pre-eminent German naturalist Bernhard Grzimek, whose fund-raising vehicle was the Frankfurt Zoological Society, founded in 1858, never wholeheartedly embraced WWF despite becoming a founding trustee of WWF-Germany in 1963 and a board member of WWF International in 1966.[9] This was only in part due to the fact that the German naturalist was, in the eyes of WWF's first director general, Fritz Vollmar, 'too much of an individualist and well aware of his own position and achievements'.[10] For, also in terms of conservation policy, Grzimek differed in an important aspect from the British founders of WWF, namely the stance taken on hunting, especially in Africa.[11] Grzimek's first film on African wildlife, *No Place for Wild Animals* (1956), denounced European and American tourists who came to Africa to shoot big game. In a deliberate attempt to shock a middle-class, animal-loving audience, Grzimek began his film with an impressive montage of wildlife scenes, shooting sounds and the killing of an elephant combined with an aggressive text praising the excitement of 'danger-free' hunting safaris to be bought for a mere 8,000 Deutschmarks.[12] In a pre-video age Grzimek's audience could not rewind the film to verify that the elephant presented as a safari trophy at the beginning was shown again at the end as an example of an animal that had to be put down by a game warden because it had been wounded in a poacher's trap. *No Place for Wild Animals* won two major German cinema prizes in 1956 and was successfully exported around the globe.[13]

Grzimek's message fell on fertile ground with many of his admirers, including Victor Stolan. The first memorandum the Czech-born naturalist drew up for Max Nicholson in January 1961 urged the main architect of WWF to 'secure the cooperation of Dr. Bernhard Grzimek, whose influence – both literary and scientific, and in specialised film production, radio and television, combined with his office of Director of the Frankfurt Zoo (the leading institution in Germany) – would make him invaluable for our purposes'. Stolan's suggestions for the conservation of African wildlife also included a fundamental hunting critique along the lines of that of his German hero. He argued that 'hunting licences should be granted exclusively to expert shots but not at all if it does not appear necessary to eliminate animals affected by decease [*sic*], or, in some districts, outgrowing the desirable balance. Pleasure killing should be stopped completely.'[14]

Steller's Albatross (Diomedea albatrus) – Pacific

Arabian Oryx (Oryx leucoryx) – Asia

Kashmir Stag (Cervus elaphus hanglu) – India

Mountain Gorilla (Gorilla gorilla beringei) – Africa

Pigmy Hippopotamus
(Choeropsis liberiensis) – Africa

WWF's first publication, the brochure *Save the World's Wildlife*, included a 'danger-list' illustrated by Barry Driscoll. The Arabian oryx (*Oryx leucoryx*) was successfully saved from extinction in 1962

Although Max Nicholson let himself be inspired by Stolan's suggestions in more than one way, the architect of the World Wildlife Fund made sure that WWF documents never included a fundamental, Grzimek-style opposition to hunting. In his article in *The Times* announcing the creation of WWF in June 1961, for instance, Nicholson deplored various ways in which wild animals lost their lives at the hands of human beings but explicitly excluded those killed 'for food or sport'.[15] By refusing to condemn hunting on moral grounds Nicholson made sure that WWF did not alienate those who enjoyed this activity. He knew perfectly well that in the UK 'sportsmen' – another English term for which there is no adequate translation in any other European language – were not only among the first people to complain about the negative effects of toxic chemicals on wildlife because it poisoned their game.

Bernhard Grzimek and a galago during the filming of *Serengeti Shall Not Die*, 1959

They had also been the driving force behind one of the most influential conservation organisations with an interest in Africa, the Fauna Preservation Society (FPS). Founded in 1903 as the Society for the Preservation of the Wild Fauna of the Empire to combat the rapid disappearance of game from colonial hunting grounds, FPS paid tribute to its hunting origins by entitling a book celebrating its 75th anniversary in 1978 *The Penitent Butchers*.[16] While Max Nicholson never hunted, another key member of the London Preparatory Group, Peter Scott, had been a keen sportsman until he gave up shooting in the early 1950s. As his biographer Elspeth Huxley put it when writing about her subject in the 1930s: 'While Peter loved his birds with passion he continued to kill them with relish.'[17]

WWF's refusal to condemn hunting was aimed at potential supporters who were still active sportsmen in 1961. As the American zoologist Harold Coolidge, one of the initiators of IUCN and a keen supporter of the WWF project, put it in a letter to Gerald Watterson in August 1961: 'If the intention is to eliminate all

Saving the World's Wildlife

sport shooting under any circumstances we will lose the backing of some of our finest "repentant butchers."' [18] Apart from Coolidge himself, who in 1927 had shot a mountain gorilla in the Belgian Congo to provide Harvard's Museum of Contemporary Zoology with a specimen, this included the American biologist Ira Gabrielson and the president of the German Bundestag, Eugen Gerstenmaier.[19] Both hunters ended up heading the WWF appeals in their countries.[20] Yet the benevolent stance on hunting was above all aimed at the two royal patrons of WWF, Prince Bernhard and Prince Philip. In addition to hunting in Europe, both princes also carried out one of the most traditional royal pastimes overseas. By hunting big game in Africa Prince Bernhard continued a tradition begun by his father, who in 1904 had published an account of his hunting adventures in present-day Tanzania.[21] Prince Philip, on the other hand, made headlines by shooting a tiger during a state visit of Queen Elizabeth II to India in January 1961. While Prince Philip remembers that 'this was part of the entertainment laid on by the Indian Government and it would have been difficult to reject their hospitality', this did not prevent criticism at home.[22] A photograph of the royal hunting party distributed by a major Fleet Street press agency was entitled 'Phil's tiger haul' and mentioned the fact that 'the skin will be sent to Windsor Castle'.[23]

The Duke of Edinburgh took a great interest in WWF's stance on hunting. In July 1961 he provided Peter Scott with a long list of criticisms of the World Wildlife Charter. In its first draft it called for 'an end to cruelty to wildlife',[24] a point the prince particularly disliked: 'This is ridiculous and smacks of the League against cruel sports!' He suggested replacing the passage with a call to protect wildlife from 'unintentional or wanton destruction'.[25] Although Peter Scott thought it 'a great bore that [Prince Philip] suggests so much alteration', he made sure that the royal criticism was integrated into the final version of the charter.[26] How alert the prince remained to hunting-related statements made in connection with WWF, whose UK president he became, is reflected in his reaction to the shock issue of the *Daily Mirror*. Although the biggest publicity coup of the London Preparatory Group was written and illustrated on the basis of WWF's first publication, Prince Philip interpreted it as an attack on sportsmanship. In a very angry note he told one of his senior employees: 'I hope you will give this chap a proper stick about the leading article in Monday's Daily Mirror!

The least he can do is to point out that only shooting and hunting people are in the least concerned about conservation because they want to go on hunting and shooting and *fishing!*[27] The secretary of WWF-UK, Rear-Admiral Cecil Parry, to whom the note was forwarded, saw no other option than to claim: 'Unfortunately this newspaper was expressing a point of view over which we have no control.'[28] Parry hastened to add that, because of the article in the *Daily Mirror*, 'we have been submerged beneath an avalanche of letters, some 30,000 to date'.[29]

Their hunting interests led both Prince Bernhard and Prince Philip to suggest that WWF should establish close ties with the Conseil International de la Chasse (CIC), an international hunters' organisation aimed at the conservation of game animals founded in Hungary in 1928.[30] While these suggestions were tactfully ignored – probably because many non-royal trustees of the fund saw CIC as a 'group of rich sportsmen, and many of them might be people whom one would not want to have'[31] – WWF could not overlook the negative publicity caused by the fact that their royal patrons continued to hunt.

A year after the launch of WWF, Aubrey Buxton, trustee of WWF-UK and a personal friend of Prince Philip, asked in an internal memorandum: '[I]s Prince Philip an asset to the cause, or is he becoming a liability?' Buxton asserted that 'the position is more serious than we admit' and explained: '[A]lmost anything we mount or arrange in connection with the W.W.F. or conservation is smoke-screened by innuendos about stags or sport, and therefore the effort is neutralised.'[32] In order to counteract the negative publicity Buxton 'placed' a series of newspaper articles in British papers in which journalists argued the compatibility of hunting and conservation.[33] Prince Philip was delighted: 'This is splendid stuff. I think copies of this might come in useful when people write in about this subject.'[34]

Although WWF's first report emphasised that 'the ethics of taking animal life should not be confused with the ethics of exterminating species' and therefore called on 'sportsmen and non-sportsmen [...] to combine together in a common crusade', hunting became increasingly incompatible with holding office at WWF.[35] In 1965 the board of trustees endorsed a proposal by Prince Bernhard 'that no Trustee or Officer of the WWF or one of its National Appeals or anyone who in the public eye was connected with the WWF should ever accept an

Royal hunting party, Ranthambore, India, 26 January 1961.
During a state visit by Queen Elizabeth II to India, Prince
Philip was invited to shoot a tiger. The Maharani Gayatri
Devi of Jaipur, standing next to the Queen, became a
trustee of WWF International in 1971

Max Nicholson

Daily Mirror

3d. Tuesday, October 3, 1961. No. 17,97

● The Duke, pictured with one of his cameras.

A book of bird snaps —taken by the Duke

A BOOK of bird photographs taken by the Duke of Edinburgh is to be published next spring.

This was announced yesterday by Longmans Green, the publishers.

They say the photographs were taken by the Duke during overseas tours in 1956 and 1959.

Islands

On the first tour he visited the Falkland Islands in the South Atlantic—home of many rare birds. In 1959 he visited the Ellice and Gilbert Islands in the Pacific.

The book includes about sixty or seventy pictures. And the Duke has written the accompanying text.

It is expected that the proceeds of the book—the Duke's third—will go to charity. ? *

His first book, published in 1957, was called "Selected Speeches, 1948-55."

The next, "Prince Philip Speaks," also a collection of speeches, was published last year.

News of the Duke's skill in photography came as a surprise. He has often been seen with a movie camera, but it was generally thought that his interest was merely that of an amateur "dabbler."

LIC

A YOUN marri gave up moon for lion cub. After the Luton reg childhood

* who?

invitation to hunt in areas set aside for posterity with WWF money because of the possible repercussions on the reputation of the WWF as a conservation organization'.[36] In addition both royal patrons, while continuing to hunt in Europe, gave up their hobby overseas. One of the daughters of Prince Bernhard, Princess Irene, remembers that at some point her father 'stopped hunting in Africa to only take pictures and film',[37] a decision also taken by Prince Philip. In view of the tiger he shot in India at the beginning of 1961, WWF appreciated a first African photo-safari by the Duke of Edinburgh in December 1961 as 'a very welcome reversal of policy'.[38] One year later Prince Philip published a book about the birds he had observed and photographed while travelling on board the royal yacht *Britannia*, a further move away from the hunter image in which the prince was assisted by Aubrey Buxton.[39]

A key to the success of WWF was that its leaders quickly developed a strong sense of identity. While their global ambitions, laid down in the deed of foundation, set them apart from national and regional competitors, it was their commitment to the ideals of the business world which differentiated WWF from other international conservation organisations. This was particularly important vis-à-vis the fund's hunting-inspired competitors, the Fauna Preservation Society and the Conseil International de la Chasse, whose self-image was strongly influenced by the aristocratic, landowning background of their founding fathers.[40] Early WWF documents, including Victor Stolan's first memorandum, are peppered with terms such as 'businesslike' or 'business world',[41] and whenever there was a personnel problem at a WWF national appeal, for instance in the Netherlands in 1963, the solution was to recruit 'additional businessmen as Trustees' in order to put the appeal on an 'entirely new and business-like basis'.[42]

At the beginning, WWF's 'key business man' was Guy Mountfort, whose advertising background exposed him to all sorts of companies and their management.[43] Subsequently the business identity of WWF was strengthened by the recruitment to the board of an impressive array of internationally renowned

Newspaper clipping from the estate of Max Nicholson announcing a book of bird photographs taken by Prince Philip, 3 October 1961

bankers, among them Samuel Schweizer, president of the Swiss Bank Corporation (1963), the British merchant bankers Henry F. Tiarks (1965) and Ernest Kleinwort (1968), and indeed Hermann Josef Abs, for decades the dominant figure at Deutsche Bank (1966).[44] The identification with the business world not only allowed WWF to differentiate itself from older conservation organisations, it also reflected the fact that during the post-war economic boom in both western Europe and North America leaders of industry and commerce were held in much higher social esteem than in times of economic difficulties such as the 1930s. In other words: the business identity of the early WWF was very much in line with the *Zeitgeist* of the 1960s.

WWF's identity was sharpened by the close but complicated relationship with IUCN. The first serious trouble broke out shortly after the successful launch of the fund because the union wanted to use some of the money raised to cover a debt of $20,000 incurred with a printer when IUCN was still located in Brussels.

The WWF leadership at a conference in Amsterdam, April 1967. From left to right: Luc Hoffmann, Prince Philip, Prince Bernhard and Peter Scott

Guy Mountfort was so upset that he threatened to resign: 'Surely we cannot use WWF funds, which are for saving animals, to pay off organisational debts.'[45] The financial situation also became tense, however, because at a first WWF board meeting in November 1961 Max Nicholson massively overestimated the amount of money the fund would be able to raise in the course of 1962, which led to more money being allocated to IUCN projects than in fact became available.[46] To make matters worse this went hand in hand with the outbreak of a highly personalised internal dispute within IUCN embroiling the president Jean Baer, the director general Gerald Watterson and the staff ecologist George Treichel. Max Nicholson later remembered that the foundation of WWF, created in order to save the union from bankruptcy, coincided with 'a spell of virtual insanity on the part of more than one of the senior [IUCN] staff'.[47]

As a result of the chaotic situation WWF feared that IUCN were a bunch of scientists incapable of running an international organisation properly. In December 1961 Nicholson complained that the union failed to produce 'businesslike financial arrangements and statements' and felt 'a strong urge to separate the WWF as soon as possible and as completely as possible from the "contaminating" contact with IUCN'.[48] Half a year later the trustees of WWF endorsed Nicholson's plan by supporting 'a clearer separation between the Fund and IUCN. The Fund was an independent organization whose main purposes were money-raising, money-management and money-spending, and IUCN was its impartial adviser on scientific and technical questions.'[49] Once the union had sorted out its internal disputes, however, by appointing, in 1962, a new director general, the British ornithologist Hugh Elliot, and in 1963 a new president, the French ecologist François Bourlière, the two organisations were able to build up a sound and complementary working relationship.[50] WWF referred all project proposals to two independent referees and to IUCN or, in ornithological matters, to the International Council for Bird Preservation. Their feedback was collected in so-called 'green books' listing the projects according to their scientific priority, which became the principal guideline for the trustees of WWF, who twice a year took the final decision in allocating the available funds.[51]

While WWF and IUCN closely and successfully collaborated for decades, attempting a merger in the 1980s and sharing office space in Switzerland until 1992, conflicts also broke out on a regular basis. The disputes were usually about money and always linked to the different identities of union and fund. This is not only a core theme of the detailed history of IUCN written by one of its former director generals, Martin Holdgate, but also features prominently in the memories of key WWF personalities.[52] Prince Philip, for instance, remembered in 1997: 'What struck me from the beginning was how different the cultures were. People in IUCN were academics, or from technical research laboratories. The people in WWF were from a business culture.'[53] Fritz Vollmar, WWF's first director general, remembers IUCN as an 'ivory tower', often complaining about the fund's 'Madison Avenue methods'. They included tuning up IUCN projects in need of funding into 'shopping lists' which 'in order to attract donors [...] had to be as "sexy" as possible and contain attractive titles'.[54]

WWF's business identity manifested itself in a first structural reorganisation implemented in 1968. By then the board of WWF International, in an effort to include representatives from all over the world, had grown to 24 trustees and 14 substitutes 'representing five continents [...] and ten different countries'.[55] Since there were plans to expand the board to 40 members, also in view of 'the desirability to have women on the WWF Board of Trustees',[56] meetings became increasingly inefficient. Based on suggestions by the British banker-trustee Ernest Kleinwort, WWF decided to create an Executive Council (EXCO) 'consisting of a relatively small number of men [sic] who are able to follow the Fund's affairs

Thomas and Sonja Bata, Bonn, Germany, 1973

closely'. While being 'under the ultimate responsibility of the Board', EXCO was to consist of no more than seven trustees and had to contain 'at all times a majority of men [sic] of practical business experience'. Responsible for 'finance, fund-raising and the allocation of funds collected', the latter in consultation with the Conservation Committee, the council was destined to become a governing body with far-reaching powers.[57]

Once the reform was implemented at the end of 1968 decisions taken by EXCO were usually nodded through at full board meetings. At those women began to participate in 1970. The first five female trustees were Prince Bernhard's eldest daughter, Princess Beatrix, the Maharani Gayatri Devi of Jaipur, the German-Hungarian Countess Margrit Batthyany-Thyssen, residing in the Swiss canton of Ticino, the American novelist and former US ambassador to Italy, Clare Boothe Luce, who lived in Honolulu, and Sonja Bata-Wettstein, Swiss-born wife of the Czech-Canadian shoe manufacturer Thomas Bata.[58] A driving force behind the establishment of WWF-Canada and elected to the fund-raising committee of WWF International in 1971, Sonja Bata was the most active member of the group. In 1972 the trained architect was elected to EXCO, which thereby ceased to be an all-male body.[59]

Despite its entrepreneurial self-image, WWF was of course not exclusively governed by business people; on the contrary. WWF's First Vice-President Peter

Scott, who ran much of the organisation in the first decade, was an artist and never managed a company. The fund's Second Vice-President was Luc Hoffmann, who, despite attending all board meetings of Hoffmann-La Roche, had chosen a career in practical ornithology instead of joining the family business. Two further key figures from outside the business world were Prince Bernhard and Prince Philip, whose world-famous personae provided the new charity with extremely valuable international prestige. As European royal families had been, ever since the nineteenth century, very efficient patrons of philanthropic and charitable organisations, the two princes were also expert fund-raisers and thus a key asset to WWF.[60] In addition, they put first-rate social and diplomatic contacts at the disposal of the fund, which not even the most important banker-trustees had access to. Prince Philip, for instance, used a 1962 visit to Buckingham Palace by former US president Dwight D. Eisenhower to recruit him as Honorary President of WWF-US.[61] Like all trustees of the fund, neither Prince Bernhard nor Prince Philip ever received a salary for their work for WWF.

Overleaf: Fritz Vollmar, White Bengal tiger (*Panthera tigris tigris*), New Delhi Zoo, January 1973

The Morges Secretariat and the first national appeals

In the first ten years, WWF supported 550 conservation projects in 59 countries.

Much of WWF's energy in the first decade was devoted to building up an international secretariat in Switzerland and a network of national fund-raising organisations. While during its first row with IUCN the fund had toyed with the idea of setting up offices in Zurich, in 1962 WWF decided to host its international secretariat also in Morges.[1] The search for a secretary general began in November 1961. Hans Hüssy, who served the fund as legal counsel, suggested the Swiss economist Fritz Vollmar, whom Hüssy had met in the army and who also came from the canton of Aargau.[2]

'Les Uttins', the villa in Morges, Switzerland, where IUCN sublet office space to WWF

Although Vollmar's CV showed that he had worked as a freelance journalist and for the Red Cross during the Hungarian refugee crisis before joining a metalwork company in Thun as a 'director's secretary', WWF's first report called him a 'young Swiss businessman'.[3] After Ian MacPhail, who continued to work in London, Vollmar became the second full-time employee of WWF in March 1962. The office of the secretary general, who received the more businesslike title of 'director general' in 1971, consisted of two small rooms sublet from IUCN. The union had settled into a small villa called 'Les Uttins' which had previously been used as a hotel.[4]

A first priority of the Morges secretariat was to build up an 'Operations Intelligence Centre' documenting the most urgent wildlife emergencies and displaying them on a world map.[5] Peter Scott, who had done active military service in the Second World War, believed that a '"War Room" type of operations centre' would enable WWF to 'direct the funds we can raise into the places where they are most urgently needed'.[6] What proved more useful in the long run, however, were IUCN's publications on endangered species, the Red Data Books which Peter Scott helped to develop.[7] In combination with the photo library initiated by Fritz Vollmar in 1963, the books provided the media with valuable raw material for wildlife stories.[8] The WWF secretariat also produced, 'almost on a daily basis', as Fritz Vollmar remembers, news bulletins aimed at creating environmental awareness, a qualification which 'at the beginning of the 1960s [...] was largely lacking both with governments and the general public'.[9] Although environmental education had not been the prime objective of the founders of WWF, preoccupied as they were with wildlife emergencies, the fund quickly realised the importance of participating in public debates. In 1964 the board of trustees noted: 'A very stimulating by-product of the establishment and the publicity campaigns of the WWF had been its growing general influence on the public opinion particularly in countries where National Appeals are operating already and on governments and authorities concerned in those countries where conservation problems had to be solved.'[10]

Fritz Vollmar, director general of WWF International from 1962 to 1977

The prime aim of the early WWF was the establishment of as many new national appeals as possible. The fund made sure that its publicity material was 'so designed that it can be easily produced with the wording in any language' and 'International Campaigns Director' Ian MacPhail paid regular visits to nascent WWF organisations around the world.[11]

In 1965 WWF published a 'Blueprint for setting up a National Appeal', which described all necessary steps from 'picking the team' headed by a VIP president, 'one of the six most distinguished and best-known people in the land', to a long list of 'fund-raising ideas', including wildlife exhibitions, fancy-dress balls and football pools.[12] In the first decade, 21 national appeals were launched. In three places – the UK, the USA and Switzerland – it was possible to set up an appeal in 1961. The original three were followed by the Netherlands (1962), Germany and Austria (1963), Belgium and Italy (1966), France and Canada (1967), South Africa (1968), Spain (1969), India, Pakistan, Japan, Luxembourg, Norway and Sweden (1970), Malaysia (1971) and Denmark and Finland (1972).[13]

Despite the detailed guidelines for setting up national appeals, because of cultural and legal differences between the countries in which WWF began to operate, the fund ended up appealing to potential donors in a great variety of

Bazaar organised by WWF-Switzerland, Zurich, 1965

Bazaar organised by WWF-UK, c. 1962

ways. Major differences existed, for instance, regarding membership schemes. Although the blueprint for setting up a national appeal stressed that WWF 'is not a membership organisation', of the founding three only one, WWF-US, did not attempt to acquire any members until the 1980s.[14] While the Americans mainly relied on direct mailings, the British preferred to raise funds via media-driven public relations campaigns, but in addition also developed a successful youth service based on membership. By 1964 there were already 40,000 British 'Wildlife Rangers'.[15] WWF-Switzerland took the legal form of an association and was therefore a membership organisation by default. By 1971 it had 21,000 members paying an annual fee – the main reason why WWF-Switzerland was able to raise more than one million Swiss francs per year.[16] The fourth national appeal, WWF-Netherlands, also owed much of its success to a broad membership base. The Dutch had 16,000 'regular supporters' by the end of 1970 and were soon raising the equivalent of half a million Swiss francs per year.[17]

The agreements between WWF International and its national branches usually allowed for one third of the money raised to be retained and spent locally, while two-thirds had to be transferred to Morges, where the funds were allocated to projects worked out by IUCN. Thrilled by the launch of WWF-UK, which managed to raise £70,000 in eight months, the founders of WWF firmly believed that this success could be repeated elsewhere.[18] Max Nicholson had high expectations regarding large and wealthy countries such as the USA, Germany and France, but suggested neglecting 'side shows which cannot really affect the main issue such as the Netherlands, Scandinavia and others'.[19] The figures published in WWF's first annual reports show that these assumptions were quite mistaken, both in terms of the absolute amounts of money raised by national appeals and the percentage they transferred to Morges. 'Side shows' like the Netherlands or Switzerland raised considerable amounts of money and handed over most of it to WWF International. WWF-US also managed to raise substantial sums from the very beginning but spent most of it at home. In France a national appeal was started in 1967 which raised practically no money, temporarily ceased to exist, and had to be relaunched in 1973. WWF-Germany also had a difficult start. In 1968, EXCO called for a meeting with founding trustee Bernhard Grzimek 'to clear all outstanding difficulties and to bring the Appeal in Germany to produce results in accordance with the importance of that country'.[20] The German figures duly improved, but much of the money was in fact raised and spent by Grzimek's Frankfurt Zoological Society. The funds were channelled through the WWF accounts only in order to make the results of the German national appeal look less miserable.[21] (See charts on page 341.)

An in-depth analysis of the strikingly different performances of WWF's national appeals would require archival research on a scale far beyond the scope of this book. Yet it is clear that in no country was a single reason responsible for either the performance or the spending policy of the local WWF organisation. While the fiscal situation in some countries, notably the USA, made it difficult to transfer tax-deductible money to WWF International, in other countries, such

Hans Hüssy and the Swiss TV presenter Heidi Abel at a fund-raising event in Basle, 1 May 1966

as India, no money could leave the country at all. Why some appeals did better than others also depended on a wide range of factors, including the quality and the devotion of the local board and the degree of competition from other environmental organisations. In Britain, one of the best-performing WWF countries, the television star Peter Scott put all his prestige and much of his time into building up the fund and continued to be a most active supporter until his death in 1989, a level of commitment Bernhard Grzimek only ever gave to the Frankfurt Zoological Society. The strong performance of WWF-Switzerland, on the other hand, was due not only to Luc Hoffmann, who as a major donor convinced other affluent individuals and companies to join him in supporting the new charity.[22] The Swiss success was also a result of the enthusiasm developed by Hans Hüssy and Fritz Vollmar. In a very hands-on manner the two Aargauers approached all sorts of notables to serve on the Swiss board, including the former federal councillor and president of the Swiss Confederation Philipp Etter.[23] Vollmar and Hüssy also developed one fund-raising idea after another. They ranged from an

Saving the World's Wildlife

auction of artworks to be donated by the likes of Chagall and Picasso – Luc Hoffmann promised to contact the latter – to the sale of WWF merchandise.[24] In 1964 the board of WWF International learned that in Switzerland 'within a few weeks 10,000 copies of the Panda-toy had been sold bringing in substantial royalties'.[25] Two years earlier Hüssy and Vollmar, who prior to being involved with WWF had no experience in either fund-raising or conservation, had gone on their first, privately financed 'business trip' to East Africa – a memorable experience which confirmed their devotion to the cause.[26]

WWF-Switzerland, teddy bear panda, c. 1970

In the first ten years WWF supported 550 conservation projects in 59 countries with a total of 31.5 million Swiss francs.[27] Projects differed widely in terms of content. Apart from 'last-minute actions of the fire-brigade type',[28] for instance buying land to conserve ornithological habitats threatened by drainage, or the emergency breeding of severely endangered species, WWF funded long-term ecological research, gave grants to environmental organisations, above all IUCN, and supported projects as diverse as reforestation in Greece, educational booklets in India, an anti-poaching unit in Kenya and radio communications for the Wildlife Department in Ceylon.[29] Given the obstacles in building up an unendowed international environmental fund-raising organisation from scratch, this was a remarkable achievement. Peter Scott: 'We thought we should just have to tell people the story and the money would come rolling in. Unfortunately it wasn't quite like that.'[30]

Rather surprisingly, the 'biggest single achievement' of an organisation created in response to wildlife emergencies in Africa was saving the wetlands of the Guadalquivir in Spain. A pet project of three funding trustees, Luc Hoffmann, Guy Mountfort and the Belgian Charles Vander Elst, the 65-square-kilometre Coto Doñana natural reserve was also the single most expensive WWF project

Overleaf: Squacco heron (*Ardeola ralloides*) in Coto Doñana National Park, Spain, July 2000

of the 1960s – the fund's commitments amounted to more than 1.8 million Swiss francs.[31] In a complicated process which included WWF's promise to buy part of the land with money they had not yet raised, large interest-free loans by Luc Hoffmann and a major donor from Belgium, letters from Prince Bernhard to General Franco and financial assistance provided by the Spanish subsidiary of Hoffmann-La Roche, the Spanish government was persuaded to create the Coto Doñana National Park in 1965 – 'one of the most valuable nature reserves in Europe', as Peter Scott proudly noted in WWF's second report.[32]

The know-how acquired in Spain proved useful to WWF in many other wetlands projects, for instance at Lake Neusiedl in Austria, at Federsee in Germany and in New Jersey, where a wetlands reserve of 5,000 acres was established in 1968. For this project WWF-US raised the equivalent of 1.5 million Swiss francs, almost the same amount which was spent on Coto Doñana.[33] When announcing the possibility of WWF support for a recently established national park at Lake Nakuru in Kenya in 1969, Peter Scott, himself very keen on preserving wetlands because they were the habitat of his beloved wildfowl, proudly noted: 'WWF has found itself specialising on the acquisition & development for research, education & conservation of wetlands all over the world, & is ready to continue in this field.'[34]

In addition to funding practical conservation work WWF also began to influence government decisions in favour of the environment by means of the so-called 'High Level Representations'. The second report of the fund was already able to state that the organisation was using 'its growing influence' to make 'recommendations to governments and other authorities concerned'.[35] Often these diplomatic initiatives involved WWF's well-connected royal patrons, for instance in Ethiopia. In 1965 a visit of Prince Philip to the East African country encouraged the 'establishment of a Wild Life Conservation Department in Addis Ababa'.[36] Four years later, Prince Bernhard's letters to Emperor Haile Selassie combined with a visit by the Dutch prince encouraged the establishment of Ethiopia's first national parks.[37] In one of his letters to Bernhard the emperor wrote: 'We should like to thank you for your continued interest in the conservation of Our country's valuable wildlife resources and for the advice and encouragement which you have offered Us in your capacity as President of the World Wildlife Fund.'[38]

Saving the World's Wildlife

Although 'Africa was the great challenge facing the World Wildlife Fund when it was founded in 1961', well over half the money the fund raised in the first decade was spent on conservation projects in Europe and North America.[39] This phenomenon reflected a donor preference for domestic projects rather than a change of priorities on the part of the WWF leadership. When in 1969 Africa attracted only 8.2 per cent of the funds, much less than Europe (26.4 per cent) and North America (39.7 per cent), WWF's annual report explained: 'Even if this percentage is perhaps not what the founders of the WWF had in mind at the time of its inception, it is clear that if the WWF wishes to raise considerable funds in future it has to show tangible results in the countries in which money is available *now*.' It was hoped that once the fund had won the trust of its donors by supporting sound conservation work in their home countries 'the present geographical table of projects supported should look quite different'.[40]

Despite the relatively small amount of money spent in Africa, the post-colonial scenarios of doom invoked in 1961 failed to materialise. While the 'dedicated effort of international conservationists', which WWF liked to invoke, certainly contributed to this success, the relatively stable political situation in key wildlife countries such as Kenya and Tanzania was probably decisive.[41] In 1964 Mewyn Cowie, a white settler in Kenya who retained his job as director of the country's national parks, told Peter Scott: 'Not much to report from this end. We are no longer "Royal". [...] The new African Government is treating us well. I still have hopes of getting some financial assistance from the World Fund!'[42] Even in the Congo, the civil war ended when General Mobutu came to power in 1965. While the political and economic stability he initiated endowed the Congolese dictator with considerable domestic popularity by the early 1970s, Mobutu was also particularly good at using conservation to curry favour with Western governments and NGOs.[43] Having announced the creation of two new national parks during an international conservation conference held in the Congolese city of Goma in 1967, WWF's board of trustees sent Mobutu a congratulatory telegram.[44] Four years later the fund noted 'that the overall conservation situation in the Congo was well under control, thanks to the personal interest of the President, General Mobutu'.[45]

On 11 September 1971 WWF celebrated the tenth anniversary of its foundation with a gala event held at the hotel Beau Rivage in Lausanne. Organised by the newly elected trustee Sonja Bata, the event was 'attended by over 500 personalities representing 45 different countries and including heads of state, government ministers, ambassadors and representatives from all fields of business and public life'.[46] One of the guests at the anniversary dinner, whose key VIPs were the king and queen of Nepal, was Victor Stolan. During the festivities in Lausanne he was made a WWF Member of Honour 'in recognition of his role in inspiring the establishment of the World Wildlife Fund'.[47] Stolan certainly appreciated this symbolic gesture, for ten years earlier he had bitterly complained about 'having been pushed out' of the WWF project in a long letter to Max Nicholson: 'Since your by now almost legendary Champagne party on December 6th 1961 I have heard neither from you nor from the headquarters of the World Wildlife Fund. No invitation, no circular – nothing.'[48] In the documents consulted for this book the last trace of Victor Stolan, whose year of death could not be established, is contained in a letter

Prince Bernhard congratulating Victor Stolan upon becoming a WWF Member of Honour, Lausanne, Switzerland, 11 September 1971

Max Nicholson received from the director of WWF-UK shortly after the tenth anniversary celebrations: 'I have had a call from Victor Stolan after his return from Lausanne. He went and stayed a few days in Morges and had talks with Fritz [Vollmar]. He has lots of ideas and wants to help us further.'[49]

Max Nicholson also became a WWF Member of Honour in 1971 'in recognition of his successful promotion of international research and conservation and his leading role in the establishment of the Nature Conservancy of the United Kingdom, the World Wildlife Fund and the International Biological Programme'.[50] Unlike other members of the London Preparatory Group, notably Peter Scott and Guy Mountfort, Nicholson had decided not to become a trustee of WWF and had retreated from the affairs of the fund once it had been successfully launched. In December 1961 Peter Scott wrote to Prince Bernhard: 'As I think you know, the planner behind W.W.F. is Max Nicholson [...] who, partly because of his position as a Senior Civil Servant and partly because of his own particular predilection, always prefers to be a "back-room boy" and to take no nominal part in the development of his brain-children.'[51] While Nicholson was certainly pleased to learn that ten years after its foundation WWF was second only to the RSPCA in terms of public awareness among UK environmental charities, he was uninterested in receiving credit for the organisation's success.[52] In an obituary of Max Nicholson, who died in 2003, the Royal Society for the Protection of Birds noted that the initiator of several successful environmental initiatives had stubbornly 'refused a knighthood several times over'.[53]

The director's photographs

Studies by Fritz Vollmar

Fritz Vollmar was one of the first people I went to see in the course of researching this book. The fund's first director general invited me to his home in Tolochenaz near Morges. There he told me that it was his friendship with Hans Hüssy which brought him to WWF almost by accident. Hearing Fritz Vollmar speak, however, it quickly became clear that the fifteen years spent at the fund were the most important period of his professional life. His youthful enthusiasm for building up an international environmental fund-raising organisation was still palpable. Looking around, I noticed that the house was filled with animal artwork, mainly depicting elephants, and I asked Fritz Vollmar whether he had ever taken pictures of WWF projects. Of course he had, and in no time we were up in the attic, where hundreds of slides are kept, each of them meticulously inscribed with detailed captions. They had once been part of the WWF picture library, much of which has recently been lost – in the course of a digitisation project, most of the older photographs were deemed uninteresting and therefore returned to the photographers or sometimes even thrown away. While Fritz Vollmar's photographs represent only a small fraction of the visual memory of WWF, clearly they are one of its key component parts. Taken with a Hasselblad, in view of their usefulness for the fund's public relations, they celebrate either WWF's success and achievement around the world or the aesthetic beauty of the wildlife it set out to preserve. Unlike a professional wildlife photographer, Vollmar didn't mind taking a portrait of a tiger in a zoo; a nice close-up could always come in handy when someone wanted to write about Operation Tiger. Yet what really fascinated Vollmar, as for countless other WWF staff and supporters, was observing animals in the wild. In 1969 the Kenya-based ornithologist John Hopcraft told Peter Scott: 'Fritz and Danielle Vollmar were out here in February and we had them up at Nakuru for a day. He just could not stop taking photographs! He described his time at Nakuru as the highlight of his East African tour.'

Overleaf, left: Fritz Vollmar, African elephants (*Loxodonta africana*), Amboseli Game Reserve, Kenya, July 1973; right: Fritz Vollmar, giraffes (*Giraffa camelopardalis*), Arusha National Park, Tanzania, February 1967

Fritz Vollmar, rifles confiscated from poachers, Khao Yai
National Park, Thailand, February 1971

Fritz Vollmar, Bengal tiger (*Panthera tigris tigris*),
New Delhi Zoo, India, January 1973

Fritz Vollmar, bearded vulture (*Gypaetus barbatus meridionalis*), Simien Mountains National Park, Ethiopia, February 1969

Fritz Vollmar, Lake Abiata, Rift Valley National Park,
Ethiopia, November 1972

Fritz Vollmar, Sally Lightfoot crab (*Grapus grapus*), James
Island, Galápagos, Ecuador, January 1974

Fritz Vollmar, Galápagos sea lion (*Zalophus wollebackei*),
Ferdinanda Island, Galápagos, Ecuador, January 1974

Overleaf: Fritz Vollmar, birdwatching at Las Nuevas, Coto
Doñana National Park, Spain, May 1972

Growth of the WWF family

'WWF's activities to save endangered habitats and species will not be of great value if man continues to destroy everything around.'

In 1969 WWF's Executive Council was pleased to note 'that the South African National Appeal had very quickly produced encouraging results'.[1] This was the achievement of Anton Rupert, an Afrikaner entrepreneur who began manufacturing cigarettes in 1941 and ended up with a global business empire that made him one of the richest men in the world. Originally active only within South Africa, Rupert's Rembrandt Group acquired the British cigarette manufacturer Rothmans in the 1950s and in due course not only became an important global player in the tobacco industry but also in the liquor and luxury goods market. While Cartier was Rupert's key acquisition of the 1970s, by the time he united his brands into the Geneva-based Richemont Group in 1988, he also owned the French fashion house Chloé and the German pen manufacturer Montblanc.[2] Luc Hoffmann, who served with Anton Rupert on the WWF board for over two decades, remembers about the man who was only seven years older than himself: 'In WWF he had the role of the wise elder man. During board meetings it was possible to discuss many things and people talked a lot. But when Anton Rupert spoke he was always to the point and that was it.' To Hoffmann, whose family fortune is based on the fabrication of pharmaceuticals, Rupert's professional career remains 'in many ways […] an enigma. I see him as one of the people with the highest moral qualities I have ever known. But he made his empire on tobacco and alcohol. I have never quite understood this.'[3]

Largely thanks to the Kruger National Park, the second national park to be established in Africa, in 1926, South Africa enjoyed a high reputation in conservation circles.[4] The incorporation of the country into WWF was thus a priority of the fund's leadership. In February 1962 Peter Scott contacted the Minister of Lands in Pretoria, Paul Sauer, in an obvious attempt to prepare the ground for a South African national appeal. Scott praised South Africa as 'a pioneer in the conservation movement – having some of the oldest game reserves in the world' and promised: 'May I conclude, Mr. Minister, by saying that I shall lose no opportunity of expressing in my TV broadcasts and books, my admiration for the lead which South Africa has given, and is giving in the field of wildlife conservation.'[5] As WWF was always looking for businessmen with an interest in conservation, Anton Rupert was their obvious choice in South Africa. He sat on the National

Parks Board of South Africa, whose director, Rocco Knobel, was one of the signatories of the Morges Manifesto.[6]

Anton Rupert, trustee of WWF International from 1968 to 1989

In January 1964 an invitation by Prince Bernhard immediately convinced Rupert of the WWF project, but a diplomatic initiative by WWF shortly thereafter temporarily blocked the launch of a South African national appeal. In view of plans to introduce ethnic homelands in Namibia, the former German colony administered by Pretoria ever since the end of the First World War, Prince Bernhard wrote several letters to the South African government expressing fears that the project threatened wildlife reserves, especially the Etosha National Park in northern Namibia.[7] Although in December 1964 the WWF board decided 'not to take any further action for the time being in view of the rather difficult situation in South Africa and in order not to compromise the establishment of the South African National Appeal', Prime Minister Hendrik Verwoerd was so irritated by Bernhard's interference that he actively opposed the establishment of WWF in South Africa.[8] Only after the death of Verwoerd, who was assassinated in 1966, and once Anton Rupert had convinced the South African Wildlife Society established in 1926 that WWF would not become a competitor by reneging on an individual membership scheme, was WWF-South Africa launched in 1968.[9]

WWF-South Africa was in many ways a special branch of the fund. Instead of appealing to the general public it derived its income from corporate members. Seventy-two companies joined within a year thanks to Anton Rupert's active canvassing among the South African business community. And contrary to most other WWF national organisations, which were primarily engaged in conservation projects at home, the main focus of WWF-South Africa lay beyond its national borders. In its first five years the organisation supported conservation projects in Malawi, Botswana, Angola, Swaziland, Lesotho, Rhodesia and Mozambique.[10] The transnational scope of the organisation was reflected in its name, 'Southern African Wildlife Foundation', which in 1972 became 'Southern

120

African Nature Foundation' (SANF).[11] By 1986 the 200 corporate members of SANF had supported 145 projects in 13 African countries, spending more than 5 million rand, the equivalent of more than 4 million Swiss francs.[12]

While the declared aim of Anton Rupert was 'conserving the natural heritage of Southern Africa for future generations', his passion for conservation was rooted in his identity as an Afrikaans-speaking South African.[13] He grew up in one of the oldest European cities on the cape, Graaff-Reinet in the Karoo semi-desert, and Rupert's first nature experiences were 'long walks across the veld' together with his father.[14] While he started off as an Afrikaner nationalist, joining the secret Afrikaner Broederbond as a student, later, after the election victory of the National Party in 1948, Rupert became a prominent '*verligte*', i.e. enlightened, Afrikaner.[15] He and other open-minded individuals saw the political aspirations of their people fulfilled and thus opposed the imposition of apartheid by their brethren of the '*verkrampte*', i.e. reactionary, kind.[16] In 1958 Rupert broke with the hard-line prime minister, Verwoerd, and in the 1960s openly clashed with him over the Sharpville massacre and other apartheid-related issues.[17]

By the time WWF got in touch with Anton Rupert he thus no longer cherished a narrow Afrikaner identity based on the desire to protect his people's language and culture but a much wider South African one in which the country's natural heritage played a central role.[18] The historian Jane Carruthers has shown that common pride in South Africa's unique natural heritage, enshrined in the Kruger National Park, was one of the key elements which integrated Afrikaners and English-speakers into a (white) South African nation following the Anglo-Boer war and the establishment of the Union of South Africa in 1910.[19] As the country became increasingly isolated when apartheid was introduced in 1948, for South Africans like Anton Rupert, who did not endorse the racist state ideology but retained a great pride in their country, conservation was an ideal field of patriotic endeavour.[20] As Prince Bernhard put it in his first letter to Rupert: 'South Africa has made an outstanding contribution to the techniques of wildlife conservation and was in the forefront of the National Parks Movement. This should be more widely recognised than it is at present, and South Africa's part would be highlighted were a National Appeal for WWF to be formed there. The subject of wildlife conservation is basically non-controversial and engenders a good deal of international sympathy and goodwill; it has ethical, aesthetic, scientific and economic overtones of considerable significance. I am sure that a South African National Appeal would succeed if you could be its leader and I very much hope you may be able to accept this invitation.' [21] Anton Rupert's reply was short but unequivocal: 'Dear Prince Bernhard, I have read your letter of 17th January with great interest and shall be honoured to accept your invitation to act as President of your World Wildlife Fund in South Africa and to launch its South African Appeal.' [22]

Anton Rupert became a trustee of WWF International in 1968 and retired from the board at the end of 1989. For over twenty years he was both a generous donor to the organisation as well as a major influence on it. Rupert's first substantial gift to WWF International was, in 1970, 100,000 Swiss Francs a year to help 'existing small or newly developing National Appeals to get properly organised on a business-like footing'.[23] Based on his experience of building up a global business empire Rupert repeatedly emphasised the need to train WWF staff.[24] An offer to provide the fund with 'a guest house and a training centre near Cape Town' for annual meetings of WWF executives 'was gratefully accepted' in 1973.[25] Unlike other self-made men who used philanthropy to gain social and media attention, Anton Rupert always kept a low profile at WWF, at least outside of his home country. According to Prince Bernhard the businessman was 'acutely conscious of the stigma of his South African citizenship during the apartheid era'[26] and in 1972 even thought about resigning in order to spare WWF negative publicity linked to his nationality.[27] In view of the economic sanctions imposed against the apartheid regime in the 1980s, WWF-South Africa adopted the same low-key approach within the WWF network. In 1988 Anton Rupert described the American and the South African WWF organisations as 'victims of history' and explained: 'Just as Latin America was very sensitive to domination by the US and preferred to work with neutral international institutions, WWF-South Africa preferred to provide conservation assistance in countries in Southern Africa through the WWF International programme rather than in its own name.' [28]

Anton Rupert's most important legacy to WWF was the establishment of a capital fund, the interest on which allowed the organisation to cover its

Saving the World's Wildlife

administrative overheads and tell potential donors 'that 100 per cent of the money donated to the international secretariat for conservation is spent on conservation projects'.[29] Like any other unendowed charity WWF knew that 'the best money [...] has no strings attached', but was faced with the dilemma that it was much easier to obtain earmarked donations for specific projects rather than money to pay for its administration.[30] The idea for solving this problem by means of a capital fund was first suggested by the banker-trustee Samuel Schweizer in 1964.[31] Yet until the arrival of Anton Rupert WWF had only done extensive research about how to obtain tax exemptions in various countries and revived a plan devised by Max Nicholson, who in 1961 had envisaged creating an exclusive club for super-rich WWF supporters.[32]

Anton Rupert, centre, visiting Peter Scott, right, Slimbridge, Gloucestershire, 1971

When Anton Rupert became chairman of the newly created Fundraising Committee in January 1970 he learnt that the aim was to raise a capital fund of US$10 million. He discussed this plan with one of his employees, Charles de Haes, an economist and lawyer who had previously set up and managed cigarette factories for Rupert in the Sudan and Kenya. Rupert and de Haes decided to approach 1,000 individuals for a donation of US$10,000 each and that de Haes should get 'carte blanche' for achieving this within two years while remaining on Rupert's payroll.[33] Charles de Haes, son of a Belgian father and a South African mother, was born in Antwerp but grew up on a farm in the Eastern Cape. He had discovered the beauty of East African wildlife when working for his pilot's licence in Kenya, which allowed him to fly over national parks, but he took the job for other reasons: 'It was the challenge of raising the ten million. It wasn't because I was passionate about wildlife.'[34]

Having submitted their plan to the WWF executives Peter Scott and Fritz Vollmar at a meeting in Slimbridge, the centre of Scott's wildfowl conservation activities in Gloucestershire, Rupert and de Haes decided that the 1,000 donors should be personally invited by Prince Bernhard to join him in forming 'The 1001 – A Nature Trust'. With logos and stationery for the trust prepared at the Rothmans head office in London, where designers normally working on cigarette packets came up with a globe and the gold-embossed letters '1001', Rupert and de Haes

went to see Prince Bernhard in the Netherlands. The prince liked the logo and agreed to make Charles de Haes his 'honorary personal assistant' responsible for setting up The 1001.[35] In November 1970 the plan won the approval of the WWF board and was completed by the end of 1973.[36] While companies were allowed to pay the US$10,000 on behalf of key representatives, membership was restricted to individuals, and in the brochures of the trust members were listed only by name and country of residence.[37] The 1001 came from over fifty countries, the top five being, in 1978, the USA with 177 members, followed by the UK (157), the Netherlands (107), South Africa (65) and Switzerland (62).[38]

Pins for members of The 1001 – A Nature Trust. For female members the logo was attached to a feather

Charles de Haes began his search for The 1001 among executives and suppliers of Anton Rupert's various businesses and among WWF board members in countries with national appeals. Pins for The 1001, made by the London jeweller Garrard, were an effective means of exerting peer pressure on reluctant trustees at board meetings. Later de Haes developed a sort of 'snowball-system', asking each new member for addresses of potential new donors and travelling around the world trying to meet them.[39] A membership list of The 1001 recruited in Switzerland shows that most of them came either from the Lake Geneva region, where WWF International was based, or from around Basle, where, thanks to Luc Hoffmann, Charles de Haes was able to persuade many other affluent individuals or companies to support the WWF capital fund.[40] While the marketing of The 1001 was clearly inspired by the symbolism of an upper-class golf or country club, in order to keep donations tax exempt the membership fee did not come with any benefits, such as a clubhouse or free entrance to WWF-sponsored wildlife reserves. For the benefit of The 1001, social gatherings, usually hosted by a local member, were organised in cities such as Los Angeles, London or Geneva, while exclusive wildlife holidays could also be booked. One of the first 1001 tours was a safari in East Africa for which twenty members signed up and paid in 1974.[41]

Saving the World's Wildlife

Axel Amuchastegui, American bald eagle, lithograph, 1971.
Each member of The 1001 – A Nature Trust received this
picture from Prince Bernhard

While WWF started off as an environmental fund-raising organisation domin-ated by businessmen and their ideals, with Luc Hoffmann it had a professional biologist on board who provided valuable scientific know-how. Deeply involved not only in the creation of the Coto Doñana National Park but also in setting up WWF national organisations in Austria and France, Hoffmann was the key figure in WWF's Conservation Committee, created in 1965. In 1971 he increased his commitment by accepting the job as WWF's second executive vice-president. Luc Hoffmann agreed to work three days a week in Morges, without, of course, asking for a salary, and moved his family home from La Tour du Valat in the South of France to a village near Geneva.[42] Hoffmann's main role was that of a liaison officer with IUCN, on which WWF continued to rely for scientific expertise. At the fund's tenth anniversary event, Hoffmann compared the close but complicated relationship with IUCN to a marriage in which the projects are the children, IUCN the mother and WWF the father: 'It is him who has to earn the bread to make the family live.'[43]

WWF trustees with less practical experience in scientific project management than Luc Hoffmann were inclined to see the relationship with IUCN in a less romantic way, especially in view of the rather complicated bureaucratic proced-ures which developed over time. The American aviator Charles Lindbergh, elec-ted to the international board in 1966, was more than irritated when Fritz Vollmar told him that before WWF could approve any project, 'it must be screened by the IUCN committee and recommended to WWF by IUCN'. As Lindbergh had received this answer in reply to a request for an additional US$1,000 for an existing rhino project in Indonesia, he told Peter Scott: 'Effective results simply can't be obtained if the transfer of funds is delayed for weeks or months while slow organizational machinery is functioning.'[44]

Operation Tiger, WWF's most prestigious campaign of the 1970s, owed its existence to a WWF trustee with a similar hands-on approach to conservation to Charles Lindbergh's. In 1969 Guy Mountfort learned at the IUCN general assembly held in Delhi that numbers of the Indian tiger had shrunk from 'about 40,000' in 1930 to 'an estimated 2500' and that the animal was also severely threatened in its other Asian habitats.[45] The main reason for the dwindling numbers appeared to be poaching. The Calcutta-based naturalist Anne Wright, founding trustee of WWF-India, discovered that by the late 1960s India was officially exporting many more tiger skins than the number of shooting permits given out each year.[46] Upon returning to Europe, Guy Mountfort was informed that WWF was unable to fund a tiger project because of the lack of scientific evidence proving the endangered state of the species. Well aware of the amount of time it took Morges to set up a new project, Mountfort decided to act alone.[47]

Indira Gandhi with a tiger cub, India, November 1967

In April 1972 Guy Mountfort, accompanied by Charles de Haes, travelled to India, Bangladesh and Nepal, trying to convince their governments to set up tiger conservation programmes.[48] The most enthusiastic reply came from the Indian prime minister, Indira Gandhi, who had banned all tiger hunting in 1970, prompted by a paper by the Indian naturalist Kailash Sankhala. According to Guy Mountfort, Gandhi regarded the tiger 'as a national symbol of India',[49] while Anne Wright remembers: 'If it was for wildlife, you could count on Mrs. Gandhi at any time, and she always took action.'[50] In his meeting with the prime minister Guy Mountfort explained that if the Indian government were to install reserves 'in areas where tigers were still relatively numerous', IUCN would provide their 'scientific management', while WWF 'would raise the equivalent of a million dollars [...] so that the reserves could be equipped to the highest standards'.

Charles de Haes, 'with his wisdom in negotiations of this kind, was quick to remark that such a programme could only succeed if directed and coordinated by the highest authority'. To the delight of Mountfort and de Haes, Gandhi 'agreed without hesitation. "I shall form a special committee – a Tiger Task Force," she said, "and it will report to me personally."'[51] Although no project had been approved let alone developed by IUCN, upon returning to Morges the

Overleaf: Bengal tiger (*Panthera tigris tigris*) in Ranthambore National Park, Rajasthan, India

WWF board was faced with a 'fait accompli' because the press had already been briefed.[52] Approving Mountfort's tiger project, the board could only note that 'similar operations should first be checked with IUCN and the WWF secretariat before being officially announced to the public'.[53]

In autumn 1972 the Indian government appointed Kailash Sankhala as director of Project Tiger and established nine tiger reserves, each containing 'a substantial area to be kept completely free from human disturbance'.[54] Simultaneously WWF launched Operation Tiger, a network-wide campaign to raise the million Mountfort had promised to Indira Gandhi. Carefully prepared by Britain's top advertising executive, David Ogilvy, and supported by an enormous wave of goodwill from people ranging from renowned British nature artist David Shepherd, who donated a limited edition of a tiger painting, to 'youngsters in the United States [...] hissing women who wore tiger-skin coats, so that very soon it became socially unacceptable to do so', Operation Tiger was very successful.[55] Guy Mountfort: 'In eighteen months the campaign raised nearly £800,000 ($1,700,000) the largest contributors being Switzerland, the United States, Great Britain and the Netherlands, in that order.'[56] Similar results were obtained by a network-wide campaign to save Lake Nakuru in Kenya, for which 2.5 million Swiss francs were raised in 1972 alone.[57] Children were especially active fund-raisers in saving this important bird habitat, known to them as 'the lake of the flamingos', because young fund-raisers could win a place on a children's safari.[58] Since little Swiss naturalists proved to be particularly efficient fund-raisers, WWF-Sweden offered two of their tickets to Africa to their colleagues in Zurich.[59]

WWF was very proud of the 'new form of integrated campaigns, with full coordination on the basis of concrete programmes' exemplified by Lake Nakuru and Operation Tiger.[60] And while the Nakuru project temporarily ran into difficulties because the Kenyan government allowed the construction of a chemical plant threatening the ecosystem of the lake,[61] Operation Tiger became the fund's long-term showpiece. Annual report after annual report praised the achievements of a campaign which led to 'a spectacular increase in the population of Tiger in all the Tiger Reserves'[62] and was still in 'full swing' years after its launch.[63] In 1981, when WWF had just spent another US$100,000 on Operation Tiger, the fund declared that the tiger population in the reserves had 'more than doubled over the past seven years'.[64] The triumphalist rhetoric of the reports and of a book published by Guy Mountfort in 1981 suggested that 'the battle to save the tiger' had effectively been won.[65] The initiator of the project concluded: 'The tiger is part of everyone's heritage and I, for one, am proud to have played a part in the crusade to save it.'[66] Events in the 1990s were to show that, for a variety of

Fritz Hug, Lake Nakuru, lithograph dedicated to Vreni Berger, 1972. Each child who sold 120 stamps at two Swiss francs a piece received this picture from WWF-Switzerland

reasons, such declarations of victory were premature (see below, Chapter 11).[67]

Throughout the 1970s the 'WWF family', a term used in internal documents from 1974 onwards,[68] steadily increased the total amount of money spent on conservation, arriving in 1980 at the staggering rate of 54 per cent, reaching a total of $9.5 million.[69] This growth was mainly due to national appeals created in the first decade of the fund's existence. In 1980, for example, the four oldest members of the WWF family – the USA, the UK, Netherlands and Switzerland – were responsible for 75 per cent of the money raised, followed by South Africa and

Sweden.[70] New family members, on the other hand, became more difficult to acquire.[71] In Peru and Portugal, national appeals set up in 1973 failed to take off and had to be closed down again.[72] By the time the fund celebrated its twentieth anniversary in 1981, there were 26 national branches, only five more than in 1972, the newcomers of the second decade being Kenya (1973), New Zealand (1975), Turkey (1976), Australia (1978) and Hong Kong (1981).[73]

In 1975 WWF ceased to publish detailed accounts of its national branches – apart from the desire not to embarrass weaker members, probably also because different systems of accounting and increasing exchange-rate fluctuations after the collapse of Bretton Woods made figures increasingly difficult to compare. Nevertheless, it is clear that some countries, notably France, Germany and Japan, still underperformed, at least in the eyes of the international board.[74] The reasons for this intrigued even the businessmen among the fund's leadership. While a broad membership base was identified as a key to success, in 1980 WWF-US, by then one of the best money-earners, still 'felt that it would lose more than it would gain by becoming a membership organisation'.[75] Also, cultural explanations were only of limited use. The assumption, for instance, that in Catholic countries 'charitable efforts had for centuries been channelled through the Church' was useful to explain the miserable situation in France[76] but clearly failed to explain why, from 1970 onwards, WWF-Italy suddenly began to acquire a very large membership. This surprised even Marchese Mario Incisa della Roccetta, president of the Italian national appeal: 'Such a boom had not been expected.'[77]

In 1977 WWF stopped calling its local branches 'National Appeals' and began using the term 'National Organisations' (NOs). This illustrates the fact that some of the larger members of the WWF family had grown from fund-raising tools run by dedicated volunteers to environmental organisations in their own right which began to carry out campaigns with full-time staff.[78] This also applied to WWF International, whose staff was considerably increased in the course of the 1970s. As in all large families, each constituent part of WWF had its own characteristics. WWF International strengthened its business identity through new trustees, such as Anton Rupert or the Belgian Louis Franck, a retired merchant banker and commodity specialist who served on the board from 1975 to 1985 and who looked after the fund's assets at his own risk.[79] When problems arose, Morges began using management consultants, McKinsey offering their services free of charge for the first time in 1970.[80] The business identity of WWF International is reflected in the photographs it chose for its twentieth anniversary brochure. Each member of EXCO was shown in suit and tie, and only the portrait of Peter Scott made reference to his passion for nature. The leather strip of a pair of binoculars hanging around his neck is visible in his portrait. The representation of the 'management team' around the director general shown on the next page consisted of one blouse-wearing woman and eleven men in suit and tie working at office desks. Only the 'conservation division' of two were shown outdoors, with binoculars and without ties.[81]

The respectable image of WWF International, which was mirrored in the exclusive, upper-class membership of The 1001, contrasted starkly with the identity of some national organisations, which in the course of the 1970s began to embrace environmental activism, including Italy and the Netherlands, but starting in Switzerland. Hans Hüssy took the key decisions at Zurich-based WWF-Switzerland, first as secretary of the board and later as its president.[82] In 1968 he hired a first full-time director with the help of Luc Hoffmann, who raised the necessary funds by appealing to leading Swiss companies, especially in the pharmaceutical industry.[83] Instead of choosing an experienced businessman, as other WWF leaders would have done, Hans Hüssy selected a 25-year-old journalist, Roland Wiederkehr.[84] A member of the generation linked to the student protests marking the year in which he took up his job at WWF, Wiederkehr and a growing team of young peers had plenty of ideas about both fund-raising and environmental politics. As Swiss teachers were reluctant to let their children be used by yet another charity to raise funds through selling tokens, for example, Wiederkehr designed attractive wildlife stickers which children enthusiastically sold in their free time, initially during the Lake Nakuru campaign of 1972.[85] And apart from classical WWF themes centred on endangered species, WWF-Switzerland also began to address more complex environmental themes such as urbanisation, pollution, waste and consumption.[86] The covers of *PANDA*, the Swiss membership magazine, were thus decorated with either classical wildlife imagery or innovative environmental designs, including a Noah's ark stuck in a sea of waste or a scared human being faced with the nightmare of an urban traffic jam.[87]

The tone and content of Roland Wiederkehr's contribution to WWF's tenth anniversary report show the extent to which the Swiss differed from other national appeals, such as WWF-UK. One of the highlights of their report was praise for the 'tremendous effort' made in 1971 by the British 'anniversary girl', former Miss World Eva von Rueber-Staier: 'Introduced to the press in April, Eva [*sic*] appeared in numerous newspaper stories in the national and provincial press, on TV, radio, and in magazines, and travelled through Britain attending regional events.'[88] Roland Wiederkehr, instead of dwelling upon anecdotes of past achievements, wrote a call to action: 'WWF's activities to save endangered habitats and endangered species will not be of great value if man continues to destroy everything around. It's time to do both: to protect (and bring the money in to do so), and to try and change man's attitude towards nature – World Wildlife Fund Switzerland's activities in 1971 show both approaches.' Wiederkehr pointed out that his organisation, which had an income of over 3 million Swiss francs in the financial year 1971/72,[89] covered its administrative overheads entirely through the sale of merchandise and had gained a first political victory by collecting 360,000 signatures for a referendum against 'speculators' held responsible for a 'construction boom' in the Engadine valley, at the heart of which lies St Moritz, playground of the super-rich.[90]

Roland Wiederkehr, director of WWF-Switzerland from 1968 to 1987

What made WWF-Switzerland seem like a 'radical organisation' in the eyes of both the Swiss establishment and many a trustee of WWF International was, however, its opposition to nuclear energy.[91] As the historian Patrick Kupper has shown, for a variety of reasons, including the aesthetic desire to protect landscapes from cooling towers and a fundamental critique of the capitalist economy, nuclear energy, socially rather well accepted for many years, suddenly became a hotly debated topic dividing Swiss society from 1969 onwards.[92] The opposition centred on plans to construct a nuclear power plant in Kaiseraugst

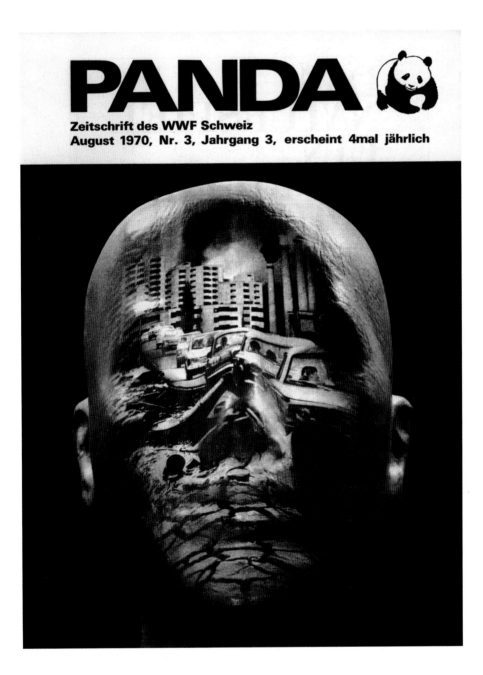

WWF-Switzerland membership magazine *PANDA*,
August 1970

near Basle, and WWF joined other environmental organisations in their anti-nuclear campaign in 1973.[93] While the construction site at Kaiseraugst was occupied by 15,000 protesters in 1975, three years later WWF-Switzerland and five other environmental organisations published an elaborate energy manifesto. It began with a statement: 'Our energy policy is a mirror of our relationship to the environment: ruthless exploitation or preservation of nature?' The 200-page book discussed nuclear energy in the context of all other forms of power, including coal, criticised for its potential of bringing about climate change, and argued strongly in favour of renewables, above all solar energy.[94]

While WWF-Switzerland reached the threshold of 100,000 members in 1980, making it the most important environmental organisation in the country,[95] its activism did not sit well with the board of WWF International, who regularly met on the shore of Lake Geneva. Swiss-born president of WWF-Canada, Sonja Bata, for instance, was irritated by questions 'about WWF-Switzerland's political involvement and I must confess that I was very surprised by some of the highly critical remarks not only by business people but also teenagers who seem to be confused about what WWF stands for. I was particularly upset when some German friends recently tried to draw comparisons between the work of the World Wildlife Fund and the Grüne Partei.'[96] In view of such criticism, Hans Hüssy, elected to the international board in 1980, summarised the Swiss position on nuclear energy in a seven-page memorandum to his fellow trustees in December 1981. Hüssy listed every environmental, technological and moral reason for supporting the anti-nuclear movement in an effort to explain why WWF-Switzerland had decided to engage in political controversy. Yet the man who had legally founded WWF in 1961 also insisted on the fact that the deed of foundation obliged the organisation 'to conserve nature in all its forms' and that WWF thus had to develop comprehensive policies which went beyond trying to save endangered species: 'WWF-Switzerland's concern with environmental problems is the performance of a duty in trying to seek the roots of problems instead of curing symptoms.' Hüssy ended by stating his 'credo' that WWF as a whole 'will not grow internationally either in figures or as a moral force by avoiding problems. In trying to achieve our objectives we should not be afraid of hurting vested interests. [...] It would be much too simple and mere alibi just to raise funds for the panda and elephant while lying over conservation issues at home by keeping polite silence on them. If we wished that to be our policy, we might just as well raise funds for dogs' and cats' homes.'[97] The board, however, remained largely unimpressed and refused to give up the 'neutral position on the question of nuclear energy' adopted by EXCO in 1979.[98] While Sonja Bata declared herself not to be 'a believer in confrontation' and thus objected to the 'activist part' played by WWF-Switzerland, Guy Mountfort told Hans Hüssy: 'I strongly believe that it is better to educate and to cooperate with industry and governments than to fight them.'[99]

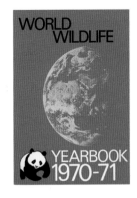

WWF International,
Yearbook 1970–71

The positions adopted by WWF-Switzerland were linked to a well-documented if as yet little-explained historical phenomenon which occurred around 1970, namely the fact that on both sides of the Atlantic environmentalism suddenly began to matter in public debates much more than ever before.[100] This '1970s watershed', a useful term coined by the environmental historian François Walter, did not go unnoticed outside of WWF-Switzerland; on the contrary.[101] In 1968 Prince Bernhard showed himself impressed by the 'remarkable awakening of public awareness in support of nature'[102] and WWF-US spoke of an 'explosion of conservation consciousness on a scale which hardly could have been anticipated' in 1971.[103] In the same year, the cover of WWF's annual report displayed a NASA photograph of Earth seen from space taken during one of the Apollo missions.[104] For the trustees of WWF, as for countless other naturalists, these photographs perfectly illustrated the fragility of life on Earth: 'This little jewel whirling around in the universe looks very small from out in space. And that thin, very thin – very fragile envelope of atmosphere is all there is – there ain't no more!'[105]

There were three main reasons why WWF International was reluctant to broaden the appeal of the fund by embracing environmental activism the way the Swiss did. On the one hand, many board members feared that tackling complex environmental issues went beyond the limited means of the fund. While in principle approving a proposal made by Guy Mountfort in 1969 that WWF should 'broaden its appeal and include in it traffic disturbance, noise, air, water and soil pollution, etc., as well as wildlife',[106] the board 'also recognised that practically speaking the enormous cost of anti-pollution projects made it very difficult for a private organisation to achieve noticeable results'.[107] On the other hand, the conservation successes obtained by lobbying governments, as in the case of Operation Tiger or in Canada, where the 'pragmatic approach' of WWF influenced legislation on the protection of seals, seemed to confirm that cooperation brought better results than confrontation.[108] Finally, in the course of the 1970s WWF learned that its traditional 'species approach' could also be used to address more complex ecological issues.[109] After the relative failure of a 1977 marine campaign entitled 'The Seas Must Live' centred on an ecosystem without making reference to a specific species or region,[110] WWF concluded: 'People can relate to an endangered whale or tiger more than to fundamental conservation problems such as deforestation or desertification. Consequently, these species serve as pegs on which to hang public interest, which can lead to broader public understanding of the basic conservation issues. Further, most species-oriented projects have a significant benefit to other components of the life support system.' To this day WWF – and other environmental organisations – regularly place charismatic megafauna, such as tigers, whales or pandas, which depend on a complex ecosystem for their survival, at the heart of their campaigns.[111]

The different positions adopted by WWF-Switzerland and WWF International in the nuclear energy debate show that twenty years after its foundation WWF was anything but a monolithic organisation with a top-down command structure. Despite the business identity adopted by its international board, WWF did not function like a multinational corporation such as Rothmans or Hoffmann-La Roche. Rather, there were many ways of being WWF. Each national organisation was largely autonomous, both in terms of fund-raising methods and environmental policy, and even those with a modest income were proud of their achievements – 'Small is Beautiful', declared a self-confident WWF-Finland at an international WWF meeting in 1981.[112] The diversity of the WWF family was not least due to the fact that each member had to operate within a specific cultural context which varied greatly even within western Europe. When, for example, WWF-Denmark reported at an international WWF meeting that it had successfully introduced collecting boxes for foreign coins at airports, an experience shared by Dutch, Austrian and Finnish delegates, WWF-Norway reported 'that they had tried it, but the box had been stolen twice'.[113]

Overleaf: Autumn view of the lakes of the Engadin valley. In 1971 WWF-Switzerland collected 360,000 signatures to protect this landscape from property speculators

Following page: WWF's Coral Triangle Initiative, begun in 2007, aims at conservation on a much larger scale, covering six million square kilometres of marine, coastal and small island ecosystems in Indonesia, the Philippines, East Timor, Papua New Guinea, the Solomon Islands and Malaysia. Ranger station surrounded by Tubbataha Reefs Natural Park. Palawan, Philippines, April 2009

WWF, the corporate world and European royalty

'There is no end to the moral judgements one is able to apply to donors of any charity.'

In the course of the twentieth century, and especially during the unprecedented economic boom following the Second World War, corporations began to use an ever greater share of the world's natural resources.[1] Any conservation organisation with a global agenda was thus faced with the question of how to deal with business and industry. According to Luc Hoffmann, the corporate policy adopted by WWF differed significantly from that of other environmental organisations. Instead of being 'antagonistic' the fund 'can cooperate with industry and commerce, even in areas where approaches do not match, and the business world perceives WWF as an equal partner'.[2] Given the business ideal of the founding fathers the choice of a cooperative attitude towards corporations is not surprising. Yet as the interests of companies geared towards making a profit and the goals of an environmental organisation trying to save life on Earth are not necessarily compatible, it is remarkable that this attitude should have worked out in the long run. An analysis of WWF's well-documented interaction with the oil industry can shed light on the complex way in which the fund's special relationship with the business world developed over time.

Unlike environmental organisations rooted in the protest movements of the late 1960s and founded after the '1970s watershed', notably Greenpeace, which originated in Vancouver around 1971 in opposition to US nuclear arms tests, the conservative, upper-class naturalists who founded WWF ten years earlier did not have a problem with approaching oil companies for funding.[3] While Greenpeace raised the funds for its first campaign through a rock concert and to this day refuses to accept money from corporations, WWF's earliest corporate sponsor was the petrochemical giant Royal Dutch/Shell.[4] In 1961 it gave WWF-UK the remarkable sum of £10,000.[5] The person responsible for this deal was Guy Mountfort. The advertising executive quickly had to learn that accepting money from a multinational was far from easy and straightforward. A precondition for Shell's gift to WWF-UK had been the fund's promise that no other national appeal might approach a Shell subsidiary in any other country. Mountfort told WWF's PR executive Ian MacPhail: 'Shell happen to be clients of mine in my business capacity and I would be embarrassed if there were any hitch in this, having given my personal assurance that we would respect the stipulations.'[6] It was probably because of a second personal link between a high-ranking WWF executive and Shell that the oil company gave up its one-off attitude towards the fund. Prince Bernhard was well acquainted with Shell's long-term director general, the Dutchman John Loudon, and it is most probably because of their friendship that Shell donated the services of the Dutch writer and advertising specialist Leonhard Huizinga to WWF-Netherlands when it was set up as the fourth national appeal in 1962.[7]

WWF's first corporate donor influenced the way in which the most important environmental debate of the early 1960s was led within the fund, namely the negative effects of agrochemicals on wildlife. After the Second World War Shell had invested heavily in chemical research, and by the 1950s possessed the exclusive rights to the 'drin family of chlorinated hydrocarbon pesticides. Thanks to a recent, primary-source-based company history, we know that these substances were 'by far the most profitable products of [Shell's] range of chemicals'.[8] When in 1962 pesticides such as Aldrin, Dieldrin and Endrin were among the agrochemicals criticised by Rachel Carson's environmental best-seller *Silent Spring*, Shell, together with the rest of the pesticides industry, 'reacted indignantly to the charges levelled by Carson's book'.[9] Their 'counter-attack' consisted of questioning the scientific credentials of the author, mobilising other scientists in defence of agrochemicals, and lobbying governments.[10] Based on their analysis of the Shell archives, the historians Stephen Howarth and Joost Jonker conclude that, in contrast to the progressive environmental policies adopted in other fields of activity, the company's attitude towards the toxicity of agrochemicals amounted to 'a stubborn policy of denial'.[11] Shell stopped selling the profitable 'drins only when the US and other governments began to ban them from the mid-1970s onwards.[12]

John Loudon, president of Royal Dutch/Shell from 1951 to 1965 and president of WWF International from 1977 to 1981

It was the Shell director John Loudon himself who in 1963 caused a lively debate about agrochemicals within WWF by writing a paper which Prince Bernhard distributed among board members.[13] In view of *Silent Spring* Loudon

Saving the World's Wildlife

summarised Shell's position on the 'drins and tried to divert WWF's attention away from them. He stressed the humanitarian usefulness of the substances, arguing that they helped to prevent famine, and asked the WWF board 'whether there might not be other more valuable fields of study for promoting human happiness & well-being than the present subject'.[14] Despite the generous support received from Shell, WWF's first vice-president Peter Scott did not hesitate to write an elaborate rebuttal of the Loudon paper. He began by pointing out that Rachel Carson's alarmist tone, which Loudon criticised, amounted to the same 'shock tactics' WWF had used in its first fund-raising campaigns. Scott went on to dissect every single argument brought forward by Loudon and identified industrial 'greed' and 'total disregard of the natural environment' as major threats to life on Earth. Nevertheless, Peter Scott urged WWF to adopt a 'realistic' stance. Instead of confrontation, his proposed recipe for change was to 'persuade the leaders of industry and public life that the philosophical case for giving high priority to the conservation of nature is not only as good but much better than the case for many other activities to which the resources of modern society are unquestioningly devoted'.[15]

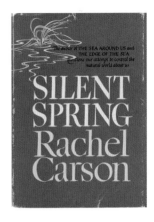

Rachel Carson, *Silent Spring*, Houghton Mifflin, Boston, 1962

Although Peter Scott wanted WWF 'to take its stance in the controversy', a majority of trustees preferred to delegate the matter to IUCN.[16] The scientists were asked for 'views and comment', while WWF decided to reconsider the question 'at a later date'.[17] It is unlikely that agrochemicals were discussed again at board level as subsequent board minutes are silent on the issue. Thus while in 1961 both the Morges Manifesto and WWF's first brochure had discussed the environmental problems caused by agrochemicals, in the wake of the publication of Rachel Carson's book one year later WWF's proximity to its first corporate donor induced the fund to keep quiet about *Silent Spring*. It was left to the British Nature Conservancy under Max Nicholson – who by then was no longer actively involved with WWF – to issue a report urging the UK government to ban agrochemicals, including those produced by Shell, in 1963.[18]

WWF's link to Shell intensified in 1966 when John Loudon, who had retired as president of the company the year before but remained chairman of the Shell board for another eleven years, was persuaded by Prince Bernhard to become a trustee of WWF International.[19] For almost two decades thereafter the cautiousness adopted in the debate about agrochemicals marked WWF's cooperative approach to the oil industry. While in 1971 EXCO decided to regard the 'highly controversial question' of an oil pipeline in Alaska 'as a purely American issue, leaving it to the WWF-United States to make a statement of their own if it felt advisable',[20] in the wake of the 1967 *Torrey Canyon* disaster, the first ever shipwreck of a supertanker affecting some two hundred miles of coastline in Britain and France and killing about 15,000 seabirds, WWF International decided not to endorse a resolution adopted by IUCN 'as this might compromise further fund-raising efforts and approaches to certain industries, particularly in the United States'.[21] The fund's reaction to the oil spill was thus confined to a 'seabird appeal' organised by its British branch, which raised more than £5,000, mostly used 'for the rescue, cleaning, translocation and rehabilitation of affected birds'.[22] The organisation's problematic closeness to the oil industry was underlined by the fact that John Loudon served as president of WWF International from 1977 to 1981.

WWF's special relationship to the business world made it relatively easy for critics to accuse the fund of being biased in favour of its donors. The first time this kind of criticism was noted by WWF executives was when the British satirical magazine *Private Eye* published an article entitled 'Lowlife fund' in August 1980.[23] Like most contributions to the magazine, which specialised in attacks on the establishment, the article on WWF was published anonymously and contained well-researched but polemically interpreted facts. *Private Eye* claimed that some 'supporters and officials in the WWF [...] are afraid of losing their share of public donations' because 'militants like Friends of the Earth and Greenpeace [...] have seized the initiative in wildlife conservation'. The magazine blamed WWF's cooperative approach to industry, which differed markedly from the confrontational activism of their left-wing competitors, for the perceived loss of donor goodwill, and claimed that this mistaken policy was due to the support the fund was receiving from The 1001. Based on a 'highly confidential' membership list of 1978, *Private Eye*'s claim was that, apart from prominent businessmen active in environmentally sensitive areas such as the oil, chemical or mining industry, The 1001 also comprised individuals who had gone bankrupt, were charged with a crime or showed other 'anomalies' deemed incompatible with the aims of the fund. The American 'mega-millionaire' Daniel K. Ludwig, for instance, whose fortune was in part based on building supertankers, was charged with 'devastating a large slice of the Brazilian rain forest', and Zaire's President Mobutu was accused of having 'presided over one of the greatest slaughters of elephants in Africa'.[24]

While WWF International decided 'not to respond'[25] to the article, WWF-UK prepared answers for worried supporters who contacted them in view of the 'attacks [...] embedded in a piece of thoroughly unpleasant and inaccurate journalism'.[26] In its replies the British national organisation (NO) pointed out that WWF was raising more money than ever before and that the organisation was working 'closely' with Greenpeace, Friends of the Earth 'and several other conservation organisations', notably on whaling, a cooperation which was largely due to the efforts of Peter Scott.[27] About the background of the money received from The 1001, WWF-UK noted: 'It is certainly true that some "1001" club members made their money in ways we'd not approve. But by making their donations they are expressing a commitment to the cause of conservation. There is no end to the moral judgements one is able to apply to donors of any charity.'[28] Two years later WWF International confirmed this attitude. At an EXCO meeting the British advertising executive David Ogilvy, acting as a consultant to the fund, enquired 'whether WWF would assess the environmental responsibility of each corporation, and refuse its donation if it was considered irresponsible'. EXCO discussed 'the concept of refusing donations from "irresponsible" companies and agreed that it would be difficult, if not impossible, to make such judgements since every business polluted the environment to some extent'. After repeating the cooperative approach to companies aimed at 'converting them to the conservation cause', the main governing body of WWF closed the subject on an ambivalent note: 'It was observed that no church refused donations from sinners. On the other hand, the danger of companies trying to buy respectability, while continuing to behave irresponsibly, was recognised.'[29]

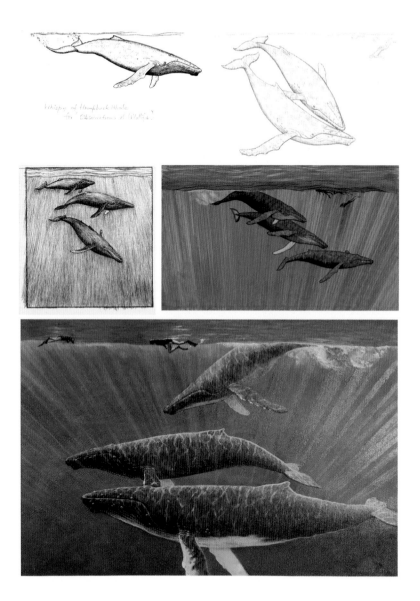

In the summer of 1976 the proximity of two key WWF board members to the business world caused the organisation a great deal of negative publicity. While the Seveso disaster in Italy put WWF's executive vice-president Luc Hoffmann under considerable pressure to resign, the Lockheed scandal eventually forced Prince Bernhard to step down as president of WWF International. The chemical plant responsible for the dioxin contamination in the northern Italian town of Seveso near Milan on 10 July 1976, which damaged the health of hundreds of people and caused widespread death in wildlife, belonged to Hoffmann-La Roche. Because of terrible crisis management on the part of both the Italian authorities and the Swiss owners of the factory, who eventually paid damages of 200 million Swiss francs, the Seveso accident turned into one of the most publicised industrial disasters of the twentieth century.[30] WWF-Italy, at least as radical as WWF-Switzerland, repeatedly called for the resignation of Luc Hoffmann, who while not being personally involved in running the family business was a major shareholder of Hoffmann-La Roche.[31] Supported by a unanimous EXCO decision asking him to stay, Hoffmann decided not to resign. In a letter to the president of WWF-Italy he wrote almost a year after the accident: 'For my part, I have asked myself whether I should resign, despite the decision of the committee.' Luc Hoffmann professed to understand the anger of the general public but blamed the media for having 'deliberately distorted the truth', making it 'difficult for the Italian public to inform itself objectively' – a view shared by the leading Swiss business newspaper, the *Neue Zürcher Zeitung*.[32] As a judicial inquiry into the employees personally responsible for the accident was under way, and believing that his resignation would only 'intensify the attacks' on WWF, Hoffmann decided to stay: 'If one does not feel guilty, better than losing one's head is to let the storm pass.'[33]

The Lockheed scandal involving Prince Bernhard and several other public figures in Europe and Asia began in 1975 when the US Senate initiated an inquiry into illegal payments made by the American aircraft manufacturer in connection

Peter Scott, humpback whales, no date. In 1979 Scott swam with humpback whales off the Hawaiian island of Maui – 'probably the most exciting natural history experience of my life'

with foreign government deals.[34] When the US inquiry brought forward evidence that Lockheed had also paid bribes in the Netherlands and mentioned Prince Bernhard, the Dutch government set up an inquiry commission of its own. Their 240-page report was published in August 1976 and concluded, among other things, that Bernhard, for years an active lobbyist for Dutch industry and commerce, had asked Lockheed in writing for a commission of one million dollars to be handed over to WWF if the Dutch government were to buy a fleet of Lockheed aircraft.[35] Widely reported by the international press, the report forced

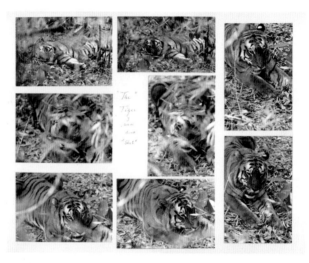

Extract from Prince Bernhard's photo album documenting a trip to India in 1976. In the course of his presidency of WWF, the prince gave up hunting overseas and began to take pictures instead

Prince Bernhard to give up all his state and business posts with immediate effect, including his job as inspector-general of the Dutch army.[36]

Initially Bernhard wanted to remain president of WWF International but was forced to step down at the end of 1976 because EXCO wanted him to go. This can be deduced from a letter by Peter Scott to the prince written two and a half weeks after the publication of the Dutch government report. As the incriminating correspondence with Lockheed was the key evidence against the prince, Peter Scott began by saying that 'however ill-advised certain letters may have been, I cannot

Saving the World's Wildlife

and do not believe you have done anything dishonourable or wicked'. While this was also 'the attitude of all the members of EXCO', Scott had the difficult task of telling Prince Bernhard that 'because of the publicity, and the nature of WWF as a fund-raising organisation, all of us felt that no other course of action was available to you or to us. That *had* to be our reply.'[37] As the board of WWF-Netherlands had unanimously decided to 'continue with PB as President',[38] Scott concluded: 'We are all acutely aware of the tremendous work you have done for conservation and for the Fund in the short period of its existence, and nothing can ever take away those great achievements, nor our gratitude to you for them. I am convinced that public attitudes will greatly improve with time, and in the meanwhile your Presidency of the Netherlands Appeal will provide the continuing link.'[39]

According to Niels Halbertsma, director of WWF-Netherlands from 1974 to 1990, the Dutch NO suffered only 'a minimal loss of donors on account of the Lockheed affair', and the 1977 'Geef on de Natuur' campaign centred on the scandal-ridden prince was very successful.[40] While WWF International thus appears to have overestimated the negative effects of the Lockheed affair on Prince Bernhard's fund-raising capacity, his resignation threw WWF into a grave leadership crisis as no precautions had been taken for a sudden departure of a president on whom much of the publicity and fund-raising effort had been centred. Apart from being the *raison d'être* of The 1001, Prince Bernhard was also at the heart of an elaborate honours system which WWF, following a practice employed by all modern monarchies, had introduced for elite bonding in the years prior to his resignation.[41]

The WWF honours system included Gold Medals awarded to outstanding contemporary conservationists from 1970 onwards and a Roll of Honour initiated in 1973 to commemorate deceased champions of environmentalism. One of the first names on the roll was Rachel Carson, who had died shortly after the publication of *Silent Spring* in 1962,[42] while in line with WWF's business identity the real gold used for the Gold Medal was donated by the South African chamber of commerce and came together with a Rolex watch.[43] The first three recipients of this valuable gift were Bernhard Grzimek, Julian Huxley and the Belgian director of the Congolese national parks, Jacques Verschuren. The latter was praised for his role in the transition of the Congo to post-colonial rule because he had 'heroically stayed on as the only European in the Albert National Park, when order collapsed in the Kivu and the province passed into turmoil for long periods'.[44] The most important decoration linked to WWF was, however, the Order of the Golden Ark. Created by Prince Bernhard in 1971, the three-graded

Order of the Golden Ark founded by Prince Bernhard in 1971

Dutch order was awarded 'in recognition of special service to the conservation of the world's flora and fauna'.[45] While the decoration was given out at Bernhard's 'sole discretion', a confidential agreement drawn up by Peter Scott made individuals eligible for it if they had given WWF 'donations in excess of $100,000 in cash or in kind'.[46] The Order of the Golden Ark could therefore be used to reward both key volunteer supporters such as Max Nicholson or Julian Huxley and major donors, among them the American philanthropist Laurance Spelman Rockefeller.[47]

By the time Prince Bernhard was forced to resign as president of WWF International the organisation had unmistakably acquired a number of symbolic elements characteristic of a modern constitutional monarchy. Not only was the persona of Bernhard, like that of a sovereign in any monarchy, one of the most important means of collective WWF identification. Royal patronage and symbolism were also the rule in all NOs in countries with a crowned head of state. A picture taken during a WWF event in London in 1970 and proudly reproduced in the annual report showed 'Prince Henrik of Denmark, Prince William of Gloucester, Crown Prince Harald and Princess Sonja of Norway, King Constantine of Greece, the Duke of Edinburgh, and the Grand Duke of Luxembourg', who were patrons of WWF in one way or another, as attentive listeners in the front row of the conference hall.[48] In former monarchies such as Germany, Italy or Austria the local WWF board tended to have a strong aristocratic note, and even in republican Switzerland Hans Hüssy had initially opted for princely support – Henry of Liechtenstein was a founding patron of WWF-Switzerland.[49] In view of the Lockheed scandal WWF-Germany was thus certainly not the only member of the royally inclined WWF family fearing 'that there is no one who can replace Prince Bernhard and the many advantages he is able to bring to the WWF'.[50]

Saving the World's Wildlife

The former Shell boss John Loudon succeeded his 'old friend' Prince Bernhard to the presidency of WWF in 1977.[51] Unlike his royal predecessor, the businessman failed to leave a lasting mark on the organisation he headed for four years. Minutes of board and Executive Council meetings contain no statements which go beyond his role as chairman, and it is probably no coincidence that the only substantial document of Loudon's presidency which surfaced in the course of this research is a report about finding a suitable – and royal – successor.[52] As we shall see below, Prince Philip, who became president of WWF in 1981, was not only to serve a much longer term than John Loudon, but was also to play at least as active a role as the first royal president of the fund. At a ceremony held in London's Wembley Stadium coinciding with the celebrations of WWF's twentieth anniversary, John Loudon handed over the presidency to the Duke of Edinburgh. The 76-year-old Dutchman left the organisation hoping 'that, during his time in office, he had shown that oil-men, like hunters, could be good conservationists'.[53]

The changes at presidential level were accompanied by changes at the international secretariat. Because of his impressive fund-raising achievement with The 1001, and following a recommendation by McKinsey, the international board appointed Charles de Haes director general jointly with Fritz Vollmar in 1975.[54] De Haes's salary was no longer paid by Anton Rupert, whose company he ceased to work for, but by a group of sponsors, among them Luc Hoffmann.[55] While de Haes was responsible for fund-raising and public relations, Vollmar was in charge of conservation, education and representing the fund abroad.[56] The two men did not, however, form the 'harmonious and effective team' as which they were announced by Luc Hoffmann.[57] Looking back, the former journalist Fritz Vollmar, who had completely espoused the business identity of WWF, remembers with consternation that 'the creation of such a split leadership for the operational management of WWF was contrary to all principles of organisational science and the leadership handbooks and was sooner or later doomed to failure'. Vollmar particularly objected to the increasing importance given to fund-raising at the expense of environmental education. In 1977 he brought the 'double-headed monster' to an end and became director general of the World Scout Foundation in Geneva.[58] Vollmar's resignation brought him 'up to 200 thank-you and appreciation letters from all over the world, and in particular from all WWF national appeals'.[59]

Upon becoming the only director general of WWF in 1977, Charles de Haes presented EXCO with an ambitious plan for the future: 'One private international conservation organisation, raising money from the general public to achieve conservation, will sooner or later come to be recognised as the pre-eminent organisation in this field. This organisation could be WWF.'[60] While de Haes admitted 'that the task of re-organising the WWF Headquarters and of getting the 26 National Organisations to improve their performance was a gigantic one', the 39-year-old left EXCO with no doubt that he was the man for the job.[61] His fourteen-page 'strategic considerations' amounted to an elaborate 'management plan'. Its essence was to strengthen the international secretariat by hiring new staff and to streamline national organisations in order to raise more money. According to de Haes, who in the course of setting up The 1001 had visited all

national branches of WWF, many NOs 'have tended "to go their own way"' and often 'confused activity with achievement'. Although the new director general knew that 'WWF does not control its N.O.'s in the sense that a company controls its subsidiaries', he believed that with professional management and marketing experts at the centre, NO performance could greatly improve. The marketing executive de Haes also insisted that a common policy on 'controversial conservation issues' had to be adopted by the entire WWF family: 'It is clear that organisations using the same name and symbol cannot take conflicting stands on identical issues.' Positions should be agreed within a 'global strategy [...] from which N.O.'s may not deviate'.[62]

A cornerstone of the de Haes plan was to move the secretariat to a new location. While Fritz Vollmar had worked for years with minimal staff in Morges, occupying rooms in a romantic villa that used to be a hotel, de Haes needed not only more space for his growing team but also a different environment. He told EXCO: 'Morges is really a most stultifying place for any dynamic, *marketing-type* person. It lacks the stimulus of a competitive, fast moving, new-ideas environment and the sooner we can get within really easy reach of Geneva the better.'[63] A new building housing WWF and IUCN had been planned for years thanks to a 1970 donation of 10 million Swiss francs by the German entrepreneur Helmut Horten. He had moved to Switzerland in 1968 making a lump-sum tax deal which allowed him to make maximum profit when selling the department stores he owned in Germany, a fact deplored by the German left.[64] According to Luc Hoffmann, Horten wanted to 'show his gratitude to Switzerland', which in turn led Horten's banker, the WWF trustee Samuel Schweizer, to suggest the donation of a building for WWF and IUCN.[65] Initially, the plan was to buy the eighteenth-century Château de Prangins, which today belongs to the Swiss National Museum, but in 1971 a property of 30,000 square metres was bought at a prime location in Geneva adjacent to both the lake and the botanical garden.[66]

WWF board of trustees, Slimbridge, June 1978. From left to right: Syed Babar Ali, David Munro, David Ogilvy, Luc Hoffmann, Charles de Haes, John Loudon, Peter Scott, Louis Franck, Prince Bernhard

Because of a series of planning mistakes, squabbles with IUCN and fierce opposition by WWF-Switzerland, raising moral objections to taking money from Horten, more than eight years after the donation no new headquarters were in sight. While Hans Hüssy believed Horten to be an outright 'Nazi' because he had begun amassing his fortune in the 1930s by buying department stores from hard-pressed Jewish owners, the German millionaire himself became increasingly irritated with the lack of progress the headquarters project was making and the criticism about his Swiss tax deal.[67] Eventually Horten 'asked for his money back, promising that he would consider helping WWF [...] if it came up with a firm proposal which could rapidly be implemented'.[68] In 1979 Charles de Haes found a suitable office block in Gland near Geneva, but because of objections by the Swiss Bank Corporation in charge of administrating the Horten donation he could not go ahead with the purchase. Prince Philip commented: 'Your accommodation problems are becoming rather like a long-running soap opera.

"Will the World Wildlife Fund get Gland or will the Swiss Bank Corporation pull out? Tune in next week for the next thrilling instalment!"' [69] One month

later the building was bought and Prince Philip cabled to Charles de Haes: 'Splendid news. Delighted last act cliff hanger is so satisfactory.' [70]

WWF headquarters, Gland, Switzerland, 1980

Saving the World's Wildlife

WWF-UK, panda collection box, c. 1980

Overleaf: Dunes and an acacia tree, Temet, Northern Aïr,
Niger. In the 1980s WWF became involved in firewood
projects in the drought-ridden Sahel

Broadening the scope

'We have a clear responsibility for all life on this planet
both for its own sake as well as our own.'

In 1981, the year in which WWF celebrated its twentieth anniversary, the organisation launched its first-ever panda campaign. The idea originated with Nancy Nash, a Hong-Kong-based public relations expert. During a consulting assignment at WWF International in Switzerland she asked the obvious question: 'Since you have the panda as a symbol, why aren't you in touch with China about a panda study?'[1] Thanks to Nash's excellent connections, WWF was the first Western NGO to be invited to China in 1979, and a delegation headed by Peter Scott and Charles de Haes travelled to Peking. They were delighted to learn that China would join IUCN and was ready to conclude a series of international environmental treaties.[2] On a subsequent trip to China undertaken by Peter Scott alone, the Chinese authorities came up with the idea of a research and conservation centre in the Wolong Panda Reserve in Sichuan – the same area in which Walther Stötzner had first seen an Ailuropoda – provided that WWF 'would contribute 50 per cent of the cost, estimated at US$2 million'.[3]

Although Peter Scott had no mandate to allocate funds of this magnitude – in 1979 the entire WWF family spent a total of $3.8 million – he promised the Chinese finance for the research centre. Niels Halbertsma of WWF-Netherlands remembers: 'He came back full of enthusiasm and then said. "I have been a naughty boy: I promised them one million dollars ..." That is why we suddenly had to go into the Panda campaign!'[4] While EXCO was worried about the open-endedness of the agreement and wanted to limit the financial liabilities of the project, from a conservation point of view the Chinese plan to build an expensive research centre with breeding facilities looked like a prestige site to show off with and not necessarily the best way to save the panda.[5] Peter Scott readily admitted that the main reason for his promise was that the panda had 'for almost 20 years, been the symbol of WWF'. He also argued that there 'was a real chance of the WWF/China initiative collapsing altogether' unless a centre was built and that Charles de Haes had told him on the phone that he did not doubt that the million could be raised 'and probably twice as much'.[6]

Despite WWF's special relationship with the animal of its logo, the financial results of the panda campaign, carried through by all national organisations bar the US, were 'rather disappointing'.[7] While the million pledged to the Chinese could eventually be raised, in 1983 WWF decided to abandon its network-wide annual campaigns, which had started with Project Tiger in 1972.[8] The end of the 'integrated campaigns' was not only due to the relative failure of the panda campaign but also reflected the fact that by the early 1980s WWF International found it increasingly difficult to convince national organisations to go along with decisions taken at Gland. This problem was linked to an intensifying internal debate about broadening the scope of the fund. While as early as 1972 EXCO had agreed that 'WWF objectives should remain flexible, admitting a general trend from the narrower Wildlife issue to a broader environmental approach',[9] the negative reaction of the board to the nuclear-power debate initiated by WWF-Switzerland shows that at the beginning of the 1980s it was far from clear what this should mean in practice. The only obvious conclusion was that wildlife conservation of the panda-project type, focusing on the construction of concrete buildings with expensive equipment, was not the way forward. In the first ten years of its existence only two captive-bred pandas were born at the Wolong research station.[10]

The most influential text highlighting the need to broaden the scope of WWF came from Max Nicholson. At a conference organised by WWF-UK marking the twentieth anniversary of the fund, its key architect argued that most conservation efforts undertaken so far had been quite futile. According to Nicholson they had failed to address three major causes rendering species endangered, namely development, energy and population growth: 'So here we are, well justified in congratulating ourselves on the vast and successful efforts we have made to save tigers and rhinoceroses, yet still hesitating to take on the three Nasty Giants which are undermining the future of life on earth, for us as well as animals. These are the giants of Reckless and Harmful Technological Development, Profligate Waste of the world's readily available energy reserves and Senseless Multiplication like crazy rabbits. The sad truth is that someone will have to tackle those three big nasties, and if it isn't to be us, who will?'[11]

Guy Mountfort repeated Nicholson's arguments at the next board meeting of WWF International, which caused 'a lively discussion'.[12] In the same year, Peter Scott remarked at an EXCO meeting that the success of WWF-Switzerland 'probably owed much of its success to its uncompromising attitude in tackling what it perceived to be the causes of environmental problems, not just the symptoms'.[13] In 1982 Luc Hoffmann again made reference to the Nicholson lecture and emphasised to EXCO the need to broaden the scope of the fund.[14] As a result the organisation's most important governing body noted 'that it was pointless to treat symptoms while ignoring the disease, and that WWF must therefore address the root causes which threatened the survival of nature, and hence of man'.[15]

Despite this decision, the best way to address the root causes of environmental problems remained very much disputed. National organisations with a broad membership base such as WWF-Switzerland and WWF-Netherlands were proud of their 'grass-roots support' and emphasised 'that their members saw WWF not simply as a fund-raising organisation but rather as an environmental movement'.[16] They and others had no problem cooperating with Greenpeace, whose trademark was seaborne protests against nuclear arms and whaling. WWF-Netherlands, for example, in 1978, gave Greenpeace a grant for its first and most famous vessel, the *Rainbow Warrior*,[17] while in 1980 Peter Scott, the WWF representative at the International Whaling Commission, persuaded Gland to co-sponsor a Washington-based secretariat coordinating efforts for a whaling moratorium together with Greenpeace.[18] Yet while EXCO knew that 'most NOs felt it was entirely appropriate to work with Greenpeace, and to fund the organisation for specific, approved projects', the international board did not approve of the methods and style employed by Greenpeace.[19] While Sonja Bata had had negative experiences with the organisation in Canada, Anton Rupert was especially outspoken on the subject.[20] In 1986 he declared: 'Our chief task remains to raise more money. Activist issues should therefore be raised in other fora.'[21] Three years later Anton Rupert objected to WWF 'becoming a broader "Greenpeace" style organization'.[22]

In early January 1982 key representatives of WWF-UK, WWF-Netherlands and WWF-Switzerland met at Hans Hüssy's Zurich office and 'decided that there

Max Nicholson, birdwatching at the seaside

Wolong Panda Reserve, Sichuan Province, China

Overleaf: Giant panda (*Ailuropoda melanoleuca*), Wolong
Panda Reserve, Sichuan Province, China

Giant panda (*Ailuropoda melanoleuca*), Wolong Panda
Reserve, Sichuan Province, China

had to be a revolution'.[23] All three NOs were in favour of taking up uncompromising environmentalist positions and were disappointed with the cautious stance adopted by WWF International. While Hans Hüssy was just being rebuffed by the international board for his paper on nuclear energy, Niels Halbertsma, director general of WWF-Netherlands, objected to the fact that Anton Rupert had bullied him into accepting a WWF agreement with Fiat about a car called Panda in 1980: 'In Holland we had never wanted to make a deal with a car company because this did not fit with our image of nature conservation.'[24] Sir Arthur Norman, chairman of WWF-UK, 'wanted to create a worldwide organisation which would have the support and influence of the equivalent of the Red Cross movement – no holds barred!'[25]

The criticism focused on the new director general, Charles de Haes. According to Claude Martin, in 1982 one of the directors of WWF-Switzerland, the Zurich meeting was 'primarily motivated by the dissatisfaction with Charles de Haes' management style, which was considered untransparent', a view shared by Niels Halbertsma and George Medley of WWF-UK.[26] The latter remembers that the director general 'concentrated all his energies on the International Trustees, and in particular, the Chairman [Prince Philip] and ignored the very real concerns of NOs'.[27] As all three members of the WWF family had been highly successful fund-raisers even before the advent of the marketing expert Charles de Haes, they also resented his performance-enhancing drive. Niels Halbertsma: 'Gland attracted fund-raisers, PR people, special assistants etc. who were presented as "the solution" but normally disappeared after one or two years. [...] How many have I seen coming and going!'[28] Yet despite all the anger voiced at the Zurich meeting, it ended without a clear plan, and only WWF-Switzerland appears to have made legal preparations to leave WWF if necessary by creating a back-up foundation.[29] When Gland found out about the 'conspirative notion' of the meeting, it reacted by removing the perceived ringleader from the international board.[30] Sir Arthur Norman: 'Charles thought that I was a threat to his position and persuaded Prince Philip to get me to resign. I resumed the chairmanship of WWF-UK as if nothing had happened.'[31]

When Prince Philip was first approached by Peter Scott about taking over from John Loudon, the prince underlined that he 'would not like to be a purely nominal President' and surprised the board by suggesting a series of reforms even before being officially elected in 1981.[32] This set the tone for a presidency which was marked by Prince Philip's active involvement in the affairs of the fund. At WWF meetings he always stated his opinions even if they clashed with the views of others. Climate change, first discussed at board level in 1989, for instance, was an issue the prince repeatedly called a 'waste of time', not because he thought it did not exist but because he was convinced that WWF lacked both the expertise and the resources to deal with it.[33]

Like his royal predecessor from the Netherlands, Prince Philip was an expert fund-raiser and a brilliant WWF ambassador, travelling the world without ever asking for a salary. Given the hiatus of the Loudon years, his universally known royal persona was very much appreciated. A first round of trips included visits to Germany, Austria, Italy, Egypt, Oman, Pakistan and India, and led EXCO to note 'that the success of the tour in publicity, fund-raising and conservation terms had been truly remarkable'.[34] In his first presidential message, like all of his speeches written by the prince himself, WWF's third president explained: 'We [...] have a clear responsibility for all life on this planet both for its sake as well as for our own.' Despite being aware of the 'immense task' ahead, Philip was confident that 'we can make a lasting contribution to the survival of life on earth'.[35]

The Duke of Edinburgh found an ideal partner in Charles de Haes, whose declared aim was to turn WWF into the 'pre-eminent' conservation organisation.[36] After initial irritation caused by a *Private Eye* article criticising the director general for his provenance from Rupert's business empire – it made the palace wonder whether 'de Haes is someone [Prince Philip] can trust and work with' – the two men formed a great team.[37] In 1982 Luc Hoffmann wrote to the Duke of Edinburgh: 'I am so glad you feel that Charles de Haes is doing a good job. I feel the same way but he gets sometimes carried away by urgent problems and does then not properly balance his priorities. This results generally in neglecting major new initiatives which we so urgently need. I believe we can help him overcome this difficulty by insisting on a carefully monitored annual management plan which provides the background against which a balanced approach to the main priorities can be judged.'[38]

In the wake of the crisis caused by the 1982 meeting of dissatisfied NOs in Zurich, WWF International initiated a series of reforms to appease national organisations, giving major NOs a seat on committees dealing with programme and finance and creating an Advisory Council where representatives from all national organisations could voice their opinion. These changes, however, went hand in hand with reducing membership of the international board, a cornerstone of the reforms initiated by Prince Philip to address what he identified as the 'structural problems' of WWF.[39] As the board had become too large to be efficient, not least because of the inclusion of women, personalities from the Third World as well as major donors such as Helmut Horten, Prince Philip wanted a smaller and more effective governing body whose members were 'chosen for their ability to assist with the management of WWF, and not for their wealth, influence, etc.'.[40] In a letter to his predecessor, John Loudon, Prince Philip sketched out the bottom line of the reforms that were to be implemented in 1982: 'The important point is to give the National Organisations some opportunity to express their opinions while retaining the power of the Board to select Trustees.'[41]

Charles de Haes and Prince Philip, president of WWF International from 1981 to 1996

While this led to the creation of Annual Conferences during which 'all NOs could meet together and discuss policy', key decisions continued to be made mostly within EXCO.[42] Like the board, it was reduced in size and, apart from the president and the director general, who became a full member in 1985, contained only four more trustees, among them almost all the time Anton Rupert and Luc Hoffmann.[43]

Under Charles de Haes WWF slowly began to transform itself from a fundraising agency into an environmental organisation in its own right. Irritated by the fact that environmentalists criticised WWF for its lack of scientific expertise in conservation matters, in 1978 de Haes hired a first staff ecologist to supplement the services rendered to the organisation by Luc Hoffmann. De Haes chose the American biologist Lee Talbot, who had previously been among the most severe critics of WWF, thinking: 'It's better to have the skunk in the tent pissing out, than outside the tent pissing in.'[44] Owing largely to the input provided by Lee Talbot, WWF was able to provide more than just financial help to the World Conservation Strategy worked out by IUCN and the United Nation's Environment Programme (UNEP). Launched in 1980, the strategy put the concept of sustainable development at the heart of conservation efforts. The environmental historian John McCormick notes that this innovative paper marked 'a shift from the traditional focus on cure rather than prevention – away from a concentration on wildlife preservation toward a concern for the wider pressures affecting the natural environment – and despite many omissions, it confirmed a growing belief that the assimilation of aims of both conservation and development was a key to a sustainable society'. The new approach was particularly relevant in the Third World, where traditional conser-

Launch of the World Conservation Strategy with representatives of IUCN, WWF and UNEP, Brussels, 1980

vation programmes such as fenced-in national parks had often been at odds with the need for economic and social development in view of rapid population growth and urbanisation.[45]

The fact that Charles de Haes began to build up the conservation skills of WWF inevitably led to frictions with IUCN, on which the fund had previously relied for scientific expertise. This eventually culminated in WWF creating a Project Management Department, taking over all field projects previously managed by the union in 1985.[46] The union's financial dependence on WWF, however, and the cultural differences between the two organisations, also contributed to the growing tensions. While the fund became increasingly affluent (in 1981 Charles de Haes announced that WWF had raised more money in the first four years of his directorship than in the previous sixteen years of its existence), the union stumbled from one financial crisis to the next and several times had to be saved from bankruptcy by WWF.[47] The fund resented the union's perceived negligence in financial matters, the key theme again being that the scientists of IUCN were not 'businesslike' enough.[48] IUCN staff, on the other hand, often overestimated the wealth of WWF and muttered that the fund had, after all, been created to finance the union.[49]

In an atmosphere of mutual distrust, living under the same roof in Gland became increasingly difficult. The situation did not improve when, because of the limitations of space, IUCN's director general, Kenton Miller, moved his office to a red-painted building next door – in Gland jargon it immediately became 'The Kremlin' as opposed to 'The White House' of Charles de Haes.[50] In 1986, Prince Philip informed the WWF board that in the five years of his presidency countless initiatives to improve the relationship with IUCN, including McKinsey studies and the introduction of joint accounts, had come to naught. Sonja Bata added 'that some of these problems had been discussed when she joined the Board fifteen years ago, and emphasized the need to look at innovative solutions'.[51] Having to decide between a complete merger, continued cohabitation or a neat separation, WWF opted for the latter. IUCN moved to a new building in 1992, but a nasty divorce could be avoided, not least because Charles de Haes and the union's new director general, Martin Holdgate, who took up his job in September 1987, 'got on well together'.[52]

One of the keynotes of Charles de Haes's term as director general was marketing. Acutely aware of the value of trademarks because of his experience of working for Rupert's empire of brands, de Haes told EXCO in 1979 'that the greatest care should be taken to protect the integrity of WWF's trademark' and got their approval to examine ways to strengthen Gland's legal hold over NOs in this matter.[53] A particular irritant to de Haes was that while most national organisations had a formal agreement with WWF International regulating the use of the trademark and the way in which the money raised was to be spent, with WWF-US there only was a 'gentlemen's agreement' drawn up in 1962.[54] Concluded at the time in order to get the US appeal tax exemption, the agreement left the Americans more freedom than other NOs to decide what to do with the money they raised. It also gave them a claim to the trademark, a key legal asset which the founders of WWF had forgotten to think about and which had only been registered country by country in 1964.[55] In 1982, the trademark issue was discussed for the first time at board level with the president of WWF-US, the lawyer Russell Train, a founding trustee of WWF-US who had been directly involved in setting up the original gentlemen's agreement. Train explained that 'the ownership of the trademark in the US was a question that would need to be decided by the WWF-US Board'. Prince Philip replied that 'if there were one or two countries where WWF International did not own the panda trademark, this could undermine the international structure of WWF'. Although Russell Train professed 'that WWF-US would not wish to do that', the trademark question was to remain unsolved for another decade.[56]

Charles de Haes also insisted on a uniform global appearance of WWF as a brand. This especially pertained to the use of the logo, where many family members had indeed gone 'their own way' in the past.[57] Since 1980 Gland had used a streamlined version of the original logo which did without the rippled outlines of the animal's coat.[58] Individual NOs, however, used the panda in all sorts of variations. The youth club of WWF-Denmark had a double panda as its logo, the Finnish Ailuropoda had a teardrop in the eye and elsewhere the panda appeared under an umbrella, reading a book or together with a cub.[59] WWF-US had even registered its own streamlined version of the original Watterson/Scott design as a trademark and was using it both at home and for projects supported in Latin America. As a uniform brand was a top priority for Charles de Haes, he was pleased to inform the international board in 1982 that WWF-US would henceforth use the Gland version abroad.[60] In order to achieve a truly global brand presence de Haes convinced the San Francisco-based design consultancy Landor & Associates, founded in 1941 by the branding pioneer Walter Landor, to donate their services for a new logo to 'provide a new and uniform identity for the WWF family'.[61]

The new logo was meant to fulfil a series of 'identity requirements' and 'design objectives'. While it had to be 'commercially attractive and marketable', it also had to be 'sufficiently close' to both the Gland and the US version 'so that existing trademark registrations and copyright user rights are not jeopardized'. It had to be flexible and adapt to all sorts of media 'at large scale on trucks, building signing, etc., as well as reduced to small sizes for postage stamps endorsements, etc.'. About WWF it had to convey 'the image of a serious, modern, dynamic, effective, well-managed organization'. What's more, there was a whole range of things the logo was *not* meant to be or express. It had to be a symbol 'and not an anatomically accurate rendition of the giant Panda species', and the impression 'that WWF is primarily involved in toy, cartoon or animal protection business' was also to be avoided. As 'WWF is not happy about the state of the natural environment, nor sanguine about the chances of halting its further degradation', the symbol 'should not be laughing, smiling or winking'. Yet as 'WWF doesn't believe its cause is hopeless', the symbol could not be 'sad, crying or morose' either.[62]

As a first step in their assignment the Landor designers went to London Zoo to study the panda 'in its natural environment'.[63] As Chi Chi, who had inspired Gerald Watterson for the sketches of the first logo, had died in 1972, the model for the new logo was a male called Chia Chia, the only panda living in the UK in 1986.[64] The most problematic aspect of the original logo were the eyes, which became distorted or disappeared altogether when the design was reduced in size. As in the American version, the Landor designers decided to 'keep the eyes black', not only because this detail 'was an unnecessary, graphic problem'

Variations of the WWF logo circulating by the mid-1980s

Nature Clubs of India
THE YOUTH MOVEMENT OF
THE WORLD WILDLIFE FUND—INDIA

WILDSCREEN'86

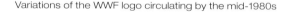

WWF IUCN

WWF
FONDS MONDIAL POUR LA NATURE

World
Wildlife
Fund
INTERNATIONAL

CLUB
WWF'85

– during their visit to London Zoo they had noticed 'that in reality the eyes *are* black'. With respect to the American panda, who appeared to be 'out of balance', whose ears looked 'rubbery' and who seemed to be holding a 'snowball' between the front legs, the Landor designers made improvements by further simplifying the logo. The elimination of the black lines defining the head and the back of the animal was particularly helpful in making the image appear less 'cartoon-like'.[65] The powerful effect of the Landor logo, however, stems from the strong glare the animal exudes from its invisible eyes in combination with the three-dimensional quality the design evokes in the eyes of the beholder.

The new logo was presented to representatives of the four major NOs – the USA, the UK, Switzerland and the Netherlands – before being approved by the rest of the WWF family in 1986.[66] It had its first public appearance during the celebrations of WWF's 25th anniversary. At the initiative of Prince Philip WWF held its annual conference at Assisi, while at the same time the abbot of the Franciscan monastery was persuaded to convene a conference of leaders of the other faiths to discuss their individual attitudes to the creation. Following its president, the board agreed that 'a sort of pilgrimage' to the birthplace of the

The streamlined version introduced by WWF International in 1980 (left) and the model used by WWF-US prior to the redesign by Landor & Associates

medieval saint known for his intense love of the natural world and involving Buddhist, Christian, Hindu, Islamic and Jewish religious leaders 'would provide an interesting focus on a moral and spiritual renewal of the conservation cause and attract public interest. It could also provide an opportunity to encourage the major world religions to make public statements in support of conservation, since the philosophy of St Francis was also of interest to other religions.'[67] As a follow-up to the Assisi event, Prince Philip created the Alliance of Religion and Conservation, which helps major religions of the world 'to develop their own conservation programmes, based on their own core teachings, beliefs and practices', an initiative which to this day involves both WWF International and WWF-UK as consultants.[68]

In the same year the fund adopted the Landor logo it also changed its name to World Wide Fund for Nature. While this particular version of a new name was suggested by the designers of the new logo, name-change discussions had been a recurrent feature at WWF meetings for over two decades. The topic was first raised at a 1964 board meeting by Hans Hüssy. He thought the original name was 'unsatisfactory', not only because 'it was almost unpronounceable in non-English-speaking countries' but also because 'it was not broad enough com-

Pilgrims on the road to Assisi, Italy, September 1986. WWF celebrated its 25th anniversary with an inter-religious conference held at the birthplace of St Francis

pared with the objects as spelt out in the Deed of Foundation which covered all nature including the protection of water, landscape planning etc. and not only wildlife, and because the WWF should, according to the deed, aim [...] to become not only one of several but the world organisation for nature conservation with the broadest possible concept and universal appeal'. Hüssy's proposal to exchange the term 'wildlife' for 'nature' was, however, rejected by the international board. It argued that 'the term "wildlife" had a certain appeal which could not be found in another

Saving the World's Wildlife

more general term, such as "nature"'. In recognition of the translation problems non-anglophone national appeals were allowed to 'find a short descriptive phrase' to add to their name.[69] When WWF made a survey of the name situation twenty years later it found that the organisation was legally registered with the equivalent of 'World Nature Fund' in French, German, Italian, Dutch, Portuguese, Spanish, Danish and Swedish, a result which overlooked the fact that in Afrikaans WWF-South Africa had always been called 'Suid Africaanse Natuurstichting'.[70]

In the mid-1980s, the time for a name change was ripe, not only because by then even the international board had accepted the need to broaden the appeal of WWF, but also because Charles de Haes wanted to have brand uniformity. In order to secure broad support for a new name, all members of the WWF family were asked to express their views on the subject in 1985.[71] Apart from old objections by non-English-speakers to 'wildlife', the term was now also seen as creating a 'wrong perception of WWF scope & objectives' when operating in the developing world. It seemed to imply that WWF was interested only in animals, not people, and thus failed to reflect the principle of sustainable development adopted by WWF in the World Conservation Strategy of 1980.[72] In late 1985 the international board decided to discontinue using the old name, to stress the acronym WWF in all communications, and to register the new name 'World Wide Fund for Nature'. As Gland could not impose a name change on the other members of the WWF family, the board decided to 'encourage all N.O.s to use the letters WWF in conjunction with the Panda symbol whenever possible so as to strengthen WWF's family identity, irrespective of what official name a particular N.O. uses in English or any other language'.[73]

In the course of the 1986 anniversary year, all national organisations went along with the name change bar two, WWF-US and WWF-Canada. Bill Reilly, then president of WWF-US, remembers objecting to the change because it was 'peremptorily executed without research or polling public attitudes' and because the original name worked well in the USA: 'There was a reason cats featured in our calendars: members loved them. And they loved wildlife, it was their way into international nature conservation. Foreign aid, biodiversity, international development – we had polled on these and nobody marched to them in our sphere.'[74]

Given the broad decision-making process, EXCO was irritated when in 1987 Bill Reilly presented 'the name change as though it had been done without adequate consultation with the National Organizations'.[75]

The Landor logo approved by representatives of WWF
International and family members from Belgium, the
Netherlands, Switzerland, the UK and the USA, 1986

From sketch to logo

How a panda conquered the world

Positive: Eyes are defined

Negative: Blind at small size

Is this line necessary to define shape?

Mouth is one sided

Looks lumpy

Nose is too soft
–Undefined
–Smashed in

Legs are too bow legged

Looks like Panda is holding something

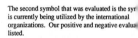

The second symbol that was evaluated is the syr is currently being utilized by the international organizations. Our positive and negative evalua listed.

General: Positive – looks more natural
– friendly, likeable image
– known as endangered species

Negative – looks old, sick, depressed
– flat, not 3-dimensional
– cuddly, toy like, not serious

Landor & Associates, comments on the Watterson/Scott
logo used by WWF International, 1986

184

Landor & Associates, sketches of Chia Chia made in
London Zoo, 1986

There are presently about 1,600 pandas left in the wild. Although I have never counted them, each WWF office I have been to seemed to be inhabited by at least as many. Apart from the inevitable soft-toy pandas sitting around on desks or shelves, they come in an incredible range of materials, shapes and sizes. While panda ashtrays tell of a time when smoking was still socially acceptable – and Anton Rupert was a major donor to WWF – lifesize panda costumes are a reminder of the fact that the organisation was created in order to raise money from the general public. How right the founding fathers were in choosing the panda as their symbol also becomes apparent when navigating the organisation's vast digital photo library. The panda logo can be applied to anything from flags and T-shirts to railway carriages and the sails of a schooner, thus providing the organisation with a picture opportunity whenever and wherever it wants. The phenomenal publicity success of the logo should not, however, distract from the key role it played for WWF's internal communications. Like a national flag, the panda logo was the single most important means of collective identification. As a symbol it was open to a wide range of individual interpretations, providing the very diverse WWF family with a useful means to foster unity and overcome internal differences. While the evolution of the logo has been documented in previous publications, the original drawings made by Peter Scott were only rediscovered, shortly before this book went into print, in the estate of the artist's late wife Philippa. They show that rather than turning one model by Gerald Watterson into a logo, Peter Scott also did his own set of sketches and preliminary drawings before arriving at the well-known prototype. The sketches contained in the Landor brochure leading to the redesign of 1986 are also reproduced here for the first time. Like many other key sources of this book, the brochure is contained in the well-kept WWF files of Prince Philip.

From left to right:
1 Bath mat, pre-1986, WWF-Switzerland
2 Tie from the wardrobe of Prince Philip, c. 1990
3 Pin, post-1986, WWF-US
4 Ashtray and matches, 1960s, WWF-Switzerland
5 T-shirt, 1970s, WWF-Switzerland

6 Pens, 1990s, WWF-US
7 Swiss Army knife, pre-1986, WWF-Switzerland
8 Poster by Fritz Hug, 1960s, WWF-Switzerland
9 WWF Gold Medal awarded to Ernst Ulrich von Weizsäcker, 1996
10 Membership button, 1990, WWF-US

From left to right:
1 WWF-China advert on a billboard in the Shanghai metro, 2008
2 WWF project worker photographing Irrawaddy river dolphins, Cambodia

3 WWF flag at the Association for Forest Development and Conservation, Ramileh, Lebanon
4 Prince Philip wearing a panda tie at a dinner in Helsinki, Finland, May 1995
5 Press event of WWF-Germany urging Vladimir Putin to ratify the Kyoto Protocol, Weimar, April 2003

6 Key ring, post-1986, WWF-US
7 Schooner *Julia*, North Sea, post-1986, WWF-Germany
8 Campaign poster 'Switch off the engine', 1972, WWF-Switzerland

From left to right:
1 Prince Bernhard wearing panda T-shirt, Virunga National, Park, Congo, 1973
2 Campaign sticker, pre-1986, WWF-Belgium
3 Car sticker, pre-1986, WWF-Switzerland
4 Fabric sew-on badge, pre-1986, WWF-Italy

5 Car sticker, pre-1986, WWF-Denmark
6 Campaign sticker to save the Bolle di Magadino, Ticino, 1979, WWF-Switzerland

7 Campaign sticker for Operation Tiger, issued jointly with the World Scout Movement, 1974, WWF International
8 Bread bag, post-1986, WWF-Netherlands

9 Campaign sticker 'La mer doit vivre', 1977, WWF-Switzerland
10 Oilskin jacket, pre-1986, WWF-Switzerland

From left to right:
1 Merchandise catalogue,
1966, WWF-Switzerland
2 Car sticker, post-1986,
WWF-Germany
3 Model railway equipment
produced by a partner of
WWF-Germany, 2006

4 Football, post-1986,
WWF-Germany
5 Appeal poster, 1962,
WWF-UK
6 Mushroom pâté
produced by a partner of
WWF-Germany, 2008

7 Soft drink bottle produced by
a partner of WWF-Switzerland,
pre-1986
8 Plush panda, 1960s,
WWF-Switzerland

From left to right:
1 Cardboard wrapping of a tie
for members of The 1001 – A
Nature Trust, post-1986
2 Tin collection box, ca. 1962,
WWF-UK
3 Sports bag for children,
1970s, WWF-Switzerland

4 Campaign button for
migratory birds, issued jointly
with the Schweizerisches
Landeskomitee für
Vogelschutz, 1986, WWF-
Switzerland
5 Pin, post-1986, WWF-
Switzerland

6 Flipflops, 2000s, WWF-
Switzerland
7 Refrigerator magnet,
2000s, WWF-Switzerland
8 Hot air balloon, Vienna,
2003, WWF-Austria

From left to right:
1 Drinking cup, 1970s,
WWF-Switzerland
2 Belt buckle, 1970s,
WWF-Switzerland
3 Foulard designed by Fritz
Hug, with autograph by Heidi
Abel, 1966, WWF-Switzerland
4 WWF performance at
Shanghai Expo, China, 2010

5 Building an ecological
corridor for pandas, Quinling
mountains, China, 2006
6 Record 'The stars sing for
the World Wildlife Fund', 1970,
WWF-UK

A family row

'WWF-US maintained their "right" to decide their programme for themselves, irrespective of what the rest of the WWF family jointly decided to do.'

Of the three WWF national organisations founded in 1961, WWF-US was the slowest to take off. The unsatisfactory performance of the American branch, especially given the size and economic potential of the country, was a permanent headache to the founders of WWF. They blamed the situation on a lack of management skills at the top. In 1966, Peter Scott discussed the problem of finding a new chief executive for WWF-US with Charles Lindbergh, who had recently become an international trustee. In one of his letters to Scott the aviator wrote: 'I fully agree with you, too, about Russell Train. He is very able, a grand fellow, and doing a wonderful job. [...] A man of Train's ability and character is just what we need for US WWF.'[1] Indeed, it was under Russell Train's leadership that WWF-US would experience a rapid and unprecedented growth, turning it into the largest member of the WWF family in terms of income, membership and staff, but this development set in only more than a decade later.

Like other key figures of WWF, Russell Train has a hunting background linked to late colonial Africa. In his autobiography he remembers a trip to Kenya in 1956: 'The safari experience was everything of which I had dreamt. It was a wonderful adventure in wild, remote country, and we spent most of our time hunting on foot with a local tribesman as tracker. The experience of a first African hunting safari, like that of a first love, can never be duplicated.'[2] In 1961 Train, then a judge at the US tax court in Washington, founded the African Wildlife Leadership Foundation which in view of decolonisation wanted to provide African states with conservation skills. In 1965 Train took over the leadership of Fairfield Osborn's Conservation Foundation (CF) and moved the policy institute from New York to Washington. Joining the Nixon administration in 1969, the Republican lawyer effectively became US minister for the environment, heading the Environmental Protection Agency from 1973 onwards. With the advent of the Carter administration, Train left politics and in 1978 accepted the presidency of WWF-US.[3]

On taking up his new job Russell Train got a call from Peter Scott, who welcomed him to WWF but also expressed his 'strong disappointment with the performance of WWF-US over the past 16 years. [...] He pulled no punches and I got the message!'[4] Train identified the fact that WWF-US was a grant-making body to other conservation organisations and did not have its own programme as the main reason for the NO's underperformance: 'We soon gave up such grants and became a project leader on our own.' As they had no conservation skills, Train hired environmental experts who often worked for rival environmental charities: '[W]hile WWF-US had supported the primatology work of Russell Mittermeier, we cancelled that grant [to the New York Zoological Society], brought Russ onto our own staff, and ran his primatology work as our own WWF project. This case can be multiplied a number of times.' The result was that 'WWF-US began to build its own identity in the field and [...] to be of more interest to the average donor.'[5] The success of a membership scheme launched in 1981, later than in most other countries, impressively illustrates this point.[6] In 1985 WWF-US had 172,000 members and five years later reached the magical threshold of a million.[7]

Meeting of the WWF board of trustees, Slimbridge, Gloucestershire, June 1978. From left to right: Russell and Aileen Train, Herta and David Ogilvy, Peter Scott, Angie Loudon

Russell Train's most important staff acquisition was Bill Reilly, a lawyer who had Train's former job at The Conservation Foundation and whom Train had identified 'as successor to me as CEO of WWF-US'.[8] Instead of poaching Reilly from CF, the two men decided to merge their organisations in 1985, incidentally a plan discussed by Charles Lindbergh and Peter Scott when they thought about hiring Russell Train back in 1966.[9] Under Bill Reilly CF was proud to rank among the 'top three most effective "lobbying" groups on environmental issues in the United States'.[10] The foundation focused on domestic issues, and CF's interest in America's natural heritage is reflected in the illustrations chosen for its annual reports. They were often masterpieces of US landscape photography, including works by Carleton Watkins, Ansel Adams and Edward Weston.[11] As CF had only a small financial base and no members, the merger with WWF gave them greater economic stability, but above all the possibility of working outside of the United States.[12] WWF-US, on the other hand, benefited

Saving the World's Wildlife

by acquiring with Reilly and his team 'a policy-making capability that it mostly lacked'.[13] After the merger in 1985, Bill Reilly became president of WWF-US while Russell Train became chairman of the US board and a member of the board of WWF International. In 1990, the year the two organisations finalised their merger, they had an annual income of $49.3 million, 89 per cent of which was provided by WWF-US. The photograph on the cover of their first joint annual report was a tiger.[14]

The meteoric rise of WWF-US went hand in hand with increasing tensions with WWF International. Apart from marketing problems concerning the ownership of the trademark and the use of the original name by WWF-US, disputes about money and programme eventually led to a bitter dispute about governance. In 1986, EXCO noted that several national organisations, among

Russell Train, president of WWF-US from 1978 to 1985 and chairman of its board from 1985 to 1994

them WWF-US, WWF-Netherlands and WWF-Italy, 'needed to be nudged into contributing to WWF International'.[15] While Gland argued that they provided services for the entire family which had to be paid for, European national organisations could bypass their financial obligations to WWF International by earmarking funds for specific projects.

The Americans, on the other hand, justified their refusal to transfer money to Switzerland by invoking their tax laws and the gentlemen's agreement of 1962. As WWF-US furthermore retained not only the capital but also the income from the money raised through The 1001, set up by Charles de Haes in order to pay for the administrative overheads of WWF International, Gland was particularly keen on getting the richest member of the WWF family to pay what they firmly believed to be their due.[16] Or, as Bill Reilly puts it: 'Much of the tension in the relationship in my view flowed from a failure of de Haes to accept that WWF-US was flourishing and failing to share its success.'[17]

The international expansion of the American conservation programme was a further cause of friction with Gland. Prince Philip remembers that WWF-US 'maintained that it had complete discretion about the use of its funds for conservation projects anywhere in the world [...] and refused to take part in any attempts by WWF International to achieve a coordinated programme of projects'.[18] A second gentlemen's agreement was able to defuse the problem only for a short while in 1982. In a Monroe Doctrine-like fashion the Americas were designated as the area for programme work by WWF-US, while the rest of the world was identified as falling under the programmatic jurisdiction of WWF International.[19] Yet as the 1985 merger with CF gave WWF-US the clear aim of being a globally active conservation organisation, it also began to develop programmes in Africa and Asia. Russell Train remembers that since their major domestic competitors, The Nature Conservancy and Conservation International, both had international programmes but 'none of the constraints which come with working within a "family" framework', WWF-US had 'no other choice' than to embark on 'a rather aggressive programmatic expansion'.[20] This necessarily clashed with the programmatic aspirations of WWF International, which in the 1980s was detaching itself from IUCN and beginning to build up its own conservation programme. Bill Reilly on Charles de Haes: 'His own preferred business model was that of a central office with access to the money of the NOs but professionally deployed by Gland. I sympathised with his plight but was repeatedly reminded that our views counted for little and also that our need for Gland was diminishing.'[21] Prince Philip, on the other hand, recalls that it was 'the refusal to take part with the other NOs in the planning of an "international" conservation programme which caused the rift. WWF-US maintained their "right" to decide their programme for themselves irrespective of what the rest of the WWF family, jointly, decided to do.'[22]

The programmatic expansion of WWF-US led to a series of disputes about 'the use of names, symbols and titles'.[23] While the adoption of the Landor logo in 1986 resolved the symbolic problem, the fact that WWF-US used the old name of the fund for its foreign programmes prevented the organisation from conveying 'the message that WWF is one integrated organisation', as Prince Philip explained in one of his letters to Russell Train. The president of WWF International

Bill Reilly, president of WWF-US from 1985 to 1989,
posing with confiscated wildlife products banned by the
Convention on International Trade in Endangered Species,
CITES

furthermore objected to the fact that the CEO of WWF-US was also called 'president': 'The point about using a common name and self-evident titles is to ensure that governments and organisations around the world know precisely with whom they are dealing when someone turns up claiming to speak for WWF.'

'Not the right man to lead WWF into the 21st century?'
Charles de Haes, 1987

[24] The title problem first came up during board meeting of WWF-US in San Francisco attended by Prince Philip in 1987. Bill Reilly has a 'vivid' memory of his clash with the prince, to whom he had the pleasure of pointing out: '[G]iven that you have abandoned the name in your organisation I am the ONLY president of World Wildlife Fund.' [25] EXCO minutes of WWF International, on the other hand, record: 'What had annoyed Mr. Reilly in San Francisco was his being told that WWF-US was unfairly benefiting from all the advantages of being associated with WWF International without giving back anything in return.' [26]

The problems between Washington and Gland were unresolved when Bill Reilly joined the Bush administration to head the Environmental Protection Agency in February 1989 and was replaced as president of WWF-US by Kathryn Fuller. The deceptively soft-spoken environmental lawyer, who took her first degree in literature, quickly disappointed hopes raised in Gland that matters could be settled if EXCO members had 'a frank talk' with her.[27] No less aware than her predecessor of the privileges the American branch of WWF enjoyed because of the gentlemen's agreement of 1962, Kathryn Fuller was clearly not a woman who could be 'nudged' into accepting anybody's point of view. To her, tension with Gland was 'unavoidable' considering 'that you had an international secretariat, and an international board, whose view was: "We are the control centre. This is where the ultimate decision making authority lies", when as a legal matter that absolutely was not true with respect to WWF-US.' [28] This view was shared by Russell Train, who took every opportunity to stand up for the rights of his NO: 'When a report from de Haes contained [...] statements regarding WWF-US that I considered incorrect I took exception by letter.

Likewise, when I received a letter from Prince Philip criticizing some action on the part of WWF-US and I considered the letter incorrect, I did not hesitate to respond to that effect.'[29]

In the course of 1990, matters deteriorated further, despite the fact that Russell Train was made a member of EXCO, the key decision-making body of WWF International. While Train insisted that 'WWF-US was not willing to take directives from Gland',[30] Prince Philip's remark that the problem was in part due to 'some kind of culture block' was very much to the point.[31] WWF-US saw the conflict with the European headquarters and its royal president to some extent as a repeat perfor-mance of their national history, especially the war of inde-pendence. While Russell Train explains his willingness to question positions of 'WWF International authorities inclu-ding royalty' by referring to his American identity, Kathryn Fuller remembers that Washington's reply to Gland's request for funds was 'the classic US rejoinder: "No taxation without representation"'.[32]

Kathryn Fuller, president of WWF-US from 1989 to 2005

In March 1991, WWF International tried to solve the prob-lem once and for all by sending a large dossier prepared by a London lawyer to Russell Train listing all grievances, explaining Gland's position and asking WWF-US to choose between making the 'necessary concessions' or 'disaffiliation'.[33] Instead of taking either of these decisions, WWF-US also took legal counsel and entered negotiations with Gland. This eventually led to a Memorandum of Understanding adopted in December 1991, the 'hammering out' of which was 'absolutely critical' to prevent WWF-US from leaving the organisation, as Kathryn Fuller recalls.[34] One reason the process worked out was that Gland and Washington delegated the negotiations to two senior staff who were personally much less involved in the dispute than the two leading tan-dems, Prince Philip/Charles de Haes and Russell Train/Kathryn Fuller. Claude Martin, former director of WWF-Switzerland and deputy director general of WWF International since 1990, recalls: 'Despite the odds we had an undeclared understanding across the green table [...] that we had to fix this problem, or we would risk years of destructive litigation.'[35] Jim Leape, an environmental lawyer who headed the American WWF delegation: 'To me, it was obvious that it would be crazy for WWF International to expel its largest member over this dispute, and equally crazy for WWF-US to give up being part of the global Network.'[36] The agreement Claude Martin and Jim Leape reached centred on the joint planning, implementation and evaluation of a global conservation programme, the perpetual lease of the panda trademark by Gland to WWF-US, and an annual contribution from the latter to WWF International for family services of one million dollars.[37]

Despite the Memorandum of Understanding there continued to be concerns at WWF-US about governance. In June 1991 Kathryn Fuller severely criticised the 'centralised control exercised by WWF International' in a letter to Charles de Haes, making a series of suggestions about how to improve Gland's relations with WWF national organisations.[38] Fuller's critique centred on the management style of Charles de Haes, which lacked 'openness' and appeared to be driven by the desire 'to control', as well as on the governance structure of WWF International, especially the composition of the board. In the eyes of Kathryn Fuller, the board was not only 'old fashioned' in its views on conservation but also lacked accountability and was thus 'not in fact representative of the institution'. While many national organisations had introduced measures to make their board both representative of its members and accountable to them, the reforms of WWF International introduced by Prince Philip in 1982 had made sure that the international board remained independent in its choice of trustees and accountable only to itself. The bottom line of the 'governance card' played by Kathryn Fuller was that WWF International 'was not a professional organisation. Our view was that the network was never going to achieve its potential unless it professionalized, unless it was accountable, unless we had governance systems.'[39]

While the critique of Gland on the part of WWF-US was largely identical to the objections raised by the European NOs present at their Zurich meeting in 1982, the fact that Kathryn Fuller's letter was distributed to all trustees at an international board meeting held in Buckingham Palace in June 1991 meant that this time the matter was discussed at the highest possible level of WWF and could not be settled behind the scenes by silencing a critical board member. Prince

Philip thought Fuller's letter was 'provocative' and that 'its recommendations put WWF at risk of becoming a less unified and effective world-wide organization'. He compared the American proposals about changing WWF's governance to the situation of a member of a club: 'If you joined, say, a golf club, you had first to pay your dues and then stick by its rules; you could not suddenly decide to play polo on the fairway or tee off from hole number 1 in the direction of hole number 4.' Russell Train replied that Kathryn Fuller had only represented 'the formal point of view of the Board of Trustees of WWF-US', which was reluctant to contribute financially to WWF International 'because it did not agree with the management structure and methods at Gland'. Charles de Haes, 'tired of unspecific criticisms of WWF International management', then offered to resign if the board felt 'that he was the real cause of the difficulties in WWF International's relationship with WWF-US'.[40]

As the German board member Hans Lange believed that the debate had become 'highly embarrassing', he invited each of the twelve trustees present at the Buckingham Palace board meeting 'to express his or her view on the issue'. Key statements came from the Swiss trustees Hans Hüssy and Luc Hoffmann. The latter emphasised the 'consensus-building' qualities of the programme coordination efforts across the WWF family, while Hans Hüssy, who of course understood the American grievances and thought that they 'had to be squarely addressed', concluded with a strong call to unity: 'Agreeing to work together according to a certain set of rules [does] not mean a loss of sovereignty for anyone.' While the British botanist Ghillean Prance 'deplored the fact that species were going extinct while the current debate continued', the Nigerian board member Chief Philip C. Asiodu also believed that 'a divorce between WWF-US and the rest of the WWF Family would be very damaging'. Asiodu also thought that governance reform had to go hand in hand with a further programmatic detachment from 'a concern with wildlife' in favour of 'sustainable development for people', because otherwise 'WWF would continue to be considered as an elitist organisation in third world countries'. At the end of the debate Russell Train stated that governance reform was not the only aim of WWF-US. He explained that 'the time had come for a change in the top management at WWF International. He felt that Charles de Haes, while deserving much credit for what he had done for the organisation in the past, was not the right man to lead WWF into the 21st Century'. After another round of highly personalised arguments during which the director general repeated his offer to resign, Prince Philip closed the debate by confirming the board's support for the ongoing negotiations for a Memorandum of Understanding with WWF-US and proposed that the governance issues raised by Kathryn Fuller be 'shelved for the time being'.[41]

If the leadership of WWF International hoped that the Memorandum of Understanding, adopted in December 1991, would allow them to postpone the governance issue for good, they were mistaken. During the same meeting in which the agreement between Gland and Washington was signed, the international board charged Hans Hüssy with revising the statutes and by-laws of the deed of foundation.[42] Passing on the lead in the governance reform initiated by WWF-US to an individual who enjoyed the trust of WWF representatives on both sides of the Atlantic was key to the success of this process. Hüssy also brought a sense of moderation into a debate which had become so antagonistic and personalised that there was a real risk of WWF disintegrating into its component parts – the Zurich lawyer repeatedly called upon a 'clear spirit of cooperation' as a necessary prerequisite for the constitutional reforms to succeed.[43] Personally in favour of greater NO participation in the matters of WWF International, Hüssy also wanted to avoid Gland becoming totally subjected to larger and more powerful members of the WWF family. When WWF-US suggested that the two NOs with the highest financial contribution to the international programme should have double representation on the international board and have more influence than others in choosing the director general,[44] Hans Hüssy concurred with Prince Philip that such a 'cash-related formula'[45] was no solution to the constitutional problems of WWF: 'There would be other considerations such as efficiency measured e.g. against overhead cost, educational effectiveness, project effectiveness, per capita performance, membership etc. If we wanted Board membership on the basis of success we would need a carefully weighted system which would need painstaking evaluation.'[46]

The new statutes and by-laws, worked out by Hans Hüssy and the Statutes Review Committee, were adopted in 1993. They brought the era of the self-perpetuating board to an end, as henceforth a majority of board members had to be people serving on the board of a national organisation. Only a minority could be co-opted as *ad personam* members if they were 'particularly competent in areas useful to the goals of the Foundation'.[47] The new statutes and by-laws were, as Hans Hüssy remembers, essentially 'a compromise' between the various views expressed in the reform process.[48] Prince Philip had to accept that while WWF International retained considerable room for manoeuvre, the independent board he had advocated at the beginning of his presidency was replaced by an executive body dominated by NO representatives. WWF-US, on the other hand, had to be content with a board that did not give extra privileges to financially successful members of the WWF family like themselves. While the Americans clearly fulfilled their most important reform goal, namely making Gland 'more representative of and responsible to the NOs',[49] the

Prince Philip, Kathryn Fuller and Russell Train, c. 1990

model was not American but Swiss. When Hans Hüssy first presented the new statutes and by-laws at an international board meeting in Oslo, he explained that the introduction of an NO-dominated board would be 'a revolutionary development [...] although it was already the practice in WWF-Switzerland'.[50] There, ever since the 1970s, cantonal sections of WWF had the right to be represented on the national board using a system of rotation and regional balance.[51]

In the eyes of WWF-US governance reform had to go hand in hand with a change of leadership at WWF International. In the run-up to an annual conference and board meeting in Buenos Aires in November 1992, Russell Train circulated a letter to all board members complaining that Gland had demonstrated a 'persistent pattern of secretiveness and unwillingness to deal in straight-forward fashion when it comes to issues of governance of WWF International'.[52] Although at an EXCO meeting preceding the Buenos Aires board meeting Charles de Haes and Claude Martin 'totally rejected the assertions contained' in Train's letter, at board level the Americans were joined by European 'change agents' in their opposition to Charles de Haes,[53] notably the key Swiss, Dutch and British participants of the 1982 Zurich meeting.[54] After a heated debate in Prince Philip's hotel suite, on 20 November 1992 the director general announced his resignation by mid-1994.[55] Prince Philip was much enraged by these developments and threatened to resign unless Russell Train stepped down as an international trustee.[56] As the latter showed no sign of obeying the prince's order, a process to remove Train from the international board was initiated at the end of November.[57] Prince Philip augmented the pressure by writing to Charles de Haes shortly before Christmas: 'You might tell Hans [Hüssy] that I will not accept a further term of 3 years from the end of 1993 unless RET [Russell Errol Train] has given a binding undertaking by 10 February 1993 that he will retire from the Board before the date of next year's Conference. There is absolutely no chance that I will change my mind.'[58] In January 1993 Russell Train announced his resignation from the international board by the end of the year.[59]

Monarch butterflies (*Danaus plexippus*), Michoacan
Province, Mexico. During Kathryn Fuller's presidency, the
conservation of the butterfly's wintering habitat in Mexico
was a key campaign of WWF-US

Operation Lock

'We are a bit confused, Sir.'

At a board meeting of WWF International held at Buckingham Palace in May 1987 the trustees were given an overview of the fund's conservation programme. The presentation by the head of the African Programme, the British biologist John Hanks, focused on the 'rhino emergency'.[1] What caused Hanks most concern was the fate of the black rhinoceros, *Diceros bicornis*. The WWF annual report of 1987/88 noted: 'Africa's black rhinos, having declined more rapidly over the past 20 years than any other large mammal, face a crisis of survival. Their total number is now under 4000, against about 65,000 in 1970 – a decline of 94 per cent.' The reason for this development had been clearly identified: 'The collapse of the black rhino is entirely due to poaching for its horn.'[2] Unlike all other animal horns, which contain a bony core, the rhino's is composed of densely compressed hair. Two markets existed for this very special material. In Yemen it was used to craft the handles of traditional *jambiya* daggers, while in traditional Chinese medicine ground rhino horn was used to alleviate life-threatening fevers.[3]

John Hanks's presentation caused Prince Sadruddin Aga Khan, trustee since 1969 and vice-president of WWF International since 1985, to query whether the fund 'had not left matters too late, when the rhino was on the brink of extinction'. Charles de Haes replied that the organisation 'had been involved in rhino conservation campaigns and actions ever since its founding' and recalled the 1961 'Shock Issue' of the *Daily Mirror*, which had displayed a rhino. The director general also explained that recent efforts had included rhino programmes in Zambia and Zimbabwe but that these had failed to prevent the decline of the species at the hands of poachers. Anton Rupert added 'that in South Africa, paradoxically, there were too many rhinos, and some of them were being sent around to other countries. To him the key problem was that of stopping the trade in rhino horn.' John Hanks concluded by noting that 'one needed to do three things: i) Prevent poaching; ii) Prevent the trade in rhino horn; iii) Tackle the middlemen, some of whom were controlled by government officials'.[4]

Two months later John Hanks, by way of George Medley, director of WWF-UK, received a letter from Colonel Ian Crooke, managing director of KAS Enterprises. The colonel suggested that his company 'may be able to assist WWF in working to protect African wildlife'.[5] KAS was a private, London-based security

firm owned by another British officer, David Stirling. Famous for having created Britain's Special Air Services (SAS) in 1941, Stirling had left the army after the war to specialise in the provision of private military assistance in the developing world. Stirling's services ranged from training foreign troops to the procurement of arms and mercenaries.[6] On 13 November 1987 Hanks met Ian Crooke in London 'to discuss the possibility of KAS infiltrating organizations of dealers in ivory and rhinoceros horn (the "Lock Project"). Hanks explains that WWF cannot fund such a project but that he knows of a benefactor who will provide the funds. Hanks and Crooke further agree that no one inside the WWF organization should be told about this project. Hanks agrees with Prince Bernhard for the latter to fund the KAS project with the understanding that WWF would have no part in the operation.'[7]

John Hanks (right) and the film-maker David Attenborough outside the office of WWF-South Africa, 1993

Exposed through newspaper articles and a book published in the early 1990s, Operation Lock was reviewed internally by WWF. Probably because the negative publicity faded away quite quickly, only some key results were communicated to the general public. In the long run, however, Operation Lock became a liability for WWF. The secrecy marking the operation from its inception led to conspiracy theories which to this day inspire not only specialised internet pages but also academic texts written about the organisation. Based on a wide range of written sources, this chapter aims to provide the first historical account of Operation Lock. Two legal texts proved to be particularly valuable. In 1993 Prince Philip commissioned the American lawyer and former federal judge Abraham Sofaer to go through all available documents and compile a chronology in order to establish all facts and allow the assessment of responsibilities.[8] One year later, the South African Ministry for Environmental Affairs and Tourism commissioned a Durban judge, Justice M. E. Kumleben, to conduct an 'inquiry into the alleged smuggling of and illegal trade in ivory and rhinoceros horn in South Africa'. In January 1996 Kumleben presented a 226-page report to President Nelson Mandela which included an entire chapter on Operation Lock.[9]

In the course of his investigations Justice Kumleben summoned 23 witnesses to give evidence, among them John Hanks. He told the court 'how Lock came about': during a field trip to Africa in early 1987, Hanks and Prince Bernhard were 'struck by the plight of the rhino on this continent'. Hanks told the 75-year-old prince 'that not enough was being done to gather information on the middlemen involved in the illicit trade in rhino horn'. This prompted Bernhard to ask whether Hanks 'knew of an organisation that could undertake the task of tracking down these smugglers and exposing them'.[10] In his testimony to the Kumleben Commission Hanks emphasised that Prince Bernhard, at the time still president of WWF-Netherlands, 'wanted to do this in his personal capacity, using his own money, because he realised that it was a sensitive topic and one that he felt should not be registered by WWF as a project'.[11] When Hanks received Ian Crooke's letter a couple of months later 'he thought that KAS would be able to do the work he and Prince Bernhard envisaged'.[12] Bernhard agreed and promised to provide the funding.[13] Justice Kumleben noted that Bernhard and Hanks were particularly impressed by the 'distinguished military record' of the former SAS officers Stirling and Crooke 'and felt sure that they could be trusted to carry out their commission. Hanks, and presumably Prince Bernhard, had no knowledge of the character or background of those recruited by Crooke, and perhaps Stirling, to complete the team. Crooke was given a free hand in carrying out the operation and, as Hanks put it, "the less that was available in documentation floating around with names of people and contact addresses, the better".'[14]

On 3 November 1987, ten days before meeting Ian Crooke, John Hanks had participated at a WWF meeting chaired by Sadruddin Aga Khan. The main topic was a paper written by Hanks in October 1987 and distributed to all NO chief executives and senior WWF International staff. It was entitled 'The Need for

Preceding page: Black rhinoceros (*Diceros bicornis*) and African elephant (*Loxodonta africana*)

a Continental Strategy for the Conservation of Rhino in Africa'. Hanks wrote that '[i]mmediate action to halt decline in the numbers of black rhino and of the northern race of the white rhino' was needed and that this should include 'a major effort to halt the illegal trade by supporting intelligence gathering and the resulting follow-up operations, combined with organising and applying diplomatic and economic pressures on the responsible countries'.[15] Reacting to Hanks's paper, Staffan de Mistura, CEO of WWF-Italy, called for 'an aggressive approach' to tackle 'those people coordinating the illegal trade'. Although John Hanks had by this point already received Ian Crooke's letter and had most probably also already made an appointment to meet him within less than a fortnight, the head of WWF's African Programme told his colleagues: 'Getting involved in tackling those people coordinating the illegal trade is not the job of WWF. It is essential that WWF encourages people to support rhino conservation, but we should not be involved in undercover-type operations.'[16]

Prince Bernhard, founder president of WWF International, with baby orang-utan, Malaysia, c. 2000

After meeting Ian Crooke John Hanks revised his rhino strategy paper. It now suggested that 'intelligence gathering' about rhino poachers and the illegal trade in the animal's horn had to be done by 'professional investigators' assembling 'comprehensive dossiers [...] on the whole illegal trade network to enable international organizations to confront Heads of State within the countries responsible with irrefutable evidence on the culpability of the traders and middlemen concerned'.[17] Deliberately avoiding any reference to 'who was doing the investigations, how it was conducted or where it was being conducted',[18] Hanks provided the WWF Conservation Committee with only a very rough outline of the undercover operation he had started: 'Professional investigations as described, funded by external sources, were initiated in November 1987. The investigating team has been provided with the information and contacts presently available to WWF. The first report from the team will be made available to WWF by 1 March 1988.'[19]

Saving the World's Wildlife

Despite this announcement, '[n]o report was ever submitted to WWF International-onal'.[20] This was due to a rather astonishing level of naivety and short-sightedness on the part of the project's sponsors. John Hanks testified in court that he and Prince Bernhard asked themselves only once KAS had begun to collect evidence about the illegal trade in rhino horn: 'what does one do with this information when you have it?'[21] As it would have been all but impossible for a respectable environmental organisation such as WWF to organise a press conference or contact government officials in Africa announcing the findings of 'an SAS team carrying out undercover operations in the cause of conservation',[22] John Hanks decided 'that there would be no purpose and nothing gained by WWF being involved in the project and having access to the first report, so it was not made available'.[23] In order to make the information gathered by KAS useful after all, Hanks decided to cooperate with South Africa's environmental police, the Endangered Species Protection Unit (ESPU), founded in 1988 to combat poaching and the trade in illegal animal products.[24]

Ian Crooke delivered a first report to John Hanks and Prince Bernhard in October 1988. It suggested on the one hand a series of 'short-term measures' to combat rhino poaching which eventually led to the training of anti-poaching units in Namibia through KAS personnel.[25] On the other hand the report focused on 'the involvement of the North Koreans' in smuggling rhino horn out of Zimbabwe. In order to combat the trade in this and other African countries, Crooke suggested 'intonat[ing]' rhino horn 'with a technical device which allows us to keep i[t] under surveillance'.[26] He assured his clients that 'a method of electronic "tagging" has been identified'. It would allow KAS agents to pose as rhino horn dealers, sell the animal parts to smugglers and, by means of the electronic tracking devices, expose both the trade routes and the buyers of the illegal merchandise.[27] John Hanks and Prince Bernhard were impressed by the 'Electronic Pursuit'[28] plan and decided that '[t]he next stage of Operation Lock should concentrate on further detailed investigations into the illegal trade in rhino horn in Zambia, Zimbabwe, Namibia, Botswana and South Africa'.[29]

The cornerstone of Crooke's plan was 'an unattributable source of rhino horn'.[30] This could be identified with the assistance of Frans Stroebel, CEO of the South African branch of WWF, the Southern African Nature Foundation (SANF).

Without informing SANF 'that the project is not connected to WWF', John Hanks introduced Ian Crooke to Frans Stroebel in November 1987, asking him to 'identify leads in South Africa and [to] help KAS with the authorities'.[31] Apart from putting Crooke in touch with the Endangered Species Protection Unit, Stroebel's introductions allowed KAS to buy a total of 110 rhino horns from two governmental conservation agencies, the Natal Parks Board in South Africa and the Namibian Department of Agriculture and Nature Conservation.[32] Stroebel also supported Operation Lock by channelling Prince Bernhard's money through the accounts of SANF. Camouflaged as funds of the 'World Wild Life Fund, United Kingdom' – a name which after the 1986 name change had no more legal meaning – the CEO of WWF-South Africa made sure that Prince Bernhard's money was able to benefit from a favourable exchange rate offered by the South African Reserve Bank (SARB), the so-called Financial Rand.[33] The chronology compiled by Judge Abraham Sofaer notes that in April 1989 '[i]n exchange for the total £150,000, the SARB pays SANF 1,002,390 Rands'.[34] In October 1989 David Stirling, the founder of KAS, became the 'second benefactor' of Operation Lock, donating £100,000, a quarter of which also passed through the accounts of SANF.[35]

In early 1989 a KAS team established itself in a 'safe-house' in Pretoria and later moved to Johannesburg.[36] Apart from the support by SANF and the South African environmental police, the main reason why British undercover agents trying to infiltrate the rhino horn trade set up their headquarters in South Africa was that during the 1980s the country became ill famed as 'the main entrepôt' and 'clearing house' for the illegal trade in ivory and rhino horn 'originating from other African countries and sent overseas, principally to the Far East'.[37] Critics of the apartheid regime suspected a link to Pretoria's struggle against the ANC and its involvement in guerrilla wars in Angola and Mozambique.[38] One of the principal aims of the Kumleben Commission, appointed by the first post-apartheid government of Nelson Mandela, was to find out whether these allegations were true and if so to what extent the South African state and its agencies were responsible.

While the Kumleben Commission found no evidence to prove that private smuggling syndicates existed nor that the Endangered Species Protection Unit

216

functioned anything but properly, it did note that it was far too easy to forge South African customs documents, which allowed traders of poached animal parts to launder their merchandise.[39] Furthermore, the commission was able to prove that the South African army, despite denials throughout the 1980s, had for almost a decade played an active role in the illegal trade in ivory and rhino horn. The army's misconduct was a result of South Africa's involvement in the civil war in Angola, which had broken out when the country gained independence from Portugal in 1975. The Kumleben Commission was able to show that between 1978 and 1987 the Military Intelligence Division of the South African Defence Force (SADF) helped the UNITA rebels of Jonas Savimbi to export ivory, rhino horn and other illegally harvested natural resources, notably teak, in return for provisions and military equipment. The merchandise was transported via Namibia to South Africa, first on SADF vehicles, later on trucks of a front company set up in Johannesburg in order to disguise the army's involvement.[40] Justice Kumleben strongly condemned the army's activities, not only because they were 'illegal' in terms of South Africa's environmental legislation – the country was a proud founding member of CITES, the Convention on International Trade in Endangered Species, set up in 1975 – but also because they had encouraged 'the large-scale slaughter of elephants and rhinoceros' in the UNITA-controlled areas of Angola.[41] Like many South Africans, Justice Kumleben had integrated conservation into his national identity, and thus particularly deplored the fate of wildlife in the Quando Cubango province, described by one of his witnesses as an animal paradise prior to the outbreak of the civil war in 1975: 'I've never seen anything like it in my life before [...] the number of animals and diversity of wildlife species was such that it put the Kruger National Park completely in the shade.'[42]

This excursion into one of the dark chapters of the history of apartheid South Africa was necessary because in the second stage of Operation Lock not only the Endangered Species Protection Unit but also the South African army became involved. The head of the environmental police, Colonel Pieter Lategan, gave evidence to the Kumleben Commission. The police officer explained that he was contacted by the KAS team in early 1989, shortly after their arrival in South Africa, and that he arranged for 'one of his own men staying in the safe-house with them to co-ordinate the work they were to do in conjunction with his investigative unit'.[43] Lategan was impressed by the 'surveillance work' and 'intelligence gathering' of Ian Crooke's men and declared that 'they helped us to gather a lot of information which we're still using today'.[44] '[W]hen they decided to take a more active part in bringing offenders to book', however, Lategan became 'disenchanted'.[45] The policeman told the Kumleben Commission: '[T]he military can't do a police investigation and they were soldiers and that's what they did. [...] Mr. Chairman, they had all sorts of weird ideas of how to deal with people. They just thought that a "shoot to kill" policy would also work and they came with various ideas which simply did not work out and which I had to veto.'[46] Lategan was also concerned about the lack of accountability regarding the rhino horn which KAS had acquired. In the course of undercover operations it often 'simply disappeared'.[47] In mid-1990 Lategan seized the remaining sixteen rhino horns he found in a KAS safe-house in Johannesburg and thus effectively brought Operation Lock to an end.[48]

In the eyes of the army, however, the military background of the KAS team was no drawback; on the contrary. The Kumleben report noted that as Operation Lock needed 'specialised military equipment, for instance night sight equipment and radios of a particular kind', in early 1989 Ian Crooke got in touch with 'elements of the RSA security Forces who saw the opportunity of using Lock for their own ends'.[49] In addition to the liaison officer of Lategan's environmental police, the army's Military Intelligence Division placed an undercover agent with the KAS team. Justice Kumleben found out that the 'security infiltrator' was 'a Mr Mike Richards, who operated under the name of Harry Stevens'.[50] His job was to make sure that Operation Lock did not by accident discover 'that the South African government is tolerating the smuggling of endangered species and wild-life products as part of the destabilisation process of its neighbouring states'.[51]

Aware of the army's sensibilities, Ian Crooke not only made sure to avoid 'any possible contact with SADF personnel involved in such activities', but also offered his services to the South African Defence Force in their struggle against the ANC and other opponents of the apartheid regime. In an internal memorandum, the army spy Mike Richards noted that one of the 'advantages' of

Operation Lock was that 'the network needed for the collection and collation of information concerning endangered species and wild-life products takes on the same format as an infrastructure which is needed for the collection and collation of intelligence directly related to the activities of anti-South African countries, forces and people'.[52]

Whether KAS ended up doing intelligence work for late-apartheid South Africa is unknown. Confronted by the Kumleben Commission with the evidence that this had been a real possibility, however, John Hanks 'was visibly astonished' and 'shocked'.[53] Justice Kumleben concluded 'that those responsible for putting Lock in place did not have the ulterior motive of Lock functioning as some sort of espionage or intelligence-collecting agency for the RSA. It was *intended* by them to be an anti-poaching or anti-smuggling operation and nothing more.'[54] Prince Philip, who thanks

WWF information panel showing wildlife ranger with poached rhino horn, c. 1970

to the chronology of Abraham Sofaer had full access to the facts, also concluded 'that all those involved went into the operation with the best intentions and that WWF behaved entirely honourably throughout'.[55] The 'fatal flaw' of Operation Lock, according to Justice Kumleben, 'was that it was a covert operation involving persons with a reputation for carrying out unorthodox exploits to achieve their goals. They were accountable to no one. Thus suspicion regarding them was inevitable particularly since there has been no disclosure of the fate of rhino horn delivered and not recovered. With the benefit of hindsight, Hanks candidly conceded that this operation was not a propitious one.'[56]

How did WWF deal with the challenges posed by Operation Lock? Initially not at all, for although John Hanks hinted at the fact that an undercover operation to stop the trade in rhino horn had been initiated in late 1987, Charles de Haes and the other staff at WWF International failed to realise that Operation Lock was proceeding until over a year later. In December 1988, Prince Bernhard and his wife, Princess Juliana of the Netherlands, gave two seventeenth-century paintings, *The Holy Family* by the Spanish painter Murillo and *The Rape of Europa* attributed to the Italian artist Elisabetta Sirani, to a Sotheby's auction in London, the proceeds of which were to be donated to WWF International.[57] The paintings were sold for '£600,000 and £10,000 respectively', the Murillo ten times exceeding its estimated value.[58] In January 1989 Tatiana Gortchacow, manager of The 1001 at WWF International, received a phone call from Prince Bernhard 'regarding the transfer of the funds to Princess Juliana's account in the Netherlands. He said he had not received anything yet and needs to have urgently £500,000 for a special project. The rest of the money we can keep. He also said that if there is any money left after the project is finished he will give it to Gland.' As Gortchacow had no idea what project the prince was referring to she asked Charles de Haes: 'Could I please know what the situation is?'[59] The director general was equally at a loss. 'We are a bit confused, Sir,' he told Prince Bernhard, and suggested a meeting to clarify the matter.[60] During their encounter on 21 January 1989 'de Haes learns for the first time of the KAS operation and of Prince Bernhard's sponsorship thereof. He is assured by Prince Bernhard that Hanks and Stroebel are providing general information and introductions for KAS, but that he, Prince Bernhard, has made it clear that WWF should not be involved in any other way. Prince Bernhard asks de Haes not to tell Hanks and Stroebel that he is aware of the project but agrees that de Haes should inform Prince Philip, President; John Nash, Treasurer; and Henner Ehringhaus, Deputy Director General.'[61]

Although the WWF leadership ought to have realised at this point that an association with an undercover operation carried out by a private security firm such as KAS could be extremely harmful to the image of an organisation whose policy it was 'not to engage in clandestine or covert operations which might be considered unethical by governments, the public, or persons who support WWF by donations and subscriptions', Gland failed to develop a comprehensive strategy dealing with the problems caused by Operation Lock.[62] Instead, over the

Elephant jawbones and rhino skulls from the 1980s, a time of intensive poaching in southern Africa, Wereldsend, Namibia

Saving the World's Wildlife

next three years, they only ever reacted to what either the original sponsors of the project or journalists decided to reveal.

At the beginning Charles de Haes thought it was possible to keep WWF separate from Operation Lock if Prince Bernhard was prevented from using the proceeds of the Sotheby's auction to fund the project. In the summer of 1989 Bernhard's wife, Princess Juliana, confirmed in writing that the funds would be donated to WWF-Netherlands and only then was the money transferred from the auction house to the princess.[63] While this made sure that no money donated to WWF was ever used for Operation Lock, the fact that the private funds of Prince Bernhard and David Stirling were transferred to South Africa via the accounts of SANF meant that WWF was nevertheless entangled in the finances of Operation Lock. When Charles de Haes discovered these transactions in April 1990, he 'expressed his great unhappiness over the matter', telling senior staff of SANF at a meeting in Pretoria: 'Because money in this context went through the hands of WWF-ZA, the whole matter can blow up in the faces of not only the SANF but also of WWF International.'[64]

Another unsuccessful attempt to limit the damage of Operation Lock was removing John Hanks from his position in Gland. In July 1989 he was informed that there was 'no future for him with WWF International'.[65] In January 1990 the CEO of WWF-South Africa, Allan Heydorn, asked Hanks whether he would consider returning to South Africa where he had been working as director of the Institute of Natural Resources, which he had established at the University of Natal before moving to Switzerland in 1985. In June 1990 Anton Rupert hired Hanks as CEO of WWF-South Africa, replacing Allan Heydorn, who retired for health reasons.[66] By the time John Hanks took up his new job, however, rumours about WWF's involvement in an undercover rhino operation were beginning to spread. In April 1991 South African journalists rang the WWF office in Stellenbosch enquiring about the 'involvement of SANF/WWF in rhino-horn trade'.[67] Two months later David Jones, a board member of WWF-UK, was worrying about 'allegations that officials of WWF might have become involved in inappropriate operations in Africa' and that 'WWF senior staff in Gland [were] employing mercenaries who worked in association with South African defence and intelligence personnel'.[68] Only then, one and a half years after Charles de

Haes had first been briefed by Prince Bernhard on Operation Lock, did the WWF leadership decide to investigate the matter thoroughly.

In July 1990 EXCO asked a London lawyer, Lord Benson, 'to undertake an inquiry into Project Lock'.[69] While Benson's report could not be located in the course of this research, the text was discussed at an EXCO meeting in October 1990 and 'the salient facts' recorded in the minutes. Without naming John Hanks and Frans Stroebel, WWF's key governing body noted that 'two officials within the WWF family made errors of judgement by personally, and without the know-ledge or approval of WWF, involving themselves in the project to a degree and in a manner which was inappropriate'.[70] As by the time of the delivery of the Benson report both men were either working for SANF or serving on its board, Prince Philip raised the matter with Anton Rupert, who at the end of 1989 had resigned from the board of WWF International but who remained president of SANF until his death in 2006. Prince Philip suggested a review of the financial assistance given to Operation Lock and 'that Stroebel resign as a member of SANF's Executive Committee and as SANF's Legal Adviser'.[71] Anton Rupert informed Prince Philip that the Financial Rand transactions 'were not in con-travention of Reserve Bank regulations', and was unwilling to distance himself from either Hanks or Stroebel.[72] While EXCO could do nothing about Stroebel, it decided to 'reprimand Hanks [...] and to inform him that he will no longer be allowed to supervise WWF International projects in Africa'.[73]

Prince Philip hoped that the actions taken at the end of 1990 'would have been the end of the matter', but later had to concede: 'Unfortunately, this did not prove to be the case since, in early 1991, a journalist called Stephen Ellis had published a story on Operation Lock and alleged that WWF's involvement was greater than it had been.'[74] Before the publication Gland made John Hanks write a statement in which he took 'sole responsibility for Operation Lock' and sent it to Ellis 'in an effort to convince him not to publish his article'.[75] If anything this probably encouraged Ellis to publish his piece, entitled 'Prince paid thousands into wildlife sting', which contained many correct details about Prince Bernhard, KAS and their cooperation with 'South African nature conservation officials'. Yet Ellis also suggested that Charles de Haes had been informed 'from the start' and that the money used had been donated to WWF.[76] While the source of this

Black rhinoceros (*Diceros bicornis*) under 24-hour armed guard because of risk of poaching. Undated photograph from WWF's digital photo library

Rangers with ivory and guns seized from poachers outside
the WWF office in Yokadouma, East Province, Cameroon,
June 2010

misinformation is unclear, within WWF it was distributed by Frans Stroebel. In January 1990, in a letter to Prince Philip, he claimed 'that WWF International did know of Operation Lock'[77] and in a letter to Lord Benson he wrote that Gland had funded the project 'through the sale of Prince Bernhard's art work'. Stroebel used the memorandum by Tatiana Gortchacow to Charles de Haes 'as evidence of this'.[78]

In February 1991 Gland once more tried to have Hanks and Stroebel removed from their WWF positions in South Africa. Prince Philip told the chairman of SANF, Gavin Relly, a former CEO of the South African mining giant Anglo-American: 'I believe it is essential that you take appropriate action in the case of Hanks and it is vital to distance SANF from Stroebel.'[79] Yet like other large and proud NOs, WWF-South Africa was unwilling to take orders from Gland. Gavin Relly told Prince Philip that while Hanks and Stroebel had been 'reprimanded', the former remained CEO of WWF-South Africa and the latter its legal adviser.[80] When in 1992 documents were leaked to the press revealing that Operation Lock had been infiltrated by the South African army, a dimension of the story which had been lacking in the first reports written by Stephen Ellis, Gland had to insist, somewhat helplessly, that John Hanks had acted 'in a private capacity'.[81] In order to keep WWF's link to South Africa out of the media, the fund's annual conference was hosted in Europe rather than on the Cape, and Prince Philip was dissuaded from visiting South Africa 'until the involvement of SANF and people related to it in Operation Locke [*sic*] has been cleared up'.[82]

In 1993, George Medley, the director of WWF-UK, had to prepare his trustees for yet another wave of bad press related to Operation Lock: 'I'm afraid we are going to be in for a rough ride on the Bonner book.'[83] In *At the Hand of Man. Peril and Hope for Africa's Wildlife* the American investigative journalist Raymond Bonner criticised the 1989 imposition of the ivory ban and argued, rather simplistically, that the CITES decision prevented local communities from reaping the benefits of their natural resources.[84] Because WWF supported the ban Bonner discussed the organisation at length. He not only suggested that WWF had changed its position on elephants under pressure from an American competitor, the African Wildlife (Leadership) Foundation, created by Russell Train in 1961, which, according to Bonner, had lobbied in favour of an ivory ban because

Saving the World's Wildlife

saving elephants was an excellent fund-raising tool.[85] Using Operation Lock as an example he also claimed 'that WWF had lost its ethical way'[86] and levelled serious accusations against the fund's management: 'It is unlikely that any other charitable organization that depends on public support operates with such little accountability and in such secrecy as WWF has under Charles de Haes. It is easier to penetrate the CIA. And when WWF has been caught in embarrassing conduct, it has engaged in damage control and cover-ups of the kind that might be expected from a company whose products have caused injury to consumers or the environment.'[87]

The problem for WWF was that Bonner's sweeping criticism was based on a wide range of high-quality sources. Apart from early WWF VIPs such as Ian MacPhail and Max Nicholson, who gave the American journalist access to his private files, Bonner's interview partners included numerous WWF leaders and staff on both sides of the Atlantic who had fallen out with Charles de Haes. While some, for example the former director of WWF-UK, Arthur Norman, let themselves be quoted, others decided to remain anonymous but provided the journalist with highly confidential documents, for instance correspondence between Charles de Haes and Prince Philip. The main reason for these leaks was the conflict-ridden relationship between WWF International and its NOs. While the pressure put on WWF-South Africa to remove Hanks and Stroebel was the reason why Bonner received Operation Lock documents slanted against Charles de Haes, the fact that the investigative journalist researched his story at the height of the conflict between Gland and Washington ensured that Bonner had a field day exposing the transatlantic 'feud' within WWF.[88]

At the Hand of Man, published by the renowned New York publisher Alfred A. Knopf in April 1993, prompted WWF to prepare a fourteen-page summary and eleven pages of questions and answers in response to enquiries by irritated supporters and the press.[89] In addition, Prince Philip asked the WWF lawyer Abraham Sofaer 'to contact Bonner's publishers to correct false statements in

Forest elephant (*Loxodonta africana cyclotis*), Dzanga-Ndoki National Park, Central African Republic. Because of poaching, elephants are nervous and run when humans are scented. Undated photograph from WWF's digital photo library

the book about WWF and its officials'. As new information indicated that John Hanks 'had been far more involved in Operation Lock than had been understood from Lord Benson's report', Philip asked Sofaer also to compile a comprehensive chronology of the facts pertaining to Operation Lock.[90] Based on the chronology EXCO decided in May 1993 that WWF needed to 'resolve whatever legal and/or moral obligations it might, directly or indirectly' have incurred through Operation Lock. It asked WWF-South Africa to clarify all outstanding questions, threatening to take 'whatever other steps it deemed necessary to meet its legal and moral obligations, including, if necessary, publication of the facts'.[91] Three weeks later the SANF chairman, Gavin Relly, wrote a memorandum, countersigned by John Hanks, containing the 'clarifications' EXCO had been looking for.[92]

Once John Hanks and WWF-South Africa had assumed the responsibility for Operation Lock, Gland was able to close the case in October 1993.[93] This was, however, not the reason why Bonner's book 'never made any headlines in Europe and the criticism even in the US ebbed away quickly'.[94] What cleared the air was the departure of Charles de Haes. Although his resignation had been decided as a result of the power struggle between Gland and its NOs at the 1992 board meeting in Buenos Aires, the enactment of the leadership change in October 1993 automatically distanced WWF from Charles de Haes. Thereafter it became irrelevant to the organisation that Stephen Ellis and Raymond Bonner not only misrepresented de Haes as one of the masterminds of Operation Lock but also demonised him as a dark force responsible for all other 'skeletons' in WWF's cupboards.[95] As this view was never challenged by either WWF or its former director general, the most enduring legacy of Operation Lock is a conspiracy theory about a key achievement of Charles de Haes, The 1001. According to Stephen Ellis and Raymond Bonner the highly successful fund-raising effort which turned WWF into an endowed foundation became an exclusive 'club' marked by 'secrecy' and a highly dubious membership, which during the apartheid era had given sixty or so white South Africans 'an opportunity to mingle and do business with tycoons, as well as with Prince Philip and Prince Bernhard'.[96]

The myth of a sinister 'South African lobby' (Ellis) whose 'clout' (Bonner) was such that they were able to manipulate the organisation into serving their political and economic interests has often been repeated, not only by authors specialising in conspiracy theories but also by academics writing about the history of WWF.[97] It first appeared in an article published in *Private Eye* in 1980. The anonymous author, whose argument Bonner and Ellis followed closely, suggested that the 'secret' nature of The 1001 was a direct consequence of the influence of another secret society on WWF, namely the Afrikaner Broederbond.[98] Founded in 1918 in order to protect Afrikaner language, culture and tradition against British dominance, and adopting secrecy soon afterwards, the Broederbond was a stronghold of Afrikaner nationalism.[99] The fact that Operation Lock was infiltrated by the South African military, who tried to use the KAS team for their own political ends, of course matched the thesis that WWF, via The 1001, had been infiltrated by Broederbonders. Yet neither Bonner nor Ellis bothered to note that Anton Rupert, while having joined the Broederbond as a student, distanced himself from their radical views and fell out with hard-line Afrikaners in the 1950s, long before joining WWF.[100] Furthermore, as we have seen above, The 1001 was not a club of shareholders who could influence the policy of WWF but a group of major donors contacted by Charles de Haes with a view to creating a capital fund. In order to keep contributions tax-free, members were not given any benefits apart from occasional drinks parties and the possibility of booking exclusive wildlife holidays.

A portrait of the environment

Brent Stirton's photographs for WWF

Ever since 2004, the South African-born photojournalist Brent Stirton has regularly documented WWF projects around the world. The award-winning photographer managed to capture the essence of the fund's transition from a fund-raising organisation based in Europe and North America to a global environmental network committed to sustainable development and local community participation. Unlike the WWF project photographs taken by Fritz Vollmar in the 1960s and 1970s, which almost exclusively focused on wildlife, in Stirton's work human beings play a central role. His photographs also testify to an awareness of the dilemmas of environmentalism which today have replaced the conservation certainties of an earlier age. The portraits Stirton took in Papua New Guinea, for instance, do not dwell on the beauty of the island's tribal culture alone. The captions make it clear that Papua's largest bird, the cassowary, provides the feathers for most of the headdresses, which immediately brings to mind the highly complex issue of tribal hunting. In Latin America, Stirton managed to capture, in a single photograph, both a new road across the Amazon responsible for deforestation and the faces of indigenous workers who need to make a living. Like many people involved with WWF before him, Stirton was impressed by the flamingo lakes in Kenya, but he also pointed out threats and possible solutions. His most impressive reportage for WWF, however, was conducted in China. Demography alone makes it clear that decisions about sustainability will be quite meaningless if their implementation is confined to the West. While this turns Stirton's images of organic farming in Hubei province or the portrait of an engineer standing on top of a windmill during its construction into symbols of hope, an aerial view of Shanghai is almost identical to the portrait of Johannesburg taken by Emil Schulthess half a century earlier. The two gloomy cityscapes underline the fact that what Max Nicholson in 1981 called the 'three Nasty Giants', namely population growth, technological progress and unsustainable use of natural resources, need to be addressed by anyone interested in saving the world's wildlife.

Brent Stirton: Leo Sunari, Sustainable Resource Trainer for
WWF-Papua New Guinea, under a
waterfall that feeds into the April river, East Sepik,
Papua New Guinea, December 2004.

Brent Stirton: the distinctive Victoria crowned pigeon
(*Goura victoria*) is ground-dwelling, but can fly short
distances if threatened. At around eighty centimetres
tall, it is the largest pigeon in the world. National Botanic
Gardens, Port Moresby, December 2004.

Brent Stirton: caged jaguar (*Panthera onca*) at the
Quistococha zoo in Iquitos, Peru, June 2007

Brent Stirton: llama herder, Andes, Peru, June 2007

Overleaf: Brent Stirton: agricultural workers on the
Interoceanica highway, a road stretching from Brazil to the
Pacific coast in Peru, June 2007

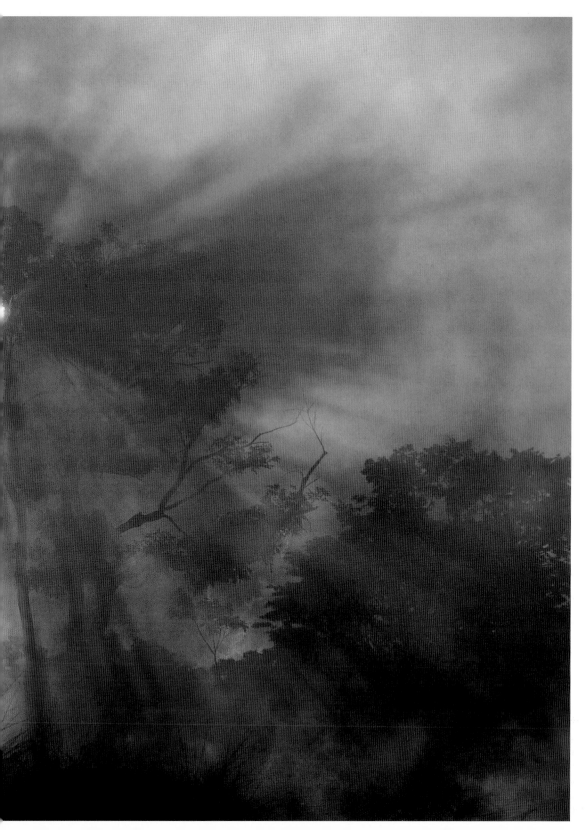

Brent Stirton: wooden carvings from Lunga Lunga
Handicraft Cooperative Society, Kenya. This illegal centre
is located in no man's land between the Kenyan and
Tanzanian borders to utilise wood from the farms and
forests of both countries, October 2005

Preceding page: Brent Stirton: smoke rising from a fire in
the Amazon, alongside the Interoceanica highway in Brazil,
June 2007

Brent Stirton: portrait of a Kenyan woman and her baby
taken at Lunga Lunga, situated on the Kenya–Tanzania
border, October 2005

Overleaf: Brent Stirton: lesser flamingoes (*Phoenicopterus
minor*) on the shore of Lake Bogoria, Kenya, October 2005

Brent Stirton: large-scale erosion forming a gully system
around six metres deep, Lake Bogoria region, Kenya,
October 2005

Brent Stirton: portrait of a worker at Golini Community
Nursery, Kwale District, Kenya, October 2005

Overleaf: Brent Stirton: farmer walking to his organic
vegetable plot, Xipanshanzhou Polder, West Dongting
Lake, Hubei Province, China, September 2008

Brent Stirton: farmers from Xipanshanzhou Polder selling
their organic produce, September 2008

254

Brent Stirton: shoppers at Carrefour supermarket,
Changsha, Hunan Province, China, September 2008

Brent Stirton: factory worker standing on a wind turbine
blade, Baoding, China, September 2008

Brent Stirton: aerial shot of tower block housing, central
Shanghai, China, September 2008

Implementing a
new mission

'WWF's ultimate goal is to stop, and eventually reverse, the accelerating degradation of our planet's natural environment.'

In June 1993 the board of WWF International elected the Swiss biologist Claude Martin as the fund's third director general.[1] He took over the organisation at a critical moment. The conflict with WWF-US had severely strained Gland's relationship with its most important national organisation, and the exposure of Operation Lock had not only damaged relations with WWF-South Africa but had also brought the organisation's conservation ethic into disrepute, at least with regard to Africa. The fact that under Claude Martin both the international status of WWF as an NGO and Gland's relationship with its NOs greatly improved was due in part to the background of the new director general. Born in Zurich in 1945, he was the first professional ecologist to head the organisation. After gaining a master's degree in biology at the University of Zurich, Martin ran a two-year field project in central India, financed by WWF-Switzerland, which in 1975 led to an ecological PhD thesis analysing the reasons for the severe endangerment of the Barasingha, the Indian swamp deer.[2] Between 1975 and 1978 Martin ran national parks in Ghana, a project also financed by WWF, and became 'deeply involved in tropical forestry', the topic of his second book.[3] In 1980 Claude Martin became a director of WWF-Switzerland and in 1990 deputy director general of WWF International, responsible for the fund's programme work.

Because of his long-term involvement with WWF-Switzerland, Claude Martin was perfectly aware of the grievances larger NOs were harbouring against Gland – he had been, in 1982, one of the participants at the 'conspirative' Zurich meeting motivated by the leadership style of Charles de Haes.[4] He was thus ideally suited to implement the constitutional changes, worked out by his former boss Hans Hüssy, which aimed at improving NO relations through revised statutes and by-laws of the deed of foundation approved by the international board in 1993. During Claude Martin's twelve-year tenure relations with WWF family members ceased to be the 'contentious and debilitating' issue about which his predecessor regularly had had to complain.[5] Of course, problems with National Organisations continued to arise, yet board and EXCO minutes show that Gland was once more able to play a constructive role in solving them. Particularly impressive was the rapid improvement of the relationship with WWF-US. This was largely due to the fact that Claude Martin had headed the Gland team negotiating the 1991 Memorandum of Understanding with Washington. The meetings had allowed him 'to re-establish a new level of trust with some of the WWF-US people', especially Kathryn Fuller, who was to remain president of the American NO until 2004.[6] Fuller remembers about Claude Martin and Jim Leape, who headed the US delegation: 'Each is really strong, really forthright, really honest, with a strong point of view, and so you can get everything out on the table without mistrust.'[7]

Claude Martin, director general of WWF International from 1993 to 2005

More difficult was the re-establishment of good relations with South Africa. The first board meeting attended by Claude Martin as director general designate, in October 1993, was marked by an 'outburst' from Gavin Relly, chairman of SANF. He resented the fact that in view of further possible revelations about Operation Lock Gland refused to consider the case closed for good.[8] Further problems related to the NO's name, which was not in line with Gland's goal of a global brand presence, and to money, as the Stellenbosch office stopped transferring funds to WWF International because of currency exchange regulations in 1992.[9] The crisis was solved only in 1994, when the Southern African Nature Foundation changed its name to 'WWF-South Africa', a move paving the way for a meeting of the WWF annual conference in South Africa one year later.[10]

Despite the reintegration of South Africa into the WWF family, Gland's relations with Anton Rupert, president of WWF-South Africa until 2002 and honorary president until his death four years later, were never again as close as in the previous decades. In the 1990s Rupert directed both his private and his corporate conservation efforts towards a new venture, the Peace Parks Foundation.[11] Established in 1997 under the patronage of Anton Rupert, Prince Bernhard and Nelson Mandela, the foundation aims at creating trans-frontier conservation areas linking ecosystems and fostering peace and prosperity. While the concept of peace parks had been developed by IUCN, Rupert concentrated on raising the funds necessary to create them in southern Africa. Apart from re-employing fund-raising techniques successful at WWF in the 1970s, especially those geared towards major donors, Anton Rupert also used former WWF staff to run the Peace Parks Foundation. John Hanks, who headed WWF-South Africa until 1997, became its first CEO (until 2000), while Frans Stroebel was a member of the board and chairman of the fund-raising committee (until 2006).[12]

The presence of key people directly responsible for Operation Lock goes a long way to explaining why Claude Martin remained non-committal to Anton Rupert's desire for WWF 'to play a more important role in the Peace Parks Foundation'.[13] The new director general believed that 'Operation Lock was in many ways a consequence of a "northern" approach to conservation, an approach that attempted to [...] impose conservation [on] developing countries without basing such measures on local knowledge and involvement. The fact that Operation Lock even resorted to paramilitary services is symptomatic of such an imperialistic approach.' To the ecologist Claude Martin, who in the 1970s had undertaken conservation work in India and Ghana and who had been running the most activist NO within the WWF family for the entire 1980s, Operation Lock was not only a 'horrendous incident' but also 'a manifestation of the thinking of the past that had nothing to do with modern conservation to which I was partisan'. He was thus bound to see Anton Rupert's new project as a top-down, park-based anachronism: 'It was inconceivable that we would have supported a "Peace Parks" initiative that was not [at] "peace" with local people and was essentially an initiative of rich wildlife enthusiasts that were willing to pay an entry price.' A seasoned diplomat, Claude Martin made sure, however, not to offend either Anton Rupert or Prince Bernhard: 'For me these two individuals played an important role in the history of WWF, but now we lived in a world with different realities, which necessitated an integrated sustainable development approach. Although I paid my respects to them, I did not expect any real input from them, nor did I discuss future strategies of WWF with them.'[14] Anton Rupert received WWF's Duke of Edinburgh Conservation Medal in 2003, and Claude Martin visited Prince Bernhard in Soestdijk Palace for the last time a few weeks before the death of WWF's founder president in 2004.

With another key member of WWF's founding generation, Claude Martin was able to intensify the relationship. Until becoming vice-president emeritus

Bengal tiger (*Panthera tigris tigris*), Kanha National Park, Madhya Pradesh, India

Barasingha (*Cervus duvaucelii*), Kanha National Park, Madhya Pradesh, India. The endangered deer is a prey of the tiger

in 1997, Luc Hoffmann was actively involved in the affairs of the fund and even thereafter remained 'a loyal ally' with whom the director general was 'in regular contact'.[15] To this day Luc Hoffmann, through his family foundation, MAVA,

Luc Hoffmann, Vice-President Emeritus, WWF International, La Tour du Valat, Camargue, France

continues to give generous support to WWF projects, and the fact that his son André replaced him on the board of WWF International in 1997 has established a trans-generational link between the Basle family and the NGO which their most eminent ornithologist member has helped to create.[16] While Claude Martin's description of Luc Hoffmann as 'one of the very few real philanthropists in the world who managed to make things move in conservation' also pertains to his other initiatives, for instance the Convention on Wetlands signed in the Iranian town of Ramsar in 1971, it is clear that, without Hoffmann's unique support combining scientific expertise, financial prowess and a deep commitment to nature conservation on a global scale, WWF would not have fared as well as it did.[17]

The most important strategy debate shaping the conservation policy of WWF in the 1990s had already taken place by the time Claude Martin became director general. In 1989 WWF International had received the Phillipson Report, a review of the effectiveness of the 1,747 conservation projects supported in the first 25 years of the fund's existence. Based on a sample of 79 projects in 26 countries, the report by the Oxford zoology professor John Phillipson and his team found that the overall success rate of WWF-sponsored projects was 73 per cent, and that while threatened species management had only the 'limited' success rate of 55 per cent, education and awareness projects had been 'remarkably successful' at 100 per cent.[18] Hand in hand with these rather impressive results, however, went severe criticism of the way in which projects had been

Saving the World's Wildlife

carried out: 'Project management leaves much to be desired, supervision is poor, reporting by executants is sporadic, true financial accountability is non-existent and file maintenance is appalling.' While Charles de Haes had to make sure that this passage was somewhat toned down before the report was made available to the press, Phillipson's critique confirmed his decision to take over project management from IUCN in 1985 as the vast majority of projects supported by WWF ever since 1961 had been both drawn up and carried out by the union.[19]

While it was thus clear that WWF had to continue transforming itself from a grant-making into a project-executing environmental organisation, what was lacking, according to John Phillipson, was 'an unambiguously worded, and widely available, WWF International policy statement'.[20] This was worked out by the Planning and Budget Committee. Initiated by Charles de Haes in 1988 in view of the mounting criticism by some of the more important NOs regarding the lack of transparency of the Gland headquarters, it contained 'the usual suspects', i.e. the CEOs of WWF-US (Bill Reilly followed by Kathryn Fuller), WWF-UK (George Medley), WWF-Netherlands (Niels Halbertsma), WWF-Switzerland (Claude Martin) and WWF-Denmark (Vibeke Skat-Rørdam).[21] Taking up discussions about broadening the scope of WWF which had been going on for well over a decade, the CEOs drew up the first mission statement to supplement the foundation's aims laid down in the deed of foundation. For an entire year the committee met once a month, each time in a different place. During this process 'we realised [...] that we wanted to be an organisation which has more than some isolated projects. We wanted to address the root causes of environmental destruction in a comprehensive way,' remembers Claude Martin.[22] Kathryn Fuller recalls that while the discussions highlighted both the drawbacks and the advantages of being part of a diverse network of environmental organisations, there was a strong desire to make real conservation progress: 'We didn't want to become the UN of conservation, just talking and not doing.'[23] The outcome of 'many a meeting, and many discussions and papers', was a short but carefully worded text approved by the board at the end of 1989.[24] It read:

WWF's mission is to achieve the conservation of nature and ecological processes by:

Preserving genetic, species and ecosystem diversity;

Ensuring that the use of renewable natural resources is sustainable both now and in the long term, for the benefit of all life on earth;

Promoting actions to reduce, to a minimum, pollution and the wasteful exploitation and consumption of resources and energy.

WWF's ultimate goal is to stop, and eventually reverse, the accelerating degradation of our planet's natural environment, and to help build a future in which humans live in harmony with nature.[25]

The process of working out the new mission statement, which in its essence is still in place today, was at least as important as the text itself.[26] For while most of the content had been up for discussion for quite some time – Hans Hüssy had raised the (nuclear) energy issue at board level as early as 1981 – the approval of the text by the international board formally endorsed a broader vision of conservation which the more traditional elements within the WWF leadership still viewed with suspicion. This became clear when a first draft was discussed by the board in June 1989. Both Prince Philip and Russell Train insisted on the centrality of wildlife and species conservation and were uneasy about becoming involved with 'human environmental problems' (Prince Philip) or extending the fund's 'constituency into new publics' (Russell Train). Also, Anton Rupert felt that WWF 'should build on what it had traditionally done and concentrate on fund raising'. The only board member who supported the thrust of the new mission without reservations was Gerardo Budowski, a former director general of IUCN: '[Dr Budowski] said that there was clearly a feeling that WWF needed to

Saving the World's Wildlife

change. He said that the Board should accept this and not act in a very conservative way and reject it. [...] The mission statement, he felt, should retain some of the more radical statements included in the draft as these were the sentiments of the younger generation within WWF.' Pointing out the generational differences between a board whose key members were born in the 1920s or earlier, and NO representatives such as Claude Martin and Kathryn Fuller, born in the 1940s, appears to have mollified the board's view on the subject. Following Budowski's remarks, Prince Philip conciliatorily declared 'that the mission statement had not been rejected by the Board' and that 'the ideas [...] were not the problem but rather the drafting'.[27]

When Claude Martin became director general in 1993 the mission statement provided the blueprint for a comprehensive repositioning of WWF, a challenge eagerly taken up by the 48-year-old: 'The Mission now emphasized a holistic approach to conservation and I was to move the programme further in that direction.'[28] In order to overcome the feeling that they were 'winning many small battles but still losing the war', WWF set out on an extensive 'exercise in prioritisation, recognising that if the available resources were spread too thinly they could not achieve the desired result'.[29] While in the early 1990s the complementing of 'the traditional scattergun approach of much conservation activity by a "silver bullet" strategy in the form of hotspots with their emphasis on cost-effective measures' was a phenomenon widespread among environmental organisations,[30] at WWF it had two effects: a) the alignment of the entire WWF family behind one common global programme based on Ecoregion Conservation and b) the development of Target Driven Activities.

The ecoregional approach to conservation was first championed by WWF-US. It summed up network-wide discussions about broadening the appeal beyond saving endangered species into a clearly defined method. An ecoregion was defined as 'a large area of land or water that contains a geographically distinct assemblage of natural communities that (a) share a large majority of their species and ecological dynamics, (b) share similar environmental conditions, and (c) interact ecologically in ways that are critical for their long-term persistence'.[31] In 1998 this part of the prioritisation exercise led to the identification of 'the Earth's most biologically valuable ecoregions', the so-called Global 200.[32] Consisting in fact of 238 geographical areas, all chosen on a scientific basis, the Global 200 allowed the representation 'of biodiversity on a global scale'.[33] Chris Hails, Global Programme Director of WWF International and thus the man responsible for the alignment of the network behind the ecoregional approach, emphasises the usefulness of the concept as a global 'organising framework' which 'recognized for the first time that it was not only coral reefs and rain forests that were important, but that deserts, Mediterranean regions, and the tundra contained unique species which, if lost, could never be replaced'.[34]

The Target Driven Activities (TDAs) were initiated by Claude Martin in 1995 in close cooperation with WWF-Netherlands, which provided most of the funding. Focusing on forests, oceans and climate change, the TDAs were 'add-ons' to the Global Programme.[35] They dealt with global issues, one of which, climate change, had so far never been addressed by the network as a whole. They included clear targets as benchmarks for success and failure, and also tried out a new management approach. Instead of running projects through committee oversight, as had hitherto been the rule, TDA managers were given 'a budget and a relatively free hand' because a 'more emphatic leadership' was believed to increase programme efficiency. Siegfried Woldhek, director of WWF-Netherlands: '[The TDA manager] is responsible for the "heart, head, and belly" of a project: the vision, the strategy, the day-to-day management, and the development of people. He or she goes to bed with the project each night, and gets up with it in the morning.'[36] Encouraged by the results of the Forest TDA, which in three years almost doubled the amount of old-growth forest lands protected from development, in 2000 the three TDAs were expanded into six Target Driven Programmes, the additional topics being freshwater, species and toxic chemicals.[37] Chris Hails: 'The TDA experiment together with the ecoregional approach allowed WWF for the first time to develop an organising framework for a global programme covering both places and processes.'[38]

While Charles de Haes had always aimed at increasing the importance of the WWF 'headquarters' – as late as 1990 he planned to hire 53 new people in Gland – under Claude Martin this trend was reversed.[39] A keynote of his term as director general was 'decentralisation', and it is no coincidence that he preferred to call his workplace the 'International Secretariat'.[40] In 1995 Martin reduced the

Gland staff 'by about 40 positions' and later imposed a hiring freeze.[41] Simultaneously the number of Programme Offices, technically subsidiaries of WWF International, drastically increased, especially in developing countries but also in post-Cold War eastern Europe: 'WWF grew from about 25 major offices in the mid-1980s to nearly 60 by the end of the 1990s.'[42] Some Programme Offices in due course became fully fledged National Organisations, for instance in Indonesia, Brazil and Russia. There were two motives for decentralisation. On the one hand Claude Martin was convinced that 'unless WWF established itself more strongly in [the developing world], and adopted a participatory approach involving local communities, we would always remain a "northern" organization with limited impact'. On the other hand, decentralisation offered a practical solution to the financial problems caused by the fact that in the 1990s it became incre-

Anti-poaching brigade supported by WWF in the Russian Far East, Bikin river, Primorye Region, September 2002. The area is the habitat of the Amur tiger

asingly difficult for Gland to attract unrestricted NO funds for programme work. The creation of Programme Offices allowed WWF International to channel NO funds directly to developing countries. As decentralisation went hand in hand with 'strong policy guidance' from the International Secretariat, the strategy was not meant to diminish Gland's power within the WWF family; on the contrary.[43] In 1994 Claude Martin told the international board: 'The challenge of successful decentralisation is in increasing the local influence and encouraging local management, by locals, while at the same time maintaining a consistent and powerful WWF global conservation programme.'[44]

The desire to cooperate with local populations, which historically had often been excluded from conservation projects and at times even physically removed from their homelands when a national park was created, pre-dated the arrival of Claude Martin as director general of WWF by almost three decades. While

WWF-Switzerland enquired about 'the possibilities to protect the Indians of Amazonia in Brazil' as early as 1964,[45] Pilanesberg National Park, opened in 1979 in the South African 'homeland' of Bophuthatswana and financed to a large extent by WWF-South Africa, was a remarkably successful pioneering attempt at indigenous people participation.[46] In the 1980s measures to augment local involvement were frequently discussed at board meetings as it became clear that conservation needed to be integrated into a social context in order to succeed. Regarding a difficult WWF project in the British Isles in 1991, Prince Philip wrote to Charles de Haes: 'As we have discovered in Africa, no conservation measure works unless the local people support it. The same applies to Scotland!'[47] One year later a workshop on people participation at an IUCN conference on World Parks in Caracas chaired by Claude Martin 'attracted so much attention that no room in the conference building was big enough'.[48] When in 2004, after the expansion of programme offices in developing countries staffed overwhelmingly with locals, an article by the American anthropologist Mac Chapin in *World Watch* magazine criticised WWF, together with its main US competitors, Conservation International and The Nature Conservancy, for showing 'a disturbing neglect of the indigenous peoples whose land they are in the business to protect', Claude Martin was understandably irritated.[49] Distributing the Chapin text at a board meeting in November 2004, the director general noted: 'While the article focuses on the important issue of indigenous people's role in conservation, it contained many inaccuracies and errors.'[50]

In a reply to the Chapin article the chief conservation officer of WWF-US, Carter Roberts, and Gland's programme director, Chris Hails, took 'exception to the misrepresentation of our on-the-ground work with indigenous peoples', but also announced an intention to 'openly re-evaluate the WWF policy on indigenous peoples and strengthen its enforcement and monitoring mechanisms'.[51] The result of this pledge was a thorough review of WWF's relationship with indigenous and local communities. A dense, eleven-page report published in 2007 is a good indication of how challenging it is to transform a simple policy decision into the complex realities of present-day conservation – in this case the need to transform WWF from a 'northern' organisation into a truly global environmental network dedicated to sustainable development. While the report makes five

Saving the World's Wildlife

recommendations, all endorsed and accepted by WWF, among them the creation of 'indigenous policy focal points' and the development of a 'broader social policy', the authors insisted that their recommendations 'represent the start of a process, not the end of it. The review is but an initial step; others must follow.' [52]

WWF's cooperative approach to business and industry became more selective under Claude Martin. In 2003 the director general told the international board: 'WWF works with progressive elements in industry to promote leadership and demonstrate corporate sustainability, develop environmental best practices, catalyse sectorial and political change and finally, to finance conservation activities.' This policy went hand in hand, however, with an increasing awareness of corporate sponsors trying to 'greenwash' themselves. Claude Martin therefore underlined that WWF 'must be vigilant and prudent in its dealings with Business and Industry' and that '[h]igh standards in terms of accountability are essential'. In practice this meant that the organisation increasingly insisted on its right to openly criticise even those companies that had given them money. This was exemplified in the case of Shell, the fund's first corporate sponsor. With Shell and its partner Enron the organisation fought 'VERY hard' over a gas pipeline constructed through the Chiquitanos dry forest from Bolivia to the Brazilian town of Cuiaba between 1999 and 2001. [53] When at the beginning of the 21st century WWF failed to identify an 'oil & gas company that is serious about being a leader in transforming their impacts on climate change and on biodiversity', the organisation began to 'phase-out [...] funding from fossil fuel companies such as BP, Shell and others' in the year 2000. [54]

While WWF's link to the oil industry ended because the fund was unable to find a corporation willing to commit itself to conservation by improving its ecological footprint – a measuring tool to calculate the environmental impact of individuals, states and corporations developed in the course of the 1990s – in the construction industry WWF found a major player who was serious about going green. [55] In 2000 the Paris-based construction giant Lafarge became WWF's

Overleaf: Emperor penguins in snowstorm, Dawson-Lambton Glacier, Antarctica

first Conservation Partner. Given that Lafarge is the world's largest producer of cement and thus a major source of CO_2 emissions, a key element of the partnership was the reduction of these emissions by 20 per cent within ten years. Further elements of the agreement were forest landscape restoration, quarry rehabilitation and the identification of performance indicators, as well as the creation of local initiatives in countries where there were both Lafarge and WWF offices. Yet what really differentiated the Lafarge agreement from earlier corporate partnerships was that instead of focusing on the transfer of money the new goal was the development of a long-term relationship in which WWF retained the ability to criticise its corporate partner. In 2003 a joint press release emphasised: 'A fundamental element of the partnership is the agreement to disagree on some issues.' [56]

Claude Martin and Bertrand Collomb, president of Lafarge, announcing WWF's first Conservation Partnership, Paris, March 2000

While the Lafarge partnership focused on a key player within the business, in another sector WWF found a way to engage with an entire industry. At the United Nations Conference on Environment and Development held in Rio de Janeiro in 1992 an attempt to curb tropical deforestation failed, not least because of a speech made by the Malaysian prime minister, Mahathir bin Mohamad, who accused the West of neocolonialism: 'When the rich chopped down their own forests, built their poison-belching factories and scoured the world for cheap resources, the poor said nothing. Indeed they paid for the development of the rich. Now the rich claim a right to regulate the development of the poor countries. And yet any suggestion that the rich

Logs at an FSC-certified timber company, East Province, Cameroon, June 2010

Saving the World's Wildlife

WWF – the first 50 years

compensate the poor adequately is regarded as outrageous. As colonies we were exploited. Now as independent nations we are to be equally exploited.'[57] Claude Martin remembers that this passage struck him 'like lightning' and that in the wake of the Rio forestry debacle WWF realised 'that we needed to influence the markets if we want to influence the way in which public resources are used. Otherwise we're always going to be "end of pipe".'[58] Together with other environmental organisations WWF established the Forest Stewardship Council (FSC) in 1993. It aimed at influencing the global timber market by establishing principles and criteria for sustainable forest management and by certifying forest companies complying with its rigorous standard. In due course FSC established itself as the key global instrument fostering sustainable forest use, a fact noted with great pride by the WWF board for the first time in 2000.[59]

A key feature of the 1990s was the 'rapidly increasing income from governments and aid agencies' (GAA), which in some NOs, for instance WWF-Germany, made up for more than half of income as early as 1993. In order to avoid being seen as an 'extension of the government's environmental arm', the international board decided to limit GAA funds to 50 per cent of any given project.[60] Claude Martin remembers that 'GAA funds became an important factor [...] when aid agencies started recognizing that NGOs had a role to play in the implementation of international conventions such as CITES and when WWF had developed field programmes that integrated development components. The introduction of the concept of "debt swaps", pioneered by WWF-US in the late 1980s, also played a role.' In 1987, WWF-US had arranged to transform a foreign debt of US$1 million into a conservation programme in Ecuador, a model subsequently repeated elsewhere in Latin America, in Africa, Asia and post-Cold War eastern Europe.[61] Rather than being the outcome of a planned fund-raising exercise, the influx of GAA money, which in 1997 made up almost 25 per cent of the fund's total income, thus appears to have been a by-product of the increasing attention given to sustainable development involving local populations.[62] Another consequence of WWF's commitment to 'biodiversity conservation within the socio-economic context' was the alliance with the World Bank on Forest Conservation and Sustainable Use concluded in 1998.[63] Through this framework the two organisations coordinated their work 'with governments, the private sector,

Saving the World's Wildlife

and civil society to significantly reduce the loss and degradation of all forest types worldwide'.[64] Until 2005 the Alliance managed to increase by almost 50 million hectares the area of protected forests, helped placing 200 million hectares of productive forest under sustainable management, and was a key facilitator of the largest tropical forest conservation initiative to date, the Amazon Region Protected Areas programme.[65]

Around the turn of the millennium WWF increasingly gained influence in international and multilateral fora which have come to symbolise the post-Cold War era of globalisation. In 2001, three years after the conclusion of the World Bank Alliance, the director general was first invited to the World Economic Forum held in Davos. The prospect of repeating this was welcomed by the international board: '[T]o have Claude as an accepted interlocutor of the WEF would lead to highly desirable networking opportunities.'[66] The focus on sustainable development and a decentralised structure combined with strong policy guidance from WWF International thus appears to have significantly increased the political prestige of the director general. Yet hand in hand with this went a gradual decrease in the significance of the presidential office. While Prince Philip had been an extremely active participant in WWF affairs until the enactment of the constitutional changes increasing the influence of the NOs in 1993, in the three remaining years of his presidency both the minutes of WWF meetings as well as the prince's personal WWF files show a somewhat reduced level of intervention. His successors left even less traces in internal WWF documents. This probably owed much to the fact that it proved rather difficult to find a new person for the job. As no external candidate was in sight in 1995, the Pakistani board member Syed Babar Ali, a former minister of finance, took over from Prince Philip *ad interim* until the end of 1999.[67] Babar Ali was followed by the former Dutch prime minister Ruud Lubbers, who failed to leave a mark because he stayed for only a year – Lubbers went on to become UN High Commissioner for Refugees in 2001.[68] Another interim president, this time the British board member Sara Morrison, took over until 2002.[69] It was thus under its first woman president that WWF celebrated its 40th anniversary with a gala event held in Seville on 11 September 2001. Although the terrorist attacks on New York and Washington prevented the fund from communicating its conservation achievements to the world, the board thought that the event was 'very successful', not least because it managed to raise 400,000 Swiss francs.[70]

At a board meeting held in Florida at the end of 2001 the international board learned that finally a presidential candidate had been found who was both 'geographically appropriate and someone with direct connections to heads of government, particularly in the developing world'.[71] The Nigerian diplomat Chief Emeka Anyaoku was the first African to serve as president of WWF. Although he held office for eight years, as in the case of his immediate predecessors but in contrast to the presidency of Prince Philip, the minutes of board and Executive Council meetings seldom note direct interventions in debates by Chief Anyaoku. And while Anyaoku did not have a global persona comparable to that of the first two presidents of the fund, the experienced diplomat undoubtedly helped WWF to gain prestige and credibility in Africa. Claude Martin: 'Emeka Anyaoku was well known in Commonwealth countries, as former Secretary General, and particularly with African Heads of State who received him with great respect for the role he played in the demise of the Apartheid regime.'[72]

Chief Emeka Anyaoku (left), president of WWF International from 2002 to 2009, representing the fund in Mali in 2004

The World Economic Forum 2002 led to a positive surprise for WWF. A New York public relations company presented a paper on NGOs as the 'fifth estate in global governance', and Claude Martin was pleased to learn that 'WWF scored very high in terms of trust in our brand. NGOs continue to score higher than Governments, Businesses and Media in Europe in terms of trust and are gaining ground in the US.'[73] Together with the results of another study which in 2001 had shown that '68 per cent of Europeans recognized the WWF logo', this seemed to confirm the communications policy pursued by Claude Martin and his team.[74] For even after the departure of the marketing specialist Charles de Haes, Gland remained 'very brand conscious', not least 'because of the increasing use of the internet and a confusing diversity of Web sites'. Claude Martin: 'We […] invested a lot in harmonizing the use of WWF's name and symbols across the family (although

Saving the World's Wildlife

we never managed to convince WWF-US to abandon the "old" name "World Wildlife Fund").' Aware of the fact that a brand 'is not just about names and marks' but also stands for the 'values and the "persona" of an organization', the 'ultimate aim' of the branding exercise was 'to reposition the organisation as a credible and reliable global conservation partner and to let these qualities be reflected through all our communications'.[75] The 'professional communications operation' initiated by Claude Martin at one point employed more than 25 staff and included the regular placement of opinion pieces by the director general in the international media.[76]

Of particular importance to the WWF brand was a dispute with Titan Sports, a US entertainment company specialising in the promotion of wrestling. In 1989 WWF-US, without informing the rest of the network, allowed Titan Sports, which traded as the World Wrestling Federation, a limited use of the term 'WWF'. When Titan Sports wanted to do a similar trademark deal with WWF International in 1991, Gland refused: 'The major concern was that both organizations were, in effect, competing for the youth audience. Titan's form of entertainment, which appears to market violence – albeit faked – was viewed by many as the antithesis of what WWF stands for.'[77] In 1994 the dispute between WWF and Titan Sports was settled, allowing the latter a limited use of the acronym. Shortly thereafter, however, WWF noticed a series of breaches of contract and again took legal action. In 2001 a London court upheld the 1994 agreement limiting the World Wrestling Federation's use of the initials WWF. Subsequently the entertainment company rebranded itself as 'World Wrestling Entertainment' and began using the acronym 'WWE'. In March 2002 EXCO, which had just been informed about the rising international levels of confidence in NGOs, was pleased to note: 'This high trust in the WWF brand makes the latest victory over the wrestlers all the more relevant.'[78]

A crisis at one of the oldest and best-performing members of the WWF family showed that, despite a wide range of impressive achievements, even after four decades the WWF project remained a fragile one. In May 2001 a dispute broke out between the CEO of WWF-Switzerland, Carol Franklin, and the Swiss board presided over by Brigitta Hellat. The conflict could not be settled and led to the board dismissing the CEO in October. As most of the staff and a minority of the board sided with the CEO and went public with a call for her reinstatement, the press had a field day exposing what looked like a bizarre civil war within Switzerland's largest environmental organisation.[79] One of the most perceptive articles appeared in the left-wing Zurich weekly *Wochenzeitung*, which published a brilliantly satirical piece about WWF-Switzerland as a Punch and Judy show.[80] In November 2001 Hans Hüssy, who had resigned from his duties at WWF-Switzerland more than twenty years earlier, had to be recalled as temporary president of the board in order to solve the crisis. A first step to calming the situation was the resignation of Brigitta Hellat as president of the board, which went, however, hand in hand with the confirmation of Carol

WWF-Switzerland, farewell panel to
Carol Franklin, 2001

Franklin's dismissal as CEO.[81] When half a year later many of the staff were still in opposition to the board and 'events had taken another turn for the worse', WWF International began to consider withdrawing the licence from one of its founding members.[82] The international board was informed that 'WWF-Switzerland is experiencing the worst NO crisis that the Director General had seen in his 30 years with WWF.' After a detailed description of events the report concluded: 'A strange irony in all of this is that WWF-Switzerland will attain this year the highest income figure in its history. Income has been increasing, primarily due to legacies. All NOs have a vested interest in seeing WWF-Switzerland pull through this crisis and return to healthy operation.'[83] Only two years after the outbreak of the crisis the appointment of a new CEO, Hans-Peter Fricker, allowed WWF-Switzerland to return to calm waters and regain its old strength.[84]

In 2002 Claude Martin, a firm believer in the necessity of organisational rejuvenation at the top, informed Emeka Anyaoku of his desire to retire. Persuaded by the president to stay on for another three years, Claude Martin eventually left WWF at the end of 2005, then aged 60.[85] With projects in over one hundred countries, an annual income of US$500 million and an estimated 5.3 million regular supporters, the WWF family was not only much larger but also much

Saving the World's Wildlife

more united than when Martin had taken over from de Haes in 1993.[86] Although 22 per cent of the network's income came from governments and aid agencies, and 6 per cent each from corporations and charitable trusts, WWF was still predominantly a membership organisation: more than half of its income came from individuals, either as donations (43 per cent) or in the form of legacies (10 per cent).[87] The substantial income derived from legacies demonstrates the ability of WWF to foster long-term attachments with supporters. Incidentally, the announcement of Claude Martin's resignation occurred during a board meeting which began with 'a moment of silence in honour of WWF's Founding President, HRH Prince Bernhard of the Netherlands, who passed away a few days earlier at the age of 93'.[88] In his will the prince stipulated that his collection of elephant artwork was to be used in favour of WWF conservation efforts in Borneo. When sold at a Sotheby's auction in 2005, Prince Bernhard's elephants raised almost 400,000 Euros.[89]

Overleaf: Aerial view of flooded forest during rainy season, Rio Negro Forest Reserve, Brazil

WWF – the first 50 years

'As a historian I find plenty to learn from it all.'

In view of its 50th anniversary event celebrated in Zurich in April 2011, WWF International asked its network of national organisations and programme offices to identify '50 big conservation wins'. Given the wide range of projects undertaken in the course of half a century, it is not surprising that Gland received a veritable avalanche of proposals. They ranged from commemorating Coto Doñana National Park as 'one of the main icons of the early history of WWF' to highlighting the achievements of the Coral Triangle Initiative, which began in 2007.[1] Supported by the governments of Indonesia, the Philippines, East Timor, Papua New Guinea, the Solomon Islands and Malaysia, and in cooperation with various other NGOs and private companies, the Coral Triangle Initiative seeks to address threats to the marine, coastal and small island ecosystems in an area of 6 million square kilometres containing '76 per cent of the world's coral species, six of the world's seven marine turtle species, and at least 2,228 reef fish species'.[2] That this and countless other conservation projects were possible is certainly the single most important achievement of an organisation which in 1961 started off as nothing more than an idea.

Despite broadening its appeal from wildlife emergencies to an ever more global and long-term perspective on conservation, species remain central to WWF. Five decades after the creation of its first logo, the panda is still the symbol of WWF, and in 2010 the tiger was again at the heart of an international campaign. Shortly before this book went to press WWF's efforts to mobilise tiger-range states and donors around a goal of doubling tiger numbers in the wild by 2022 manifested itself at a Tiger Summit held in St Petersburg. Bringing together several government leaders, including Russian prime minister Vladimir Putin and Chinese premier Wen Jiabao, the summit yielded high-level political commitment to an unprecedented global effort to save the tiger.[3] This is all the more remarkable because in the 1990s WWF had been severely criticised for its tiger work when it transpired that some Indian reserves had no more tigers living in them and that population figures had often been inaccurate and at times even fictional.[4] In 1992 Guy Mountfort was shocked to learn that a British television programme reported on 'the complete failure [...] of our Tiger Project throughout South Asia and particularly in India', and three years later in an internal memorandum WWF-UK bitterly complained about the perceived neglect of tiger conservation

by WWF International.[5] Claude Martin was well aware of the fact that for a variety of reasons, including population growth and changing political landscapes in India and an increasing demand for tiger parts by practitioners of traditional Chinese medicine, the park-based tiger conservation of the 1970s had to be replaced with a much more sophisticated approach, including the integration of local populations and the enforcement of the international ban on the trade in tiger parts. He told WWF-UK: 'We have seen 25 years of tiger crisis with successes and failures, and we will see many more. Knowing the situation in the tiger range states this crisis will unfortunately never be over. We must plan with this in mind.' [6] Once a management problem at WWF-India paralysing the NO in the second half of the 1990s was solved, WWF was again able to contribute meaningfully to the conservation of one of the most charismatic species of the animal kingdom. Nevertheless, by 2010 there were more tigers living in captivity than in the wild, and WWF's campaign again drew on a scenario of doom. Its Tiger Fact Sheet emphasises rapid habitat loss and high persecution pressure on all remaining sub-species, sketches out the fund's multilayered plan to prevent extinction in the wild, and declares that 'only such a fully integrated approach will save the tiger'.[7]

Yet WWF is not just an interesting example of an environmental organisation which in the course of five decades abandoned the belief that saving species was a battle that can be won and replaced it with the certainty that every conservation achievement is only ever temporary. Its history also offers fascinating insights into how the deliberations of a small group of British naturalists could develop into one of the world's largest and most influential environmental NGOs. The archival evidence analysed in the course of writing this book has shown that within less than a year of Julian Huxley's articles on African wildlife published in November 1960 an organisation was set up with a logo, a distinct sense of purpose and identity, a legally registered deed of foundation, two top royal patrons and a very successful initial fund-raising campaign. In the course of a decade, WWF built up an international secretariat, a network of national appeals spread over four continents, and by 1973 even had an endowment of US$10 million thanks to the establishment of The 1001 – A Nature Trust. When in 1977 Max Nicholson sent Fritz Vollmar a substantial dossier of documents pertaining to the foundation of WWF, the key architect of the organisation

Saving the World's Wildlife

looked back at the beginnings and noted: 'As a historian also I find plenty to learn from it all.'[8]

This is no less true for the following decades during which WWF transformed itself from a fund-raising and grant-making agency into a fully fledged environmental organisation implementing a global conservation programme. For me as a historian it was fascinating to discover that this process went hand in hand with strong internal tensions, which in the early 1990s brought WWF to the brink of disintegration. While the fact that a permanent split could be avoided is clearly an achievement in its own right, comparing the WWF experience with the history of other NGOs suggests that such a crisis is not as exceptional as it may seem at first sight. Médecins sans frontières (MSF), the network of medical doctors established in 1971, for instance, underwent a period of intense internal dispute in the early 1980s, during which the French founding organisation together with its Swiss branch opposed sister organisations in Belgium, the Netherlands, Luxembourg and Spain. The MSF family only made up again in 1988 by adopting a common logo and by establishing an international secretariat three years later.[9] The history of Greenpeace offers even more striking parallels. When attempts on the part of the Vancouver headquarters to assert their authority over affiliates in the USA could not be solved with the creation of new by-laws, in 1979 the Canadian founders took their San Francisco office to court in an attempt to reclaim the Greenpeace trademark. Ironically for an organisation marked by a founding group of left-wing hippies the solution came in the form of David McTaggard, a Canadian businessman. He convinced the Vancouver and San Francisco offices to drop their dispute in exchange for a merger of all national branches into Greenpeace International, led by himself and situated in Amsterdam.[10] While Greenpeace in its crisis benefited from a businessman who within a few months of taking over an unruly group of activist tribes provided the organisation with 'a sophisticated management structure' it had previously lacked, at business-oriented WWF it was lawyers who helped the organisation overcome its internal

Preceding page: Cape buffalo (*Syncerus caffer caffer*) on the shore of Lake Nakuru, Lake Nakuru National Park, Kenya

Overleaf: Adult mountain gorilla playing with youngster, Uganda

dispute. The key roles played by Russell Train, Kathryn Fuller and Hans Hüssy in WWF's family row made sure that, rather than by calling in management consultants, the problem was perceived and solved as a constitutional matter.

Since 2005 the American environmental lawyer Jim Leape has been director general of WWF International. Thanks to long-term experience at WWF-US he is well acquainted with the delicate nature of the organisation's internal relations – in 1991 he was heading the Washington delegation negotiating the Memorandum of Understanding with Claude Martin, then still deputy director general of WWF International. Like his biologist predecessor, Jim Leape has ambitious conservation goals. When asked about them four years after his appointment, WWF's first American director general underlined the need to work with governments and corporations on ever larger scales while at the same time fostering WWF's links to local communities whose trust is essential for making conservation work. At the heart of Leape's agenda are Network Initiatives. Going beyond the ecoregions targeted in the 1990s, he sees them as the logical consequence of the global conservation aims of WWF: 'The Network Initiatives are about mobilizing truly concerted action. The key is not to settle for just the "alignment" of related but often parallel activities. In the Network Initiatives, we ask the relevant offices interested in a place like the Arctic or an issue like fisheries to come together to agree on targets and strategy, and then commit themselves to mobilizing the resources and action necessary to achieve them. It is a more intensive, demanding collaboration than we have typically attempted, but it offers huge potential.' [11]

Whether Network Initiatives centred on specific world regions such as the Coral Triangle, the Congo basin or the Himalaya, or those focusing on global issues such as market transformation, climate change or smart energy, will bring the desired results is of course something that only time can tell. The same is true for a constitutional change enacted in 2010 which reduced the board from 24 to 13 trustees. As in a similar move prompted by Prince Philip in 1982, this reform was motivated by the desire to make the key governing body of WWF more effective. The new board also includes a new president. In 2010 Yolanda Kakabadse, a former Ecuadorean minister of the environment, took over from Emeka Anyaoku. After Sara Morrison, Kakabdse is the second woman president of WWF. The fact that she is also a former president of IUCN underlines the fund's strong links to an organisation whose financial problems at the beginning of the 1960s were a key reason for the creation of WWF.

Yet when Max Nicholson sat down over Easter 1961 to write up his plan for an international environmental fund-raising organisation he had more in mind than saving IUCN from bankruptcy. The ten-page document which was to lead to the formation of WWF's London Preparatory Group was entitled 'How to save the world's wildlife'. It included the vision that not only money but also people can be motivated in favour of nature conservation on a global scale: 'The will which so many possess to co-operate in saving wild life has been frustrated because no one has asked them to join in a world crusade to this end and has shown how to conduct it.'[12] Although the millions of supporters WWF now has seem to indicate that Max Nicholson was right, if anything this book has shown that the development of his bold and ambitious plan into one of the world's largest environmental organisations was anything but inevitable. More than once the survival of the WWF family looked as uncertain as the future of the endangered species the organisation set out to save.

Looking back on over two years of archival research and personal encounters with WWF staff and supporters, my personal guess as to why the organisation managed to be as successful as it was, despite all odds, is to do with the enthusiasm the WWF project was capable of fostering within a great many individuals. Preparing the WWF exhibition at the Swiss National Museum in Zurich in October 2010, I made an appeal in the membership magazine of WWF-Switzerland. I was looking for people with childhood memories of collecting money for Lake Nakuru in 1972. The emotional intensity of the responses was remarkable. Peter Weber was twelve when he sold stamps displaying the flamingos whose African habitat he had never seen: 'It was tough selling the stamps. Conservation was not yet on everyone's lips. But I was fascinated by the name of the appeal: Nakuru.'[13] And Magdalena Hilfiker, who was only seven and lived in an Appenzell village where the houses are spread out over a large area, remembers having knocked on every door because she desperately wanted to receive the flamingo picture that successful fund-raisers were eligible for: 'The lithograph by Fritz Hug still hangs in my living room today. As a child I was really proud to own a picture with my name under it! And somehow I still have a special relationship with flamingos. It always makes me happy when I see one, on photographs or in the zoo.' [14] Many people also remember that the Nakuru appeal was the beginning of a very per-

sonal relationship with an organisation that gave them the possibility of doing something for nature conservation. Cornelia Urscheler, at twelve too shy a girl to approach many people, ended up buying most of the stamps herself with her pocket money. She recalls: 'I used them on letters to my pen pals in order to make publicity for "my" WWF! And despite "ruining" myself for a while I have remained loyal to WWF until today. Probably rightly so, because WWF is one of the best organisations in the world.' [15]

WWF members
Peter Weber and
Cornelia Urscheler,
c. 1972

Saving the World's Wildlife

Kenji Tezuka (9) Japan

Erika Brunner (18) Switzerland

Ashish Sachdeva (8) India

Karin Nielsen (12) Sweden

Keita Okoro Kalu (13) Nigeria

Michaël Adriaansz (12) Netherlands

Marjatta Salmenkallio (16) Finland

Keith Alderson (11) England

Jonas Fredén (14) Sweden

Ricky Vaernewijck (13) Belgium

Nicolas Addamiano (16) France

Christiane Gysen (14) Belgium

Nizam Murshed (9) Bangladesh

Satawat Chuiynum (16) Thailand

Soma Banerjee (8) India

Kirsi Oksala (13) Finland

Nick Karalis (15) Greece

Gaute Anil Ganapata (13) India

Akila Sesharsayee (10) India

Suman Sijapati (11) Nepal

WWF-Switzerland, fund-raising stamps for Operation
Tiger, 1974. The designs were the result of an international
drawing competition for children

Overleaf: Greeting interaction between two Eastern Grey
kangaroos (*Macropus giganteus*), Australia

What if...?

Contemporary artists' perspectives

What happens if you give an army of retired panda collection boxes to contemporary artists? WWF-UK found out by asking sixteen renowned British artists and designers to transform them into new works in 2009. London-based artist Adam King created a fragile mobile from a wide array of found and second-hand objects. The sculpture slowly revolves around itself – a striking metaphor for the consumer world we live in, but by no means a negative one, due to the piece's cheerful colours and funny details. While Jim Lambie's mother-and-child panda half submerged in concrete recalls the scenarios of doom invoked by the founders of WWF, two design cooperatives focused on the intense glare of the panda. Troika inserted laser beams into the eyes of the panda cub, while Jason Bruges Studio placed servo motors into 100 collection boxes linked to a thermal camera, so that the entire group follows the movement of each passer-by. The key question of what happens to the natural world is, of course, a theme contemporary artists take up without being prompted by WWF. In a powerful video poem, for instance, the British artist Lemn Sissay combines cityscapes with melting glaciers and polar landscapes in order to emphasise the risks of unsustainable development: 'What if we got it wrong? What if we weakened ourselves getting strong?' Looking at two further contemporary artworks sheds light on a key element of the communication strategy employed by WWF ever since 1961, namely the tension between visions of doom and our collective longing for unspoilt natural landscapes. While the Swiss photographer Florio Puenter creates magnificent views of his native Engadine valley, from which all traces of human interaction have been removed, the video collage Doomed by the Australian artist Tracey Moffatt, based on a wide range of movies, shows that apocalyptic nightmares are at least as fascinating as visions of paradise.

Preceding page: Troika, Surrogate, mixed media, 2009

Jim Lambie, Sweet Bamboo, panda, concrete, 2009

304

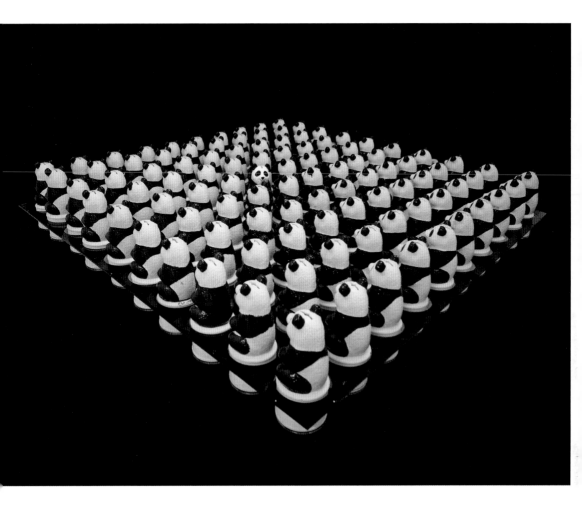

Jason Bruges Studio, Panda Eyes, panda, perspex, paint,
plywood, thermal camera, servo motors, 2009

Tracey Moffatt, Doomed, video collage in collaboration with Gary Hilberg, 2007

Lemn Sissay, What If?,
video poem, 2009

Overleaf: Florio Puenter, Lej da Segl, Cibachrome, 2009

Sources and acknowledgements

In 2008 Andreas Spillmann, the director of the Swiss National Museum, asked me whether I wanted to curate an exhibition on WWF. He explained that the organisation was founded in Zurich in 1961 and that the upcoming 50th anniversary could be an interesting opportunity for the museum to tell the WWF story. As I had just finished a major book and exhibition project, on the Swiss writer Annemarie Schwarzenbach, the proposal came at the right moment. Yet since environmental history was not my field I had to look into the existing secondary literature in order to assess the project's feasibility. I soon found out that there was no independent, primary-source-based history of WWF, and the prospect of covering uncharted territory became very tempting. I agreed to curate an exhibition if the Swiss National Museum could get unrestricted access to WWF's archives. This proved relatively easy, for the CEOs of both WWF organisations located in Switzerland, Jim Leape of WWF International and Hans-Peter Fricker of WWF-Switzerland, quickly complied with our request. In order to make sure that the history of the organisation could be told as objectively as possible, it was also agreed that WWF should not become involved in financing the exhibition.

The working title of this project was *WWF. A Biography*. It was eventually used for both the exhibition and the accompanying book in its German version. This was not only due to the fact that I was familiar with biographies as a genre, including a book on Switzerland's most famous physicist, Albert Einstein. Focusing on people rather than structures or policies also proved to be right because the sources showed that WWF was the creation of a distinct set of individuals who quickly began to refer to their organisation as a 'family'. This human dimension was, however, almost completely lacking in the few existing academic texts on WWF.[1] I found my experience confirmed by the environmental historian Frank Zelko, who recently noted: 'Groups such as Greenpeace, Friends of the Earth or the World Wildlife Fund are merely identified as "international" organizations and analysis proceeds from there. The *process* by which these organizations reach this state and the meaning attached to it by their members are elided in favour of analysis which portrays them as abstract constructs devoid of the historical forces and human beings that shape them.'[2]

A biography needs to be based on a wide range of primary sources. In the case of WWF that was not a problem. On the contrary. Each WWF national office I visited contained enough archival material for several books. Leaving portraits of individual family members to subsequent researchers, I concentrated on sources pertaining to the history of the entire WWF family. The single most important source of this kind was found in the archives of WWF International in Gland – an almost complete set of minutes of the fund's key governing bodies, the board of trustees and its executive council, EXCO.[3] Luckily for historians such as myself, the WWF leadership did not stick to a decision taken at their second meeting, namely that minutes should be 'short and precise [...] and, as a rule, not mention the participants in the discussions by name'.[4] Instead the documents quickly became long and detailed and, especially at times of internal debate or even conflict, clearly identified those who voiced their opinion. Fifty years of minutes thus ended up filling no fewer than eight large files, the analysis of which kept me busy for several months. A second key source, nine files labelled 'WWF history', are also located in the archives of WWF International. They were compiled by the first director general, Fritz Vollmar. In 1977 he contacted the founders of WWF asking them for written documents and private memories pertaining to the origins of the organisation. As most of the founders have meanwhile died, Vollmar's timely initiative was another stroke of good luck.

Further useful sources were found abroad. The estates of two important founding figures were donated to archives in the UK, Max Nicholson's papers to the Linnean Society of London, the papers of Sir Peter Scott to Cambridge University. The estate of the fund's first president, Prince Bernhard of the Netherlands, is held by the Koninklijk Huisarchief in The Hague. The WWF papers of the third president, HRH The Prince Philip, Duke of Edinburgh, are kept at Buckingham Palace, where their owner kindly allowed me to consult them. Because Prince Philip has been involved with WWF ever since 1961, his extensive and well-organised files shed light on almost every aspect of the fund's history. In one case they even contained a unique and previously unknown document without which an entire chapter of this book could not have been written, namely the chronology of Operation Lock compiled by Abraham Sofaer in 1993.

The written evidence was complemented by memories of WWF leaders who were willing to share them in interviews, by e-mail or letter. Without their generous help key questions prompted by the archival evidence could not have been answered. Many members of that group also provided the Swiss National Museum with important loans for the WWF exhibition. In the UK, I am sincerely grateful for their help and support to HRH The Duke of Edinburgh, Sir Arthur Norman and Charles de Haes; in Switzerland to Luc Hoffmann, Hans Hüssy, Fritz Vollmar, Roland Wiederkehr, Claude Martin and Jim Leape; in the USA to Russell Train, Bill Reilly and Kathryn Fuller; in the Netherlands to Niels Halbertsma and in India to Anne Wright. Additional information, much appreciated practical help and access to WWF sources, photographs and objects was kindly provided by many other former and present staff of the organisation, including, in the UK: Greg Armfield, Carrie Armitage, Georgie Bridge, Sarah Brunwin, Winnie De'Ath, Allison Jackson, George Medley and Katie Randerson; in Switzerland (Gland): Martin Atkin, Jean-François Buvelot, John Cederroth, Zorana Davis, Michèle Dépraz, Chris Hails, Tessa Kroon, Pascale Moehrle, Susanna Schultze, Rob Soutter and Naze Teo; in Switzerland (Zurich): Jacques Duméril, Rahel Gerber, Holger Hoffmann-Riem, Alfred Matthias, Gian-Reto Raselli and Franziska Zoller; in the USA: Christopher O'Leary, Dawn Pointer McCleskey and Kerry Zobor; in South Africa: Carolyn Cramer, Morné du Plessis, John Hanks and Frans Stroebel; in the Netherlands: Maarten Bijleveld, Clarisse Buma and Lot Folgering. A special note of thanks to all those members of WWF-Switzerland who shared their memories of the 1972 Lake Nakuru campaign. They provided me with a much-appreciated perspective on WWF from below.

For permission to consult WWF papers of Prince Bernhard I am indebted to Her Majesty Queen Beatrix of the Netherlands. Her sister, Princess Irene, kindly answered questions about their late father's approach to the environment. I would also like to thank the director of the Dutch Royal Archives, Philip Maarschalkerweerd, for his kind assistance, both in The Hague and when he came to Zurich bringing me a briefcase full of documents. At Buckingham Palace my special thanks go to Dame Anne Griffiths, Librarian and Archivist to HRH The Duke of Edinburgh, for her generous help, interesting lunchtime conversations and, above all, the perfectly kept WWF files of Prince Philip. I survived the freezing cold of Cambridge University's manuscript reading room thanks to the cafeteria and the most helpful staff looking after the estate of Sir Peter Scott, in particular Frank Bowles and Peter Meadows. Permission to consult the papers was kindly granted by the late Lady Philippa Scott. I also owe thanks to her daughter Dafila, who gave us Peter Scott's original drawing of the panda logo on loan, and to Philip Ball, the manager of the Photography and Illustration Service at Cambridge University, who provided scans of Peter Scott's artwork. At the Linnean Society of London I am indebted to Lynda Brooks for her generous help and to Gina Douglas for first-hand accounts of Max Nicholson's driving skills – rather than concentrating on the road, he appears to have looked out for birds all the time. It is thanks to Nicholson's son Piers that the Swiss National Museum can show the most important architect of WWF by means of a portrait bust, by Alan Jarvis.

Further information, illustrations for the book and loans to the exhibition were kindly provided by the following people and institutions: George Aman, Zurich; Judith Knight, Artsadmin, London; Deana Vanagan, Artwise Curators, London; Cornelia Zaugg, Bundesamt für Veterinärwesen, Berne; Beat Stutzer, Katharina Ammann, Bündner Kunstmuseum, Chur; Wolf-Dieter Burkhard, Landschlacht; Verena Buschle-Berger, Münchenbuchsee; Letizia Enderli, Fotostiftung Schweiz, Winterthur; Mathis Wackernagel, Global Footprint Network, Oakland; Magdalena Hilfiker, St Gallen; Dora Moor-Schär, Vordemwald; Ferdinand Damaschun, Uwe Moldrzyk, Museum für Naturkunde, Berlin; Christian Meyer, Ambros Hänggi, Eduard Stöckli, Naturhistorisches Museum, Basle; Beatrice Blöchlinger, Naturhistorisches Museum, Berne; Eugen Schmid, Zurich; Felix Schwarzenbach, Sachseln; François Schwarzenbach, Gattikon; Ed Smith, Westerham; Olivia Sophia, Roslyn Oxley9 Gallery, Sydney; Peter Weber, Wald ZH; Ernst Ulrich von Weizsäcker, Emmendingen, and Cornelia Urscheler, Schmerikon. Especially generous were Lukas Keller and Barbara Oberholzer of the Zoologisches Museum der Universität Zürich. In addition to hundreds of animals from their stacks they were also prepared to part with one of the highlights of their permanent exhibition, the baby panda.

While this book was being written I had the opportunity to present two papers on aspects of WWF history. I'm very grateful to Marja Spierenburg, Stephen Ellis and Harry Wels at the University of Amsterdam and to Tom Buchanan and Martin Conway at the Oxford University History Faculty for organising much-appreciated moments of exchange, reflection and encounter. For additional professional advice, moral support and generous hospitality during research trips I would like to thank Denise Cripps, Pietro del Favero, Bahi Ghoubril, Subha Mukherji, Peter Sarris, James MacEwen, Belinda Edwards, Regina Frey, Timothy Watkins, Todd Gambill, Philip Farha, Patrick Harries, Tobias Straumann, Patrick Kupper, Anna-Katharina Wöbse and Bernhard Gissibl. I am particularly indebted to Jane Carruthers, who helped me navigate through the complexities of South Africa's environmental history, and to Florio Puenter, who showed me the Engadin in ways I had never seen the valley before. As with all my previous books and exhibitions, the person who suffered most from my struggle with the panda was Mario Nerlich. He nevertheless supported me throughout this project, assisted halfway through by Valentin, the most lovely field spaniel in the world. Without them nothing would have been possible.

The book part of this project went through difficult stages. Without the unfaltering support of my publisher, Anja Heyne, and her director at Collection Rolf Heyne, Jürgen Welte, who believed in the book even in its darkest hour, it could not have been published. My cheerful and encouraging editor Annika Genning made sure that texts and layout were finished on time, while Sabine Schwenk managed to translate a constantly changing English manuscript into German without ever losing patience. The fact that the book comes out simultaneously in English, German and French is due to the excellent services provided, once again, by the Liepman Agency in Zurich, especially Eva and Marc Koralnik. They put me in touch with Vera Michalski, the publisher of Buchet-Chastel in Paris, and Andrew Franklin, the publisher of Profile Books in London. After an intense day of running around the Frankfurt Book Fair they both agreed to become our partners in this challenging project.

Rather than going along with a book and exhibition project initiated by the Swiss National Museum, it would have been much easier for WWF to commission an advertising company to produce a glossy anniversary publication. Instead, several members of the WWF family have taken the time to read drafts of this book: HRH The Duke of Edinburgh and Winnie De'Ath in the UK and Jim Leape, Claude Martin, Hans-Peter Fricker, Chris Hails and Pascale Moehrle in Switzerland. While they pointed out mistakes and suggested specifications on issues that had been dealt with too briefly, at no time did any of them try to influence my interpretation of the sources. This organisational openness towards the perspective of an outsider is exceptional and deserves to be acknowledged as the rarity it represents. It goes without saying that the views expressed and the errors included in this book are mine alone.

Zurich, January 2011

WWF – five decades of conservation milestones

Source: WWF International, Gland

1961
In its first decade, WWF raised over US$5.6 million – an enormous sum in the 1960s. With allocation based on the best available science, this money was distributed as grants to support 356 conservation-related projects around the world – from wildlife surveys to anti-poaching efforts to education. Many of the animals and habitats supported by these early grants went on to become iconic conservation symbols, and continue to be a focus of WWF's work. The popular fund-raising appeals also, for the first time, brought conservation into the public arena.

1962
Research station established in the Galápagos Islands
In addition to becoming a leading scientific institution that has hosted researchers from around the world, the Charles Darwin Foundation Research Station – which a WWF grant helped establish – has played a central role in raising awareness among local people and the Ecuadorean government of the importance of preserving the Galápagos's unique species. Together with other work by WWF and partners, this contributed to the passing of the Galápagos Special Law in 1998 and the establishment of the Galápagos Marine Reserve, the second-largest marine reserve at the time. WWF's early recognition of the importance of awareness-raising has contributed in no small part to the current global level of environmental consciousness.

1963
Premier school for park management opens
A WWF grant helped establish the College of African Wildlife Management in Tanzania, which has since trained more than four thousand park rangers and wildlife managers from over fifty countries in Africa and elsewhere in all aspects of protected-areas management, including ecology, range management and law enforcement. Recognising that protected areas will be successful only if they are managed effectively, WWF has invested heavily in improving management capacity and skills in many hundreds of protected areas around the world.

1965
Southern white rhino range extended
With support from WWF, the East African Wildlife Society carried out a trial introduction of southern white rhinos from South Africa to Kenya – leading to the subsequent successful introduction and reintroduction of the subspecies to several other countries. The southern white rhino was the earliest to be affected by European game hunters and poachers supplying markets for rhino horn. Fewer than twenty individuals survived in South Africa in 1895, but determined anti-poaching and other conservation efforts saw numbers increase to an estimated 17,480 in 2007. Similar efforts for other rhino species in both Africa and Asia have seen black rhino numbers increase from around 2,500 in 1993 to over 4,100, greater one-horned rhino numbers increase from 600 in 1975 to more than 2,500, and Javan rhino numbers in western Java increase from no more than 25 in 1964 to 60. While these are huge conservation successes, some rhino species, subspecies and populations are nevertheless almost extinct and poaching remains an ever-present threat, even for relatively secure populations. For this reason, all rhinos remain priority species for WWF.

1966
Wildlife survey in South America
A survey of the status of the spectacled bear in South America was among the first of many wildlife surveys that WWF has supported, and in later years helped carry out, throughout its history. These surveys have provided essential information for conservation efforts, such as the population size, distribution and ecology of particular species, as well as habitat status and threats. In some cases, these surveys have even discovered species previously unknown to science – including three large mammals in Vietnam, a fish on Fiji's Great Sea Reef and some of the 1,200 animals and plants discovered in the Amazon over the last decade.

Land bought in Spain's Guadalquivir Delta marshes

Purchased by WWF and the Spanish government, this land became Coto Doñana National Park – one of the world's first wetland reserves and an important site for migratory birds. Its establishment kicked off the protection of several other key sites along the Palaearctic bird migration flyway, from breeding areas in northern Europe to overwintering sites in western and southern Africa. Coto Doñana is also an important refuge for other species, including two of the world's most endangered, the Iberian lynx and the Spanish imperial eagle. Protected areas have formed a crucial part of WWF's work, with the organisation supporting the establishment of over one billion hectares of protected habitat around the world to date.

While WWF remained focused on species and habitat preservation **throughout the 1970s**, its approach began to change: instead of providing more or less ad hoc support to individual projects, it began encouraging more comprehensive conservation efforts for entire biomes as well as species across their range. As part of this, WWF stepped up its engagement with governments and international environmental treaties and started to tackle some of the drivers behind environmental threats.

Intergovernmental treaty for wetlands

Following several years of advocacy by WWF and others, eighteen governments signed the Ramsar Convention on Wetlands of International Importance, which remains the world's only international environmental treaty for a single biome. Aiming for both the conservation and the wise use of wetlands and their resources, the convention was also a forerunner of sustainable development principles. More than 1,900 wetlands covering a combined area of 186 million hectares are now included in the Ramsar list of Wetlands of International Importance, including the world's largest wetland, the 6.6-million-hectare Ngiri-Tumba-Maindombe in the Democratic Republic of Congo. WWF continues to support the convention, particularly by encouraging governments to list new Ramsar sites. Indeed, WWF's work at different levels has contributed to about 75 per cent of new sites since 1999.

Large-scale tiger conservation

WWF's Operation Tiger was the first-ever global campaign to save a species across its range. One of its first outcomes was the launching of India's Project Tiger, whereby a six-year national tiger conservation plan and fifteen new tiger reserves saw the country's tiger population increase by 30 per cent in just seven years. Since then, Nepal, Bangladesh, Malaysia, Thailand, Indonesia, Bhutan, Russia and China have also joined in tiger conservation efforts that continue to this day. A large-scale resurgence in poaching resurgence from the early 1990s to supply markets for tiger body parts, however, combined with continued habitat loss outside protected areas, has left no more than 3,200 tigers alive in the wild. As part of its aim to double the wild tiger population by 2022, WWF launched the Year of the Tiger campaign in 2010. This culminated with a historic Tiger Summit in November 2010, at which the thirteen tiger-range states gave crucial high-level backing – and various donors and other stakeholders pledged significant funding – to a Global Tiger Recovery Programme.

Rainforest conservation starts

WWF's Tropical Rainforest Campaign was the first-ever conservation campaign based on an entire biome rather than a single species or individual area of habitat. In addition to raising money for new rainforest protected areas in Central and West Africa, South-East Asia and Latin America, the campaign contributed to widespread recognition of the biodiversity and ecological values of rainforests and the threats they face. WWF has since played a key role in efforts to build protected area networks in priority tropical forests and achieve sustainable management of their resources.

Regulation of trade in endangered species

To support the newly created Convention on International Trade in Endangered Species (CITES), WWF and the International Union for Conservation of Nature (IUCN) jointly founded TRAFFIC, a programme to monitor trade in wildlife and wildlife products. CITES currently covers some 30,000 plant and animal species and has 175 member countries, while TRAFFIC has grown into a global network with offices on six continents. Together, these two bodies have played a crucial role in strengthening wildlife trade controls and promoting the sustainable management of a myriad of species whose populations are threatened by international trade – from orchids and mahogany to lizards and birds. For example, a ban on international trade in ivory by CITES and ongoing investigations into the illegal ivory trade by TRAFFIC have helped eliminate some of the world's major ivory markets. This led to reduced elephant poaching in Africa and the recovery of some populations following dramatic declines in the 1970s and 1980s.

By its twentieth anniversary, WWF had supported protected areas on five continents covering 1 per cent of the Earth's surface and had contributed to the continued existence of a number of species. As impressive as this was, the organisation realised that parks and crisis-led conservation efforts – while important – were not enough. Now with an expanded global presence and starting to run its own projects, WWF began more heavily promoting the ideas of its founders: that conservation was in the interest of people and needed to be integrated into, rather than viewed as being in conflict with, development. These concepts laid the foundation for sustainable development, a philosophy that now permeates conservation, development and even corporate strategies.

First global sustainable development strategy

Published by WWF, IUCN and the United Nations Environment Programme (UNEP) and endorsed by the UN secretary general, the *World Conservation Strategy* was the first document to integrate conservation and the sustainable use of natural resources. It was also one of the first to explain conservation objectives in terms of the benefits to people. More than fifty countries created their own national conservation strategies based on the strategy's recommendations, and it formed the scientific and philosophical basis of the 1987 Brundtland Report, which coined the term 'sustainable development'. In 1991 the three organisations published the follow-up *Caring for the Earth*, which fed into the 1992 Rio Earth Summit and began the mainstreaming of conservation into world politics and development. WWF has since been part of the ongoing effort to implement sustainable development in practice.

Research into toxic chemicals

Published in 1962, Rachel Carson's *Silent Spring* opened the world's eyes to the dangers posed by environmental pollution, especially pesticides. WWF supported research into the effects of pesticides on species and ecosystems throughout the 1980s. In the 2000s, the organisation raised public awareness of how toxic substances – including pesticides, industrial by-products and chemicals present in everyday items – are found in human bodies and even in animals living in pristine areas such as the Arctic. At a policy level, WWF contributed to the negotiation and entry into force of the 2001 Stockholm Convention on Persistent Organic Pollutants, successfully campaigned for the 2001 Convention on the Control of Harmful Anti-fouling Systems on Ships and campaigned for strong EU chemical legislation (REACH). WWF is also a founding partner of the Africa Stockpiles Programme, which is working to eliminate huge stockpiles of obsolete pesticides scattered across Africa.

Moratorium on commercial whaling

The Save the Whales campaigns of the 1970s made whales – victims of centuries of rampant, uncontrolled hunting – one of the most well-known and visible 'faces' of bad environmental governance. WWF had been working for a moratorium on commercial whaling by the International Whaling Commission (IWC) since 1965, and the majority of its efforts to protect cetaceans (whales, dolphins and porpoises) continue to take place within the context of the IWC. Later successes include the IWC's declaration of a whale sanctuary in the Southern Ocean in 1994, which, together with the moratorium, has contributed to some whale populations recovering, and a 2003 resolution that extended the IWC's remit to address all threats to cetacean populations, particularly incidental catches in fishing nets and climate change. Nearly two thousand whales are still hunted each year, however, despite the moratorium. WWF therefore continues to seek a resolution to this issue that will benefit whales and promote the recovery of whale populations.

Integrating conservation with development

1986

Established with the help of WWF, Cameroon's Korup National Park was one of the first to include local people in the planning process and to have a management plan that included sustainable land-use practices and rural development within local communities. Such development has included teaching income-generating activities to village women and training local people as anti-poaching patrollers. WWF has since helped develop participatory management processes for, and integrate development into the management of, many other protected areas around the world. In addition to providing park management training and alternative livelihoods for local communities, this work also includes addressing issues of governance, gender, health and education.

New mechanism for financing conservation

1989

WWF pioneered the debt-for-nature concept, in which a portion of a nation's debt is bought in return for the country allocating an equivalent amount in local currency to conservation. WWF has helped negotiate a series of such swaps for Madagascar, from the first in 1989 to the most recent in 2008, which together have generated over $US50 million to preserve Madagascar's rich biodiversity. These funds have been used to establish new protected areas, build park management capacity, promote sustainable use of the country's natural resources, and involve local communities in forest and coastal management. WWF has similarly helped facilitate debt-for-nature swaps in Bolivia, Costa Rica, Ecuador, Gabon, the Philippines and Zambia. WWF has also led the development of other novel funding mechanisms to provide long-term financing for conservation and environmental management. These include a carbon finance project, conservation trust funds, and payments for ecosystem services.

National giant panda conservation plan

1989

As the first conservation organisation invited to China, WWF has been involved in giant panda conservation since 1979. At this time, the outlook for the species looked bleak: just 1,000 individuals survived in isolated populations in a massively reduced and fragmented range. The conservation management plan developed by WWF and the Chinese Ministry of Forestry formed the basis of work to establish a connected panda landscape. This is now well under way, with 62 nature reserves covering 60 per cent of current and potential habitat linked by ecological corridors that reunite dozens of panda populations. Overall, the Chinese government has committed to protect 3 million hectares of panda forest in total – an area the size of Belgium – by 2015. WWF has also supported a number of community development projects to encourage sustainable forest use and management among the people living in panda habitat. As a result of these and other efforts, the giant panda population has increased to an estimated 1,600. WWF has been similarly involved in creating connected networks of protected areas in many other countries.

The 1990s saw more widespread acceptance of the global links between the environment, human activities and human welfare – as well as the value of biodiversity and the emerging threat of climate change. These issues were explicitly incorporated in WWF's 1990 Mission Statement, and have framed the organisation's on-the-ground and policy work ever since. Continuing the move from country-based projects to a targeted and more unified approach,

1990

WWF developed a global conservation strategy that focused efforts on the world's most critical ecoregions and in six key areas – species, forest, marine and freshwater conservation, climate change and toxic chemicals. In addition to its long-standing relationships with traditional conservation partners, WWF also began to more actively engage with business and other new partners to promote sustainable resource management.

Treaty to stem biodiversity loss
WWF was a critical player in establishing the Convention on Biological Diversity (CBD), an international treaty covering the conservation and use of biodiversity, and has since campaigned for the adoption of strong CBD targets and work plans. In 2002, WWF helped secure a CBD commitment to significantly reduce the rate of biodiversity loss by 2010, and in 2004 was part of an NGO consortium that successfully lobbied for a programme of work on protected areas which, for the first time, included concrete targets and timelines. At the latest CBD Conference of the Parties in 2010, WWF similarly contributed to the adoption of a strong new ten-year biodiversity plan that includes commitments to protect 10 per cent of oceans and 17 per cent of land habitats by 2020, as well as a focus on addressing the drivers behind biodiversity loss. It also requires countries to account for the value of biodiversity within their national assets, opening the way towards new, greener economics. Working with many partners, WWF has also helped national governments to implement their CBD commitments.

Community-based natural resource management
Launched by WWF and development agency USAID, the LIFE project empowers rural Namibian communities to actively manage their natural resources. Organised as conservancies, the communities have legal rights over the wildlife on their land – and can directly benefit from their natural resources through tourism, managed hunting and other activities. With wildlife now seen as a community resource to be protected and managed instead of a threat or competition, poaching has significantly decreased and many animal populations have increased. The conservancies also provide valuable employment opportunities to these remote areas: in 2001, for example, they collectively earned nearly US$1.5 million in the form of wages, communal income and profits on community-owned enterprises. WWF has similarly supported community-based resource management in many other countries.

Certifying sustainable commodities
WWF was a key player behind the launch of the Forest Stewardship Council (FSC), a pioneering certification scheme for forest products harvested according to strict environmental, social and economic criteria. Starting in the forest and continuing through the entire chain of custody, the certification process promotes sustainable forestry and allows end consumers to be certain they are buying environmentally sound products. With WWF support, more than 130 million hectares of forest, and 8.5 per cent of forest products in international trade, are now FSC certified. The Marine Stewardship Council (MSC) certification scheme for wild-caught seafood, launched by WWF and Unilever in 1996, is a similar success, with over one hundred fisheries now MSC certified and 7,000 certified products available worldwide.

Global efforts to curb carbon emissions begin
WWF helped design, and played a pivotal role in the ratification and entry into force of, the Kyoto Protocol, the world's first international agreement to limit carbon emissions in industrialised countries. The organisation has also secured significant private-sector commitments to reduce carbon emissions. One of the first was from cement-maker Lafarge, which in 2001 pledged to reduce its absolute gross CO_2 emissions in industrialised countries to 10 per cent below 1990 levels by 2010, as well as to reduce worldwide net emissions per tonne of cement to 20 per cent below 1990 levels. In addition to promoting energy efficiency and renewable energy sources, WWF is now working for

Saving the World's Wildlife

an effective successor to the Protocol once its first period ends in 2012. The organisation is also heavily involved in efforts to prevent greenhouse gas emissions from deforestation, which are currently responsible for 15 per cent of all emissions.

First Living Planet Report
1998

Now a biannual publication and prepared in collaboration with the Zoological Society of London and the Global Footprint Network, the Living Planet Report is one of the world's leading science-based analyses of biodiversity health and humanity's pressure on nature, or ecological footprint. The first report found that global biodiversity had declined by 30 per cent since 1970 – highlighting for the first time that while the conservation movement had won many battles, it was nevertheless losing the war. The report also showed that humanity's use of renewable natural resources exceeded the Earth's capacity to renew them by 30 per cent – a figure which had risen to 50 per cent by 2010. The reports have been instrumental in helping to raise awareness of the ongoing threats to biodiversity, the impacts of human activities on nature and the Earth's ecological limits – and the stark consequences of 'business as usual' on the future health and well-being of all people

Groundbreaking declaration for Congo forests
1999

Alarmed by large-scale illegal logging, weak forest management and widespread poaching of wildlife, WWF convened the Yaoundé Forest Summit – the first-ever meeting of heads of state from the Congo Basin on the protection and sustainable management of the world's second-largest rainforest. The resulting Yaoundé Declaration and a second summit in 2005 led to Africa's first regional treaty on sustainable forest management, together with an inter-ministerial coordination mechanism for this. Over four million hectares of new protected areas, two tri-national conservation complexes totalling almost twenty million hectares – more than 10 per cent of the Congo forest – and 4.5 million hectares of FSC-certified forests have been created to date. A third summit scheduled for mid-2011 aims for further commitments, including projects to promote the reduction of greenhouse gas emissions from deforestation and forest degradation (REDD), expansion of the protected-area network and FSC-certified forests, improved protection for great apes, and policies for the sustainable development of infrastructure such as roads and dams.

The turn of the century saw WWF vastly upscale its ambition, aiming for transformational changes that lead to lasting conservation, sustainable development and sustainable lifestyles. With twin goals of conserving biodiversity and reducing humanity's ecological footprint, the organisation is drawing on the combined strength and expertise of its global network to create innovative partnerships that integrate on-the-ground conservation, high-level policy and advocacy, and strategic private sector engagement. These efforts are particularly focused on globally important areas and species, including vast areas like the Arctic and animals and plants important both for their habitats and for people, and tackling global challenges like climate change and bringing sustainability into global markets.
2000

Large-scale initiative to save the Amazon
2002

With the world's largest tropical forest facing massive deforestation threats, WWF worked with the government of Brazil and other partners to launch a ten-year initiative to preserve 12 per cent, or 60 million hectares, of the Brazilian Amazon. The world's largest *in situ* conservation effort, ARPA (Amazon Region Protected Area) has already created more than thirty million hectares of protected areas, improved management in 62 existing protected areas, and established a US$29 million conservation fund. This and similar efforts in other Amazon countries, including extensive work prior to 2002, mean that over 80 per cent of the Amazon's original forest is still largely intact. Continued and increasing threats, however – particularly unsustainable cattle ranching and agricultural expansion – led WWF to launch the Living Amazon Initiative in 2007. Carried out in partnership with a wide variety of stakeholders, this ten-year initiative aims to conserve the entire Amazon basin through a combination of good governance, clear land tenure, sustainable commodity production, forest-friendly infrastructure development, and biodiversity conservation.

2003 Showing the economic value of nature

A WWF report estimated that coral reefs provide nearly US$30 billion in net benefits each year through their provision of goods and services to world economies, including tourism, fisheries and coastal protection. Subsequent reports looked at the value of other ecosystems to human societies: forest areas were shown to provide a cost-effective means of supplying high-quality drinking water to many of the world's biggest cities, while the annual economic value of the world's wetlands was estimated at US$3.4 billion through their provision of food, fresh water, building materials, water treatment services and erosion control services. Such research has made a vital contribution to convincing governments and local communities of the true value of ecosystems and species. It has also boosted the development of payments for ecosystem services, whereby local people are compensated for maintaining and managing natural habitats.

2008 Certified sustainable palm oil enters the market

Building on the success of the FSC and MSC, in 2004 WWF, other NGOs and the palm oil industry set up the Roundtable on Sustainable Palm Oil (RSPO) to develop standards and a certification scheme for sustainable palm oil – a key agricultural commodity whose enormously expanded production over the last few decades has come at the expense of vast areas of tropical rainforest. In 2010, just two years after it became operational, about 6.4 per cent of global palm oil production was RSPO certified – a level of market penetration that took the FSC and MSC over a decade to achieve. WWF's work on palm oil forms part of its efforts to steer fifteen key global commodity markets towards sustainability, including soy, cotton, beef and farmed shrimp. In addition to helping develop sustainable production practices and standards, WWF is also working to ensure that the main companies buying these commodities implement sustainable sourcing policies.

2009 Securing a future for the world's richest marine hot spot

In May 2009, the leaders of six nations – Indonesia, Malaysia, Papua New Guinea, the Philippines, the Solomon Islands and Timor Leste – committed to a comprehensive plan to conserve and sustainably manage coastal and marine resources within the Coral Triangle region, a vast area hosting 76 per cent of the world's coral species and the world's largest tuna fisheries. Incorporating WWF's goals for the Coral Triangle, the plan aims, among other things, to establish a region-wide network of marine protected areas, achieve an ecosystem approach to fisheries management, improve income, livelihoods and food security for coastal communities, ensure sustainable exploitation of shared tuna stocks, and implement climate adaptation strategies. WWF is now working to help implement the plan, as well as build momentum for change in fisheries capture, trade and purchase practices through new partnerships and coalitions.

2010 The world's largest environmental activism event

As part of its advocacy work, WWF harnesses the tremendous voice of its supporters to demonstrate widespread public support for WWF's goals and apply crucial pressure on key decision-makers. Earth Hour – in which people, buildings, landmarks and entire cities switch off their lights for one hour to demonstrate support for action on climate change – has become the biggest such platform. The first Earth Hour in 2007 involved 2.2 million homes and businesses in Sydney, Australia; just three years later, hundreds of millions of people around the globe joined Earth Hour 2010, which reached about one in six people on the planet. WWF is using this unprecedented show of support as part of its efforts to convince politicians, governments and world leaders to secure an effective successor to the Kyoto Protocol and start making the necessary cuts in greenhouse gas emissions.

Saving the World's Wildlife

Fritz Vollmar, Aletschwald Nature Reserve, Valais,
Switzerland, October 1972

American black bear (*Ursus americanus*) hunting salmon,
Anan creek, Alaska, 2008

Abbreviations

ARPA: Amazon Region Protected Areas Programme
BP: Buckingham Palace
CF: Conservation Foundation
CIC: Conseil International de la Chasse
CITES: Convention on International Trade in Endangered Species
EMN: Estate Max Nicholson, Linnean Society of London
EPB: Estate Prince Bernhard, Koninklijk Huisarchief, The Hague

EPS: Estate Sir Peter Scott, Cambridge University
EXCO: Executive Council, later Executive Committee
FPS: Fauna Preservation Society
FSC: Forest Stewardship Council
IRC: Information Research Centre of WWF-US, Washington
MSC: Marine Stewardship Council
PB: Prince Bernhard
PP: Prince Philip

RSPB: Royal Society for the Protection of Birds
RSPCA: Royal Society for the Prevention of Cruelty to Animals
RSPO: Roundtable on Sustainable Palm Oil
SNM: Swiss National Museum, Zurich
WWF Intl.: WWF International, Gland

Saving the World's Wildlife

The Nicholson plan

1. See Stiftungsurkunde, World Wildlife Fund, 11 Sept. 1961, EMN 4/7.
2. Hans Hüssy to Trustees of WWF, 11 Oct. 1961, WWF Intl., file 'WWF History', no. 6/1.
3. Gerald Watterson to Max Nicholson, 18 Aug. 1961, WWF Intl., file 'WWF History', no. 5/4.
4. Frank Fraser Darling, quoted in E. B. Worthington to Fritz Vollmar, 12 Jan. 1978, WWF Intl., file 'WWF History', no. 8/3.
5. Gerald Watterson to M. F. Mörzer-Bruijns, 28 July 1961, WWF Intl., file 'WWF History', no. 5/4.
6. As there is no biography of Max Nicholson, a collection of obituaries was consulted on the memorial website www.maxnicholson.com.
7. www.iucn.org, last consultation 11 Feb. 2010.
8. Martin Holdgate, *The Green Web. A Union for World Conservation*, Earthscan, London, 1999, p. v.
9. Ibid., p. v.
10. See Gerald Watterson to Max Nicholson, 21 April 1961, WWF Intl., file 'WWF History', no. 5/4.
11. Barton Worthington to Fritz Vollmar, 12 Jan. 1978, WWF Intl., file 'WWF History', no. 8/3.
12. See John McCormick, *Reclaiming Paradise. The Global Environmental Movement*, Indiana University Press, Bloomington, 1989, pp. 47–68.
13. Rachel Carson, *Silent Spring*, Houghton Mifflin, Boston, 1962.
14. Lord Shackleton, House of Lords, Official Report, 25 April 1961, BP, WWF Box 9/B1.
15. See John Robert McNeill, *Something New under the Sun. An environmental history of the twentieth-century world*, Norton, New York, 2000, pp. 269–95.
16. Theodore Roosevelt, *African Game Trails. An account of the African wanderings of an American hunter-naturalist*, Scribner, New York, 1910; Winston Churchill, *My African Journey*, Hodder & Stoughton, London, 1908.
17. See Kaj Arhem, *Pastoral Man in the Garden of Eden. The Maasai of the Ngorongoro Conservation Area, Tanzania*, Department of Cultural Anthropology, Uppsala University, Uppsala, 1985; Jan Bender Shetler, *Imagining Serengeti. A history of landscape memory in Tanzania from earliest times to the present*, Ohio University Press, Athens, 2007.
18. See Julian Huxley in the *Observer*: 'The treasure house of wild life', 13 Nov. 1960; 'Cropping the wild protein', 20 Nov. 1960; 'Wild life as a world asset', 27 Nov. 1960.
19. Huxley, 'Cropping the wild protein'.
20. On Huxley's family, see Ronald W. Clark, *The Huxleys*, Heinemann, London, 1968.
21. Huxley, 'Wild life as a world asset'.
22. On late-colonial Kenya, see Daniel Branch, *Defeating Mau Mau, Creating Kenya Counterinsurgency, Civil War, and Decolonization*, Cambridge University Press, Cambridge, 2009.
23. On British decolonisation, see John Darwin, *The Empire Project. The Rise and Fall of the British World-System, 1830–1970*, Cambridge University Press, Cambridge, 2009, pp. 610–48.
24. On French and Belgian decolonisation, see Martin Thomas, Bob Moore and L. J. Butler (eds), *Crises of Empire. Decolonization and Europe's Imperial States, 1918–1975*, Hodder & Stoughton, London, 2008, pp. 127–272, 385–93.
25. Roger Peterson to Max Nicholson, 30 July 1961, WWF Intl., file 'WWF History', no. 7.
26. Huxley, 'The treasure house of wild life'.
27. Huxley, 'Wild life as a world asset'.
28. Max Nicholson to Julian Huxley, 9 Jan. 1961, WWF Intl., file 'WWF History', no. 2/5.
29. Victor Stolan to Julian Huxley, 6 Dec. 1960, WWF Intl., file 'WWF History', no. 2/5.
30. Max Nicholson to Victor Stolan, 16 Dec. 1960, WWF Intl., file 'WWF History', no. 2/5; and see Max Nicholson, 'Money for Nature', summer 1960, EMN, 4/1.
31. Max Nicholson to Julian Huxley, 9 Jan. 1961, WWF Intl., file 'WWF History', no. 2/5.
32. Robert Lamb, *Promising the Earth*, Routledge, London, 1996, p. 29.
33. Victor Stolan to Max Nicholson, 22 Jan. 1961, WWF Intl., file 'WWF History', no. 2/5.
34. On Grzimek see the recent, rather uncritical biography by Claudia Sewig, *Bernhard Grzimek. Der Mann, der die Tiere liebte*, Lübbe, Bergisch Gladbach, 2009.
35. Victor Stolan to Max Nicholson, 30 Jan. 1961, WWF Intl., file 'WWF History', no. 2/5.
36. Max Nicholson, 'How to save the world's wildlife', 6 April 1961, WWF Intl., file 'WWF History', no. 1/1.
37. Max Nicholson, 'Earliest planning of World Wildlife Fund', 21 Dec. 1977, WWF Intl., file 'WWF History', no. 2/1. The trip lasted from 28 Feb. until 10 March 1961.
38. On Russell Train, see Russell Train, *Politics, Pollution and Pandas. An Environmental Memoir*, Island Press, Washington, DC, 2003; J. Brooks Flippen, *Conservative Conservationist. Russell E. Train and the Emergence of American Environmentalism*, Louisiana State University Press, Baton Rouge, 2006. Nicholson and Train did not meet in 1961; see e-mail, Russell Train to Alexis Schwarzenbach, 25 Feb. 2010.
39. Interview, Max Nicholson, 1991, quoted in Raymond Bonner, *At the Hand of Man. Peril and hope for Africa's wildlife*, Knopf, New York, 1993, p. 64.
40. Ibid., p. 63.
41. Max Nicholson, 'Earliest planning of World Wildlife Fund', 21 Dec. 1977, WWF Intl., file 'WWF History', no. 2/1.
42. Interview, Max Nicholson, 1991, quoted in Bonner, *At the Hand of Man*, p. 63.
43. Max Nicholson, 'Earliest planning of World Wildlife Fund', 21 Dec. 1977, WWF Intl., file 'WWF History', no. 2/1.
44. Max Nicholson to various recipients, 6 April 1961, WWF Intl., file 'WWF History', no. 1/1.
45. Max Nicholson, 'How to save the world's wildlife', 6 April 1961, WWF Intl., file 'WWF History', no. 1/1.
46. Ibid.
47. See Max Nicholson to various recipients, 6 April 1961, WWF Intl., file 'WWF History', no. 1/1.
48. Max Nicholson to Fairfield Osborn, 7 April 1961, WWF Intl., file 'WWF History', no. 3/3.
49. Max Nicholson to Ira Gabrielson, 12 May 1961, WWF Intl., file 'WWF History', no. 2/8.
50. On the RSPCA, see Edward Fairholme, *A Century of Work for Animals. The History of the R.S.P.C.A., 1824–1924*, John Murray, London, 1924.
51. On the Battersea Dogs Home, see Garry Jenkins, *A Home of Their Own. 150 Years of Battersea Dogs & Cats Home*, Bantam, London, 2010.
52. Max Nicholson to The Editor, *The Times*, 1 June 1961, WWF Intl., file 'WWF History', no. 1/1; and see Max Nicholson, SO MANY TO SAVE, no date [June 1961], ibid.
53. Holdgate, *The Green Web*, p. 77.
54. Peter Scott, *Launching of a New Ark. First report of the president and trustees of the World Wildlife Fund*, Collins, London, 1965, p. 28. Scott printed an abbreviated and edited version of the 1961 original.
55. The signatories were: 'J. G. Baer (Switzerland), C. J. Bernard (Switzerland), F. Bourlière (France), W. E. Burhenne (Germany), Charles Vander Elst (Belgium), W. Goetel (Poland), Edward H. Graham (USA), R. Knobel (South Africa), Kai Curry-Lindahl (Sweden), E. C. Nicola (Netherlands-Switzerland), Peter Scott (UK), S. K. Shawki (Sudan), E. B. Worthington (UK)'; see 'We must save the world's wild life. An International Declaration' [Morges Manifesto], 29 April 1961, EMN 4/1.
56. Ibid.
57. Holdgate, *The Green Web*, p. 76.
58. 'We must save the world's wild life. An International Declaration'.

The London Preparatory Group

1. The term was coined by WWF's first director general, Fritz Vollmar, who before leaving the organisation in 1977 made a compilation of historical WWF

documents. See WWF Intl., file 'WWF History', no. 1.

2. On Phyllis Barclay-Smith, see Catherine Haines, *International Women in Science. A biographical dictionary to 1950*, ABC-Clio, Oxford, 2001, pp. 19–20.

3. See [Fritz Vollmar], Attendance at Meetings of London Preparatory Group of WWF in 1961, [1977], WWF Intl., file 'WWF History', no. 1/0. The Minutes are kept in the same file.

4. On Mountfort, see his autobiography, *Memories of Three Lives*, Merlin, Brauton, 1991; the best-seller written with Roger Tory Peterson was *A Field Guide to the Birds of Britain and Europe*, Collins, London, 1954.

5. [London Preparatory Group], Minutes, 1st meeting, 25 April 1961, WWF Intl., file 'WWF History', no. 1/1; and see Guy Mountfort to Max Nicholson, 1 May 1961, WWF Intl., file 'WWF History', no. 2/3.

6. See Ian MacPhail, 'Public Relations for a wild life organisation', [May 1961], WWF Intl., file 'WWF History', no. 1/2.

7. [London Preparatory Group], Minutes, 2nd meeting, 10 May 1961, WWF Intl., file 'WWF History', no. 1/2; Ian MacPhail, 'Public Relations for a wild life organisation', [May 1961], WWF Intl., file 'WWF History', no. 1/2.

8. [London Preparatory Group], Minutes, 3rd meeting, 16 May 1961, WWF Intl., file 'WWF History', no. 1/3.

9. Ever since the late seventeenth century, the word 'fund' has been used to describe 'A stock or sum of money, *esp.* one set apart for a particular purpose 1694', C. T. Onions, *The Shorter Oxford English Dictionary*, Clarendon Press, Oxford, 1988 [1973], p. 817.

10. Guy Mountfort to Max Nicholson, 18 Jan. 1978, WWF Intl., file 'WWF History', no. 2/3.

11. [London Preparatory Group], Minutes, 6th meeting, 6 July 1961, WWF Intl., file 'WWF History', no. 1/6.

12. J. A. Simpson and E. S. C. Weiner (eds), *The Oxford English Dictionary*, vol. XX, Clarendon Press, Oxford, 1989, pp. 336–7.

13. See, for example, Francis M. Wyndham, *Wild Life on the Fjelds of Norway*, Longman, London, 1861; E. H. Lamont, *Wild Life among the Pacific Islanders*, Hurst and Blackett, London, 1867.

14. For the decision to use 'the letters "WWF" in all languages', see Minutes, WWF Intl., Executive Council, 14 Sept. 1979, WWF Intl.

15. Ian MacPhail, 'Public Relations for a wild life organisation', [May 1961], WWF Intl., file 'WWF History', no. 1/2.

16. [London Preparatory Group], Minutes, 6th meeting, 6 July 1961, WWF Intl., file 'WWF History', no. 1/6. Phyllis Barclay-Smith was present at the meeting.

17. Elspeth Huxley, interview, Max Nicholson, 3 Oct. 1990, EPS M.2950/34.

18. Anon., 'Meeting at Royal Society of Arts on 28th September, Proposed Arrangements and Programme', [Sept. 1961], WWF Intl., file 'WWF History', no. 4/8.

19. See George Schaller, *The Last Panda*, University of Chicago Press, Chicago, 1993, pp. 261–7.

20. '[D]er erste Europäer, der den Bambusbären lebend zu Gesicht bekommt', Walther Stötzner, *Ins unerforschte Tibet. Tagebuch der deutschen Expedition Stötzner 1914*, Koehler, Leipzig, 1924, p. 121.

21. '[W]ildaussehender', 'Drei Bambusbären auf einmal! Meine Freude kennt keine Grenzen, denn es gibt kein zweites Säugetier von gleicher Seltenheit', 'Es gibt keine zweite Gegend auf der grossen Erde, wo das sagenumwobene, merkwürdige Tier noch zu finden wäre. Nur in diesen weltenfernen, ungangbaren, einsamen Hochalpen lebt er noch als Überbleibsel aus vorgeschichtlicher Zeit', 'Die erste Aufnahme vom frischgeschossenen Ailuropus', 'Zoologische Kostbarkeit', Stötzner, pp. 120–21.

22. 'Der umgestülpte Ailuropus', Stötzner, plate facing p. 112.

23. '[E]in ganz altes Männchen', 'Ein kleines Menschenkind kann nicht sorgsamer gepflegt werden, wie von mir der possierliche kleine Bär, der wie ein Wollknäuel, aber genau gezeichnet wie die Alten, aussieht. Tapsig stolpert der kleine Bussel auf seiner weichen, warmen Tuchunterlage im Hause über die kurzen Beinchen', 'Allgemeine Trauer', Stötzner, pp. 121–2.

24. For an excellent cultural history of the panda, see Henry Nicholls, *The Way of the Panda. The curious history of China's political animal*, Profile, London, 2010.

25. See Cäsar Claude, 'Die Geschichte des Grossen Pandas oder Bambusbären', *Tages-Anzeiger*, 31 July 1972.

26. See Susan Lumpkin and John Seidensticker, *Smithsonian Book of Giant Pandas*, Smithsonian Institution Press, Washington, DC, 2002, p. 25.

27. On Chi Chi, see Nicholls, *passim*.

28. The first WWF report mentions Watterson's sketches but is silent about his inspirations. See Scott, *Launching of a New Ark*, pp. 27–8. The logo's link to Chi Chi is first mentioned in WWF International (ed.), *Twentieth Anniversary Review*, Gland, 1981, p. 10.

29. See items 110498 and 110500 of the WWF/Canon photo library.

30. Nicholson quoted in Bonner, *At the Hand of Man*, p. 64; interview, 1991.

31. For a collection of reviews of Peter Scott, *The Eye of the Wind*, Hodder & Stoughton, London, 1961, see EPS A.688.

32. Elspeth Huxley, *Peter Scott. Painter and Naturalist*, Faber and Faber, London, 1993, p. 289.

33. Niels Halbertsma to Alexis Schwarzenbach, 9 Feb. 2010.

34. [London Preparatory Group], Minutes, 4th meeting, 30 May 1961, WWF Intl., file 'WWF History', no. 1/4.

35. 'Wildlife konnte man nicht übersetzen', interview, Hans Hüssy, 9 June 2009.

36. Stiftungsurkunde, World Wildlife Fund, 11 Sept. 1961, and its literal translation: EMN 4/7. A copy of the original English version, drawn up on 25 May 1961, is contained in WWF Intl., file 'WWF History', no. 4/2.

37. Lee Talbot, 1956, quoted in Holdgate, *The Green Web*, p. 64.

38. Holdgate, *The Green Web*, p. 64.

39. Interview, Max Nicholson, 1997, quoted in Holdgate, *The Green Web*, p. 65.

40. Fairfield Osborn, *Our Plundered Planet*, Little, Brown, Boston, 1948.

41. World Wildlife Fund [1st draft, deed of foundation], 25 May 1961, WWF Intl., file 'WWF History', no. 4/2. This passage is identical to the one published in WWF's first annual report; see Scott, *Launching of a New Ark*, pp. 31–5.

42. See interview, Hans Hüssy, 4 June 2009.

43. Stiftungsurkunde, World Wildlife Fund, 11 Sept. 1961, EMN 4/7.

44. Official Deed concerning the […] 'World Wildlife Fund', 11 Sept. 1961, EMN 4/7.

45. Stiftungsurkunde, World Wildlife Fund, 29 Nov. 1973, Dossier WWF, Registre du Commerce du Canton de Vaud, Moudon. When WWF moved its official base from Zurich to Gland in the canton of Vaud, the deed was translated into French and 'natural resources' became '*ressources naturelles*'; see Statuts, World Wildlife Fund, 12 Dec. 1980, ibid.

46. See Stiftungsurkunde, World Wildlife Fund, 11 Sept. 1961, EMN 4/7.

47. [London Preparatory Group], Minutes, 4th meeting, 30 May 1961, WWF Intl., file 'WWF History', no. 1/4.

48. See Dame Anne Griffiths, Librarian and Archivist to HRH The Duke of Edinburgh, to Alexis Schwarzenbach, 9 Dec. 2010.

49. Peter Scott, quoted in Huxley, *Peter Scott*, p. 250.

50. Peter Scott to Prince Bernhard, 8 Aug. 1961, DKH, PB; further letters trying to make the prince change his mind include Gerald Watterson to Prince Bernhard, 11 Aug. 1961, and Peter Scott to Prince Bernhard, 20 Aug. 1961, ibid.

51. Max Nicholson to Jean Baer, 12 Aug. 1961, WWF Intl., file 'WWF History', no. 5/3.

52. The letter which finally convinced Bernhard to becoming president came from Peter Scott; see DKH, PB, Peter Scott to Prince Bernhard, 22 Dec. 1961.

53. Clipping of unidentified New York paper, 'Two princes in town with a plea', [8 June 1962], WWF Intl., file 'WWF History', no. 7; see also clipping 'The Duke condemns status seekers and

Saving the World's Wildlife

poachers', [*Times*], 7 June 1962, WWF Intl., file 'WWF History', no. 4/8.

54. See 'Philip and Bernhard appeal here for aid to wildlife' and 'Garden-party pastels prevail at wildlife fund dinner', *New York Times*, 8 June 1962, WWF Intl., file 'WWF History', no. 7.

55. On Hoffmann, see Alison Goddard, *The Unsung Ornithologist. A biography of Luc Hoffmann*, Oxford University Press, Oxford, forthcoming.

56. See interview, Luc Hoffmann, 17 Dec. 2009; Luc Hoffmann to Max Nicholson, 25 Aug. 1959, WWF Intl., file 'WWF History', no. 9.

57. '[V]éritable clé magique pour la protection de la Nature qui s'appelle «World Wildlife Fund »', Luc Hoffmann to Antonio Valverde, 19 Aug. 1961, WWF Intl., file 'WWF History', no. 9.

58. See Jean Stengers, 'Precipitous decolonization: the case of the Belgian Congo', in Prosser Gifford and William Roger Louis (eds), *The Transfer of Power in Africa. Decolonization, 1940–1960*, Yale University Press, New Haven, 1982, pp. 305-35.

59. Ludo de Witte, *L'assassinat de Lumumba*, Karthala, Paris, 2000.

60. On Parc National Albert, see Marc Languy and Emmanuel de Merode (eds), *Virunga. The Survival of Africa's first national park*, Lannoo, Tielt, 2009.

61. Victor Stolan to Max Nicholson, 14 Feb. 1961, WWF Intl., file 'WWF History', no. 2/5; Gerald Watterson to Fairfield Osborn, 13 April 1961, EMN 4/4.

62. Typewritten copy of K. R. S. Morris to Charles Leofric Boyle, 8 June 1961, EMN 4/4.

63. On IUCN's Africa Special Project, see Holdgate, *The Green Web*, pp. 72-3.

64. Gerald Watterson to C. Mace, Permanent Secretary, Ministry of Land and Surveys, Dar es Salaam, Tanganyika, 27 July 1961, WWF Intl., file 'WWF History', no. 3/6.

65. See list of 'signatories to the declaration', WWF Intl., file 'WWF History', no. 3/5.

66. [London Preparatory Group], Declaration of a State of Emergency, [1st draft, July 1961], EMN 4/1.

67. [London Preparatory Group], Declaration of a State of Emergency, [final version, September 1961], WWF Intl., file 'WWF History', no. 3/5. The reference to oil pollution was absent in the first draft.

68. Barton Worthington to Julius Nyerere, 1 Aug. 1961, WWF Intl., file 'WWF History', no. 3/6.

69. C. I. Meek, Prime Minister's Office, Dar es Salaam, to Gerald Watterson, 8 Aug. 1961, WWF Intl., file 'WWF History', no. 3/6.

70. Peter Scott to Max Nicholson, 23 Aug. 1961, WWF Intl., file 'WWF History', no. 2.

71. See Gerald Watterson to Julius Nyerere, 2 Aug. 1961; Prime Minister's Office,

Dar es Salaam to Barton Worthington cc Gerald Watterson, 18 Aug. 1961, WWF Intl., file 'WWF History', no. 3/6.

72. 'Arusha Manifesto', attachment to Gerald Watterson to Julius Nyerere, 2 Aug. 1961. After its presentation to the world press, the text was often reproduced, for instance in the IUCN Bulletin, no. 2, Dec. 1961, WWF Intl., file 'WWF History', no. 3/6.

73. Julian Huxley to Major I. Grimwood, 9 March 1961, WWF Intl., file 'WWF History', no. 2/2. A copy of the off-print is located in EMN 4/1. The British financial support of the Arusha conference is referred to in the IUCN document 'To all members of council from chairman', no date [1961], in EMN 4/5.

74. Max Nicholson to Fairfield Osborn, 15 May 1961, WWF Intl., file 'WWF History', no. 2.

75. [London Preparatory Group], Minutes, 5th meeting, 13 June 1961, WWF Intl., file 'WWF History', no. 1.

76. Peter Scott to Max Nicholson, 25 June 1961, WWF Intl., file 'WWF History', no. 3/7.

77. World Wildlife Fund, *Save the World's Wildlife*, Mather & Crowther, London, 1961, EMN 5/5.

78. Ibid.

79. The information regarding photographs of pandas in the wild was received from Henry Nicholls, 13 June 2010.

80. Ian MacPhail to Bernhard Grzimek, 3 Aug. 1961, WWF Intl., file 'WWF History', no. 2/9.

81. Bernhard Grzimek to Gerald Watterson, 9 Aug. 1961, WWF Intl., file 'WWF History', no. 5/6.

82. 'phantastisch gross', Emil Schulthess, *Afrika. Vom Aequator zum Kap der guten Hoffnung*, Manesse, Zurich, 1959, plate 33. The giraffe is reproduced on plate 22. The elephant bull appears on plate 119 of the first volume, Emil Schulthess, *Afrika. Vom Mittelmeer zum Aequator*, Manesse, Zurich, 1958.

83. World Wildlife Fund, *Save the World's Wildlife*.

84. See [Ian MacPhail], World Wildlife Newsletter No. 1, July 1961; [Ian MacPhail], World's Wildlife on Brink of Extinction, 21 Sept. 1961; WWF Intl., file 'WWF History', no. 4/8.

85. [Ian MacPhail], Meeting at R.S.A., at 2.30 p.m. on Thursday, 28th September, 1961, 27 Sept. 1961, WWF Intl., file 'WWF History', no. 4/8.

86. [Ian MacPhail], Meeting at the Royal Society of Arts on 28th September 1961, [no date, 1st draft?], WWF Intl., file 'WWF History', no. 4/6.

87. Max Nicholson to Heads of International Campaigns, 11 Oct. 1961, EMN 8/5.

88. *Daily Mirror*, 9 Oct. 1961, WWF Intl., file 'WWF History', no. 3/appendix.

89. Ian MacPhail, Press reaction to the World Wildlife Fund, 18 Oct. 1961,

WWF Intl., file 'WWF History', no. 4/8.

90. Max Nicholson to Heads of International Campaigns, 11 Oct. 1961, EMN 8/5.

Launching of a new ark

1. Scott, *Launching of a New Ark*, p. 18.

2. See [London Preparatory Group], Minutes, 2nd meeting, 10 May 1961, WWF Intl., file 'WWF History', no. 1/2.

3. On Operation Oryx, see Scott, *Launching of a New Ark*, p. 68. Starting with a mere three animals in 1962, the 'World Herd' of Arabian oryx in Arizona had risen to 91 animals by 1978; see Richard Fitter and Peter Scott, *The Penitent Butchers: The Fauna Preservation Society 1903–1978*, Collins, London, 1978, p. 45.

4. Guy Mountfort to Ian MacPhail, cc: Max Nicholson, 19 March 1962, EMN 8/4.

5. On the SNB, see Pro Natura, *Die Stimme der Natur. 100 Jahre Pro Natura*, Kontrast, Zurich, 2009; on the Rheinaubund, see 'Für die Gewässer und für die Heimat. Der Rheinaubund wird 50 Jahre alt und sucht sich eine Nische in der Umweltbewegung', *Neue Zürcher Zeitung*, 8 June 2010.

6. On the history of the US national parks, see Richard Sellars, *Preserving Nature in the National Parks. A History*, Yale University Press, New Haven, 1997.

7. Fairfield Osborn to Ira Gabrielson, 29 Dec. 1961, WWF Intl., file 'WWF History', no. 7.

8. See Fairfield Osborn to Peter Scott, 24 Jan. 1963, WWF Intl., file 'WWF History', no. 7.

9. See Scott, *Launching of a New Ark*, p. 11; minutes, 11th meeting of WWF Intl. Board of Trustees, 26 Nov. 1966, WWF Intl.

10. '[Z]u sehr Einzelgänger und sich seiner eigenen Stellung und Erfolge wohl bewusst', Fritz Vollmar to Claudia Sewig, 22 Jan. 2006, copy provided to Alexis Schwarzenbach by Fritz Vollmar.

11. On Grzimek's stance on hunting in Europe, which he less radically opposed than hunting in Africa, see Sewig, *Bernhard Grzimek*, pp. 241–2.

12. '[G]efahrlos' Bernhard Grzimek; Michael Grzimek, *Kein Platz für wilde Tiere*, Germany, 1956, 81 mins.

13. See Sewig, *Bernhard Grzimek*, pp. 209-10. This largely hagiographic biography fails to discuss Grzimek's montages.

14. Victor Stolan, 'A Confidential Memorandum on the rescue and preservation of Wild Life (mainly) in Africa irrespective of whatever has been said, written or done so far.', 3 Jan. 1961, WWF Intl., file 'WWF History', no. 2.

15. *The Times*, 1 June 1961, WWF Intl., file 'WWF History', no. 1/1.

16. See Fitter and Scott, *The Penitent Butchers*. The illustrations in the book were by Peter Scott, who became chairman of FPS in 1966 and whose name also appeared on the cover.
17. Huxley, *Peter Scott*, p. 86.
18. Harold Coolidge to Gerald Watterson, 2 Aug. 1961, WWF Intl., file 'WWF History', no. 5/6.
19. For Coolidge's hunting trip to the Congo, see Mark Barrow, *Nature's Ghosts. Confronting Extinction from the Age of Jefferson to the Age of Ecology*, University of Chicago Press, Chicago, 2009, pp. 135–40. For the efforts to formulate the Declaration of a State of Emergency in such a way 'that a sportsman like Gabrielson would gladly sign it', see Harold Coolidge to Gerald Watterson, 2 Aug. 1961, WWF Intl., file 'WWF History', no. 5/6. For a critique of Gerstenmaier's passion for hunting, including an African safari to the Belgian Congo for 8,500 Deutschmarks, see *Der Spiegel*, 25 June 1955. This revealing article, which may well have inspired Grzimek's opening scene for *No Place for Wild Animals*, was generously provided to me by Bernhard Gissibl.
20. For the WWF functions of Gabrielson and Gerstenmaier, see Scott, *Launching of a New Ark*, pp. 10–11.
21. Bernhard Graf zur Lippe, *In den Jagdgründen Deutsch-Ostafrikas*, Reimer, Berlin, 1904.
22. Dame Anne Griffiths, Librarian and Archivist to HRH The Duke of Edinburgh, to Alexis Schwarzenbach, 24 Nov. 2010.
23. Fox Photos, 'Phil's tiger haul', 26 Jan. 1961, Getty Images no. 3164584.
24. [Max Nicholson], Draft World Wildlife Charter, 6 July 1961, WWF Intl., file 'WWF History', no. 3/8.
25. Memorandum from H.R.H. The Duke of Edinburgh to Peter Scott, appendix to Peter Scott to Max Nicholson, 20 July 1961, EMN 4/3/1.
26. Peter Scott to Max Nicholson, 20 July 1961, EMN 4/3/1.
27. Prince Philip to Christopher Bonham-Carter [Oct. 1961], BP, WWF Box 9/B21.
28. Cecil Parry to Christopher Bonham-Carter, 18 Oct. 1961 [1st letter], BP, WWF Box 9/B21.
29. Cecil Parry to Christopher Bonham-Carter, 18 Oct. 1961 [2nd letter], BP, WWF Box 1/A1.
30. On CIC, see Conseil International de la Chasse (ed.), CIC Newsletter, 3–4 (2008), Special Edition. 80 Years of Conservation through Sustainable Hunting, 1928–2008.
31. Harold Coolidge to Jean Baer, 20 April 1961, WWF Intl., file 'WWF History', no. 3/3. Luc Hoffmann, himself a member of CIC, holds very similar views on the organisation; see interview, 17 Dec. 2009.

32. Aubrey Buxton to Trustees of W.W.F., 9 Oct. 1962, EMN 8/5.
33. Aubrey Buxton to 'Certain Friends', 8 Jan. 1963, EMN 8/5.
34. Prince Philip to Christopher Bonham-Carter, no date [1962], BP, WWF Box 9/B2.
35. Scott, *Launching of a New Ark*. pp. 38–9.
36. Minutes, 8th meeting of WWF Intl. Board of Trustees, 20–22 May 1965, WWF Intl.
37. Irene van Lippe to Alexis Schwarzenbach, 23 Oct. 2009.
38. Ian MacPhail, quoted in 'No kills for Prince Philip', *Daily Express*, 8 Dec. 1961, WWF Intl., file 'WWF History', no. 6/10.
39. Prince Philip, Duke of Edinburgh, *Birds from Britannia*, Longmans, London, 1962. The introduction thanks 'in particular Aubrey Buxton for his expert help and advice at all times', p. 13.
40. See Conseil International de la Chasse (ed.), CIC Newsletter, 3–4 (2008), Special Edition. 80 Years of Conservation through Sustainable Hunting, 1928–2008.
41. Victor Stolan, 'A Confidential Memorandum on the rescue and preservation of Wild Life (mainly) in Africa irrespective of whatever has been said, written or done so far', 3 Jan. 1961, WWF Intl., file 'WWF History', no. 2/5; minutes, 6th meeting of WWF Intl. Board of Trustees, 29 June–1 July 1964, WWF Intl.
42. Minutes, 5th meeting of WWF Intl. Board of Trustees, 3–5 Dec. 1963, WWF Intl.
43. Max Nicholson to Jean Baer, 6 Dec. 1961, WWF Intl., file 'WWF History', no. 5/3.
44. See minutes, 5th meeting of WWF Intl. Board of Trustees, 3–5 Dec. 1963, WWF Intl.; minutes, 9th meeting of WWF Intl. Board of Trustees, 18–20 Oct. 1965, WWF Intl.; minutes, 13th meeting of WWF Intl. Board of Trustees, 28 Feb. 1968, WWF Intl.; minutes, 11th meeting of WWF Intl. Board of Trustees, 26 Nov. 1966, WWF Intl.
45. Guy Mountfort to Max Nicholson, 4 Dec. 1961, WWF Intl., file 'WWF History', no. 2/3.
46. See minutes, WWF Board of Trustees, 1st meeting, 18 Nov. 1961, WWF Intl.
47. Max Nicholson to Fritz Vollmar, 22 Dec. 1977, WWF Intl., file 'WWF History', no. 8/2.
48. Max Nicholson to unidentified correspondent, 20 Dec. 1961, WWF Intl., file 'WWF History', no. 8/2.
49. Minutes, 2nd meeting of WWF Intl. Board of Trustees, 18–20 May 1962, WWF Intl. Minutes.
50. See Holdgate, *The Green Web*, pp. 92–3.
51. See ibid., pp. 84–97.
52. See ibid., pp. 79–195.
53. Prince Philip, interview, 1997, quoted in Holdgate, *The Green Web*, p. 105.

54. 'Elfenbeinturm', 'Madison Avenue methods' [*sic*], 'Um Spender anzuziehen, sollte dieses Verzeichnis möglichst "sexy" sein und attraktive Titel enthalten', Fritz Vollmar to Alexis Schwarzenbach, 9 Dec. 2009.
55. WWF Intl. (ed.), Yearbook 1968, Morges, 1969, p. 12.
56. Minutes, 13th meeting of WWF Intl. Board of Trustees, 1 Dec. 1967, WWF Intl.
57. Minutes, 2nd meeting of WWF Executive Council Group, 1 Dec. 1968, WWF Intl.; for the approved version including specifications regarding the Conservation Committee, see minutes, 15th meeting of WWF Intl. Board of Trustees, 20 Dec. 1968, WWF Intl.
58. See minutes, 17th meeting of WWF Intl. Board of Trustees, 16 Nov. 1970, WWF Intl.
59. See minutes, WWF Intl., Executive Council, 7/8 May 1971, WWF Intl.; minutes, WWF Intl., Executive Council, 4 Sept. 1972, WWF Intl.
60. On royal philanthropy, see Frank Prochaska, *Royal Bounty. The making of a welfare monarchy*, Yale University Press, New Haven, 1995.
61. The correspondence between Prince Philip and Dwight D. Eisenhower is located in BP, WWF Box 9/B2.

The Morges Secretariat and the first national appeals

1. On Max Nicholson's plan to locate the secretariat in Zurich see Max Nicholson, Summary of Recommendations, 13 Nov. 1961, WWF Intl., file 'WWF History', no. 4/3.
2. See Jean Baer to Max Nicholson, 9 Dec. 1961, WWF Intl., file 'WWF History', no. 5/3.
3. Curriculum Vitae Fritz Vollmar, 19 March 1962, in WWF Intl., file 'WWF History', no. 6/3; Scott, *Launching of a New Ark*, p. 30.
4. See WWF Intl. (ed.), World Wildlife Yearbook 1971–72, Morges, 1972, p. 11. On the first premises see Holdgate, *The Green Web*, p. 77.
5. See minutes, 2nd meeting of WWF Intl. Board of Trustees, 18–20 May 1962, WWF Intl.
6. Peter Scott, [general fund-raising letter], [Aug. 1961], WWF Intl., file 'WWF History', no. 2/4; and cf. Scott, *Launching of a New Ark*, p. 17.
7. See Holdgate, *The Green Web*, pp. 90–91.
8. See minutes, 4th meeting of WWF Intl. Board of Trustees, 14–15 May 1963, WWF Intl.
9. 'fast täglich herausgegebene Aufrufe und Pressemitteilungen' 'Zu Beginn der 1960er Jahre […] kaum präsent, weder bei Behörden noch in der Öffentlichkeit.' Fritz Vollmar to Alexis Schwarzenbach, 9 Dec. 2009.

10. Minutes, 6th meeting of WWF Intl. Board of Trustees, 29 June–1 July 1964, WWF Intl.
11. Scott, *Launching of a New Ark*, plate facing p. 33; ibid., p. 9.
12. Ibid., pp. 43–57.
13. See WWF Intl. (ed.), Yearbook 1972–73, Morges, 1973, p. 17. France is not on the 1972 list, as the organisation temporarily ceased to exist between 1970 and 1973.
14. Scott, *Launching of a New Ark*, p. 43.
15. Minutes, 6th meeting of WWF Intl. Board of Trustees, 29 June–1 July 1964, WWF Intl.
16. See minutes, 18th meeting of WWF Intl. Board of Trustees, 11 Sept. 1971, WWF Intl.
17. WWF Intl. (ed.), World Wildlife Yearbook 1970–71, Morges, 1971, p. 187.
18. See minutes, 2nd meeting of WWF Intl. Board of Trustees, 18–20 May 1962, WWF Intl.
19. Max Nicholson to Gerald Watterson, 1 Nov. 1961, WWF Intl., file 'WWF History', no. 2/1
20. Minutes, 2nd meeting of WWF Executive Council Group, 1 Dec. 1968, WWF Intl.
21. On the deal, see Fritz Vollmar to WWF President, Vice-Presidents etc., 4 Jan. 1967, EPS C.1103.
22. Minutes, 7th meeting of WWF Intl. Board of Trustees, 29 Nov.–1 Dec. 1964, WWF Intl.
23. See interview, Hans Hüssy, 4 June 2009.
24. Hans Hüssy to Trustees of WWF, March 1962, WWF Intl., file 'WWF History', no. 6/3; minutes, 4th meeting of WWF Intl. Board of Trustees, 14–15 May 1963, WWF Intl.
25. Minutes, 6th meeting of WWF Intl. Board of Trustees, 29 June–1 July 1964, WWF Intl.
26. 'Geschäftsreise' Fritz Vollmar to Alexis Schwarzenbach. The term is used in inverted commas. On Hüssy and Hoffmann's African trip, see also Fritz Vollmar to Trustees of WWF, 10 Jan. 1963, EMN 4/8.
27. WWF Peter Scott, 'World Wildlife's Ten Years', in WWF Intl. (ed.), World Wildlife Yearbook 1971–72, Morges, 1972, p. 257.
28. WWF Intl. (ed.), The Ark Under Way. Second report of the World Wildlife Fund, 1965–1967, Morges, 1968, p. 243.
29. Samples taken from the 1969 list of projects, WWF Intl. (ed.), World Wildlife Yearbook 1969, Morges, 1969, pp. 25–9.
30. Peter Scott, 'World Wildlife's Ten Years', in WWF Intl. (ed.), World Wildlife Yearbook 1971–72, Morges, 1972, p. 257.
31. WWF Intl. (ed.), The Ark Under Way. Second report of the World Wildlife Fund, 1965–1967, Morges, 1968, p. 67.
32. WWF Intl. (ed.), The Ark Under Way. Second report of the World Wildlife Fund, 1965–1967, Morges, 1968, p. 67. On the foundation of Coto Doñana, see Alison Goddard's forthcoming

biography of Luc Hoffmann, especially ch. 3.
33. For the New Jersey Wetlands Reserve see WWF Intl., Yearbook 1968, Morges, 1969, pp. 176–8.
34. Peter Scott to Merwyn Cowie, 4 May 1969, EPS D.235.
35. WWF Intl. (ed.), The Ark Under Way. Second report of the World Wildlife Fund, 1965–1967, Morges, 1968, p. 237.
36. Ibid., p. 238.
37. See WWF Intl. (ed.), Yearbook 1969, Morges, 1970, pp. 70–71.
38. Haile Selassie to Prince Bernhard, 4 July 1969, DKH, PB.
39. Kai Curry-Lindahl, 'African Decade', in WWF Intl. (ed.), Yearbook 1970–71 Morges, 1971, pp. 265–76.
40. Original italics. WWF Intl. (ed.), World Wildlife Yearbook 1969, Morges, 1970, p. 16.
41. Kai Curry-Lindahl, 'African Decade', in WWF Intl. (ed.), Yearbook 1970–71, Morges, 1971, p. 265. On post-colonial Tanzania and Kenya, see Paul Nugent, *Africa since Independence. A comparative history*, Palgrave Macmillan, Basingstoke, 2004, pp. 141–66.
42. Merwyn Cowie to Peter Scott, 28 Feb. 1964, EPS C.952.
43. On post-colonial Congo/Zaire, see Nugent, *Africa since Independence*, pp. 232–9.
44. Minutes, 12th meeting of WWF Intl. Board of Trustees, 26 April 1967, WWF Intl.
45. WWF Intl. (ed.), World Wildlife Yearbook 1970–71, Morges, 1971, p. 16.
46. WWF Intl. (ed.), World Wildlife Yearbook 1971–72, Morges, 1972, p. 16.
47. WWF Intl. (ed.), World Wildlife Yearbook 1971–72, Morges, 1972, p. 13; and see Minutes, WWF Intl., Executive Council, 9/10 Sept. 1971, WWF Intl.
48. Victor Stolan to Max Nicholson, 19 Dec. 1961, EMN 4/2.
49. Arnold Thorne to Max Nicholson, 1 Oct. 1971, EMN 4/28.
50. WWF Intl. (ed.), World Wildlife Yearbook 1971–72, Morges, 1972, pp. 12–13.
51. Peter Scott to Prince Bernhard, 22 Dec. 1961, DKH, PB.
52. See McKinsey & Company, Inc., 'Meeting the challenge of the future. World Wildlife Fund', survey, July 1971, Exhibit II, WWF Intl.; and see Max Nicholson to Fritz Vollmar, 22 Dec. 1977, WWF Intl., file 'WWF History', no. 8/2.
53. Royal Society for the Protection of Birds, Obituary, Max Nicholson, no date [2003], in www.maxnicholson.com, last consultation 9 Feb. 2010.

Growth of the WWF family

1. Minutes, WWF Intl., Executive Council, 21 April 1969, WWF Intl.

2. On Rupert, see Ebbe Dommisse, *Anton Rupert. A Biography*, Tafelberg, Cape Town, 2005.
3. 'Im WWF hatte er die Rolle des weisen älteren Mannes. Wenn die Leute im Vorstand geredet haben, dann hat man über vieles reden können, aber wenn Anton Ruppert etwas gesagt hat, hat es einfach gesessen. Er ist mir in vielerlei Hinsicht – was seine Karriere angeht – ein Rätsel. Ich sehe ihn als eine der moralisch hochwertigsten Personen, die ich kenne. Aber er hat sein Imperium mit Tabak und Alkohol gemacht. Das habe ich nie ganz begriffen.' Interview, Luc Hoffmann, 17 Dec. 2009.
4. On the history of Kruger National Park, see Jane Carruthers, *The Kruger National Park. A social and political history*, University of Natal Press, Pietermaritzburg, 1995.
5. Peter Scott to Dr Sauer, 22 Feb. 1962, WWF Intl., file 'WWF History', no. 2.
6. For an alternative suggestion about Bernhard and Rupert meeting in 1954, see Marja Spierenburg and Harry Wels, 'Conservative philanthropists, royalty and business elites in nature conservation in southern Africa', *Antipode, a Radical Journal of Geography*, 42(3), 2010, pp. 647–70. In 1964 they were certainly not yet 'friends'.
7. See Minutes, 6th meeting of WWF Intl. Board of Trustees, 29 June–1 July 1964, WWF Intl.
8. See Minutes, 7th meeting of WWF Intl. Board of Trustees, 29 Nov.–1 Dec. 1964, WWF Intl. On Verwoerd's opposition, see Ebbe Dommisse, *Anton Rupert. A Biography*, Tafelberg, Cape Town, 2005, p. 349
9. See Dommisse, *Anton Rupert*, p. 349; Frans Stroebel to Alexis Schwarzenbach, 6 July 2010.
10. On the early WWF-SA, see Dommisse, *Anton Rupert*, pp. 349–56.
11. See Frans Stroebel to Alexis Schwarzenbach, 6 July 2010.
12. WWF Intl. (ed.), WWF Conservation Yearbook 1985/1986, Gland, 1986, p. 546. For the calculation, reference was made to www.measuringworth.com.
13. Anton Rupert, quoted in WWF Intl. (ed.), Yearbook 1969, Morges, 1970, p. 249.
14. Dommisse, *Anton Rupert*, p. 33.
15. See ibid., pp. 63, 84–86.
16. See Dan O'Meara, *Forty Lost Years. The Apartheid State and the Politics of the National Party 1948–1994*, Ravan Press, Randburg, 1996, p. xxxv.
17. Dommisse, *Anton Rupert*, pp. 151–74.
18. For the history of Afrikaner identity, see Hermann Giliomee, *The Afrikaners. Biography of a People*, Hurst, London, 2003.
19. Carruthers, *The Kruger National Park*.
20. For a summary of Rupert's pride in things South African, see his *Priorities of Coexistence*, Tafelberg, Cape Town, 1982.

21. Prince Bernhard to Anton Rupert, 17 Feb. 1964, EPS M.971.
22. Anton Rupert to Prince Bernhard, 4 Feb. 1964, EPS M.971.
23. Minutes, 17th meeting of WWF Intl. Board of Trustees, 16 Nov. 1970, WWF Intl.; see also Minutes, WWF Intl., Executive Council, 14/15 Oct. 1970, WWF Intl.
24. Anton Rupert in Minutes, 27th meeting of WWF Intl. Board of Trustees, 9/10 Nov. 1978, WWF Intl.
25. Minutes, WWF Intl., Executive Council, 7/8 May 1971, WWF Intl.
26. Bernhard, paraphrased in Dommisse 2005, p. 351.
27. For Rupert's near-resignation from the board, see Minutes, 19th meeting of WWF Intl. Board of Trustees, 27 Oct. 1972, WWF Intl.
28. Minutes, 44th meeting of WWF Intl. Board of Trustees, 19 May 1988, WWF Intl.
29. WWF Intl. (ed.), World Wildlife Yearbook 1978–79, Morges, 1979, p. 11.
30. [WWF-UK], 'Financial Policy', memorandum, 25 Oct. 1961, WWF Intl., file 'WWF History', no. 4.
31. Minutes, 6th meeting of WWF Intl. Board of Trustees, 29 June–1 July 1964, WWF Intl.
32. See Minutes, 8th meeting of WWF Intl. Board of Trustees, 20–22 May 1965, WWF Intl.
33. Interview, Charles de Haes, 11 Dec. 2009.
34. Ibid.
35. Ibid.
36. See Minutes, 17th meeting of WWF Intl. Board of Trustees, 16 Nov. 1970, WWF Intl.; Minutes, WWF Intl., Executive Council, 27/28 Feb. 1974, WWF Intl.
37. Interview, Charles de Haes, 11 Dec. 2009.
38. See The 1001: A Nature Trust, [membership list], July 1978. Although membership lists were confidential, they were printed annually and distributed among members. Some of them can therefore be consulted in estates of deceased members such as Peter Scott or as circulated as scans on the Internet, for instance www.isgp.org/organisations/1001_Club_members_list.htm.
39. Interview, Charles de Haes, 11 Dec. 2009.
40. See [WWF-Switzerland], 'Herrn Hoffmann', '1001' Nature Trust Fund Members, no date [c. 1974], WWF-Schweiz, B4, Trust '1001' 1974–1982.
41. See Minutes, WWF Intl., Executive Council, 23/24 May 1974, WWF Intl.
42. See Minutes, WWF Intl., Executive Council, 16/17 July 1971, WWF Intl.; and Goddard, The Unsung Ornithologist.
43. 'C'est lui qui doit gagner le pain pour faire vivre la famille.' Luc Hoffmann, 'Une stratégie pour l'avenir', in WWF Yearbook 1971–72, Morges, 1972, p. 263.

44. Charles Lindbergh to Peter Scott, 22 June 1967, EPS C.338.
45. See WWF Intl. (ed.), Yearbook 1972–73, Morges, 1973, p. 157.
46. Anne Wright, 'History of WWF-India Eastern Region', [New Delhi], 14 May 2003, attachment to Anne Wright to Alexis Schwarzenbach, 19 Oct. 2009.
47. See Guy Mountfort, Saving the Tiger, Michael Joseph, London, 1981, pp. 80–87.
48. See Minutes, WWF Intl., Executive Council, 25/26 May 1972, WWF Intl.
49. Mountfort, Saving the Tiger, p. 89.
50. Anne Wright, 'History of WWF-India Eastern Region', [New Delhi], 14 May 2003, attachment to Anne Wright to Alexis Schwarzenbach, 19 Oct. 2009.
51. Mountfort, Saving the Tiger, p. 91.
52. Anne Wright, 'History of WWF-India Eastern Region', [New Delhi], 14 May 2003, attachment to Anne Wright to Alexis Schwarzenbach, 19 Oct. 2009.
53. Minutes, WWF Intl., Executive Council, 25/26 May 1972, WWF Intl.
54. WWF Intl. (ed.), Yearbook 1974–75, Morges, 1975, p. 165.
55. Mountfort, Saving the Tiger, pp. 101, 103.
56. Ibid., p. 105.
57. See Minutes, WWF Intl., Executive Council, 28 April 1973, WWF Intl.
58. See Charles Vaucher, Nakuru. See der Flamingos, World Wildlife Fund, Zurich, 1972.
59. Minutes, 19th meeting of WWF Intl. Board of Trustees, 27 Oct. 1972, WWF Intl.
60. Minutes, WWF Intl., Executive Council, 28 April 1973, WWF Intl.
61. See WWF Intl. (ed.), Yearbook 1977–1978, Gland, 1978, p. 258.
62. WWF Intl. (ed.), Yearbook 1978–79, Morges, 1979, p. 59.
63. WWF Intl. (ed.), Yearbook 1977–78, Morges, 1978, p. 74.
64. WWF Intl. (ed.), WWF Yearbook 1980–81, Gland, 1981, p. 333.
65. Mountfort, Saving the Tiger, p. 81.
66. Ibid., p. 116.
67. See Valmik Thapar, 'The tragedy of the Indian Tiger: starting from scratch', in John Seidensticker, Sarah Christie and Peter Jackson (eds), Riding the Tiger. Tiger Conservation in Human-Dominated Landscapes, Cambridge University Press, Cambridge, 1999, pp. 296–306.
68. See Minutes, WWF Intl., Executive Council, 27/28 Feb. 1974, WWF Intl.
69. See Minutes, WWF Intl., Executive Committee, 9 March 1981, WWF Intl. In 1980 the Executive Council was renamed Executive Committee.
70. Minutes, Joint WWF International Board/National Organisations Meeting, 26–28 May 1981, WWF Intl.
71. For a discussion of this, see Minutes, 27th meeting of WWF Intl. Board of Trustees, 9/10 Nov. 1978, WWF Intl.
72. The countries are listed as sites of full national appeals in WWF Intl. (ed.), Yearbook 1973–74, Morges, 1974, p. 18.

73. See WWF Intl. (ed.), Yearbook 1980–81, Gland, 1981, pp. 510–11.
74. See Minutes, 29th meeting of WWF Intl. Board of Trustees, 8/9 Nov. 1979, WWF Intl.
75. Minutes, Joint WWF International Board/National Organisations Meeting, 24/25 June 1980, WWF Intl.
76. Minutes, WWF Intl., Executive Committee, 20 Nov. 1981, WWF Intl.
77. Mario Incisa della Roccetta, quoted in WWF Intl. (ed.), World Wildlife Yearbook 1970–71, Morges, 1971, p. 195.
78. Minutes, WWF Intl., Executive Council, 27/28 Feb. 1974, WWF Intl.; and see WWF Intl. (ed.), World Wildlife Yearbook 1976–77, Morges, 1977, back cover.
79. See Minutes, WWF Intl., Executive Council, 9 Nov. 1978, WWF Intl.
80. See Minutes, WWF Intl., Executive Council, 14/15 Oct. 1970, WWF Intl.
81. See WWF Intl. (ed.), Twentieth Anniversary Review, Gland, 1981, pp. 21, 22, EMN 4/19/1, 2.
82. Hüssy was secretary of the 'Verein zur Förderung des World Wildlife Fund' from 1961 to 1972 and president of the Stiftung World Wildlife Fund Schweiz from 1972 to 1980.
83. Luc Hoffmann raised 450,000 Swiss francs; see interview, Luc Hoffmann, 17 Dec. 2009.
84. Interview, Hans Hüssy, 4 June 2009.
85. Telephone interview, Roland Wiederkehr, 6 July 2010.
86. See Panda 3, 1970; Panda 2, 1972; Panda 4, 1972; Panda 4, 1973; WWF-CH.
87. See Panda 2, 1973; Panda 3, 1970; WWF-CH.
88. Arnold F. Thorpe, Administrator WWF-UK, WWF Intl. (ed.), World Wildlife Yearbook 1971–72, Morges, 1972, p. 217.
89. See Jahresbericht 1971/72, Panda 4, 1972, p. 14, WWF-CH.
90. Roland Wiederkehr, Secretary of WWF-Switzerland, quoted in WWF Intl. (ed.), World Wildlife Yearbook 1971–72, Morges, 1972, p. 222; and see interview, Hans Hüssy, 4 June 2009.
91. Alan MacNaughton to W. B. Harris, cc: Hans Hüssy etc, 5 Jan. 1982, EMN 7/3/1.
92. See Patrick Kupper, Atomenergie und Gespaltene Gesellschaft. Die Geschichte des gescheiterten Projektes Kernkraftwerk Kaiseraugst, Chronos, Zurich, 2003.
93. See Panda 3, 1973, WWF-CH.
94. 'In unserer Energiepolitik spiegelt sich unser Verhältnis zur Umwelt: Raubbau oder Erhaltung der Natur?' Schweizerischer Bund für Naturschutz, Schweizerische Energiestiftung, Schweizerische Gesellschaft für Umweltschutz, Schweizerische Vereinigung für Sonnenenergie, Schweizerische Vereinigung für Volksgesundheit, World Wildlife Fund Schweiz (eds), Jenseits der Sachzwänge. Ein Beitrag der Umweltorganisationen zur schweizerischen Gesamtenergiekonzeption, Ropress, Zurich, 1978.

Saving the World's Wildlife

95. See Jahresbericht 1979/80 des WWF-Schweiz, WWF-CH.
96. Sonja Bata to Hans Hüssy, 11 Jan 1982, EMN 7/3/1. Bata explains that she had heard these questions 'During the last few months'.
97. Hans Hüssy to Board of Trustees and management of WWF International, 15 Dec. 1981, EMN 7/3/1.
98. Minutes, WWF Intl., Executive Council, 16 March 1979, WWF Intl.
99. Sonja Bata to Hans Hüssy, 11 Jan 1982, EMN 7/3/1; Guy Mountfort to Hans Hüssy, 2 Jan. 1982, EMN 7/3/1.
100. 'In contrast to the big ideas of the twentieth century, explicitly environmental thought mattered little before 1970.' J. R. McNeill, *Something New under the Sun. An environmental history of the twentieth-century world*, Norton, New York, 2000, p. 336. For a discussion of the potential reasons see Kupper, *Atomenergie und Gespaltene Gesellschaft*, pp. 131–7.
101. 'Wende der siebziger Jahre', François Walter, *Bedrohliche und bedrohte Natur, Umweltgeschichte der Schweiz seit 1800*, Chronos, Zurich, 1996, p. 184.
102. Prince Bernhard in WWF Intl. (ed.), Yearbook 1968, Morges, 1968, p. 7.
103. Herbert H. Mills, Executive Vice President WWF-US, in WWF Intl. (ed.), Yearbook 1970–71, Morges, 1971, p. 182.
104. See WWF Intl. (ed.), Yearbook 1970–71, Morges, 1971.
105. Arthur M. Godfrey, trustee of WWF International, in WWF Intl. (ed.), Yearbook 1968, Morges, 1968, p. 20.
106. Minutes, WWF Intl., Executive Council, 21 April 1969, WWF Intl.
107. Minutes, WWF Intl., Executive Council, 14/15 Oct. 1970, WWF Intl.
108. Sonja Bata to Hans Hüssy, 11 Jan 1982, EMN 7/3/1.
109. See WWF Intl. (ed.), World Wildlife Yearbook 1978–79, Morges, 1979, p. 12.
110. Minutes, WWF Intl., Executive Council, 14/15 April 1978, WWF Intl.
111. For a recent analysis of the species approach see Nigel Leader-Williams and Holly T. Dublin, 'Charismatic megafauna as "flagship species"', in Abigail Entwistle and Nigel Dubstone (eds), *Priorities for the Conservation of Mammalian Diversity. Has the Panda Had Its Day?*, Cambridge University Press, Cambridge, 2000, pp. 53–81.
112. Minutes, Joint WWF International Board/National Organisations Meeting, 26–28 May 1981, WWF Intl.
113. Minutes, Joint WWF International Board/National Organisations Meeting, 24/25 June 1980, WWF Intl.

WWF, the corporate world and European royalty

1. See Christian Pfister (ed.), *Das 1950er Syndrom. Der Weg in die Konsumgesellschaft*, Haupt, Bern, 1995; John McNeill, *Something New under the Sun. An environmental history of the twentieth-century world*, Norton, New York, 2000, pp. 296–324.
2. '[A]ntagonistisch', 'Dass der WWF mit der Industrie und dem Handel zusammen arbeiten kann, auch dort, wo es im Einzelnen nicht zusammen geht, und die Wirtschaft den WWF als gleichberechtigten Partner wahrnimmt.' Interview, Luc Hoffmann, 17 Dec. 2009.
3. On Greenpeace, see Frank Zelko, 'Greenpeace and the development of international environmental activism in the 1970's', in Ursula Lehmkuhl and Hermann Wellenreuther (eds), *Historians and Nature. Comparative Approaches to Environmental History*, Berg, Oxford, 2007, pp. 296–318.
4. See http://www.greenpeace.org/international/about/our-core-values/fundraising-principles/, last consultation 8 Nov. 2010.
5. See Guy Mountfort to Ian MacPhail, 18 Jan. 1962, WWF Intl., file 'WWF History', no. 2/3.
6. Guy Mountfort to Ian MacPhail, 18 Jan. 1962, WWF Intl., file 'WWF History', no. 2/3.
7. See Minutes, 2nd meeting of WWF Intl. Board of Trustees, 18–20 May 1962.
8. Stephen Howarth and Joost Jonker, *A History of Royal Dutch Shell*, vol. 2: *Powering the Hydrocarbon Revolution, 1939–1973*, Oxford University Press, Oxford, 2007, p. 427.
9. Ibid., p. 431.
10. Ibid.
11. Ibid., p. 433.
12. See ibid., p. 438.
13. See Minutes, 4th meeting of WWF Intl. Board of Trustees, 29 Aug. 1963.
14. John Loudon, quoted in Peter Scott, Consideration of W.W.F.'s Attitude to Toxic Chemicals in Agriculture, manuscript, May 1963, EPS A.1069. The original Loudon text could not be located in the WWF archives.
15. Peter Scott, Consideration of W.W.F.'s Attitude to Toxic Chemicals in Agriculture, manuscript, May 1963, EPS A.1069.
16. Ibid.
17. Minutes, 4th meeting of WWF Intl. Board of Trustees, 29 Aug. 1963.
18. See Howarth and Jonker, *A History of Royal Dutch Shell*, vol. 2, p. 431.
19. See Minutes, 11th meeting of WWF Intl. Board of Trustees, 26 Nov. 1966, WWF Intl.; Maarten Bijleveld to Alexis Schwarzenbach, 12 March 2010; on John Loudon at Shell see Howarth and Jonker, *A History of Royal Dutch Shell*, vol. 2, pp. 106–10, and his *New York Times* obituary published on 9 Feb. 1996.
20. Minutes, WWF Intl, Executive Council, 7/8 May 1971, WWF Intl.
21. Minutes, 12th meeting of WWF Intl. Board of Trustees, 26 April 1967, WWF Intl.
22. WWF Intl. (ed.), The Ark Under Way. Second report of the World Wildlife Fund, 1965–1967, Morges, 1968, p. 73.
23. See Minutes, WWF Intl., Executive Committee, 12 Sept. 1980, WWF Intl.
24. 'Lowlife fund', *Private Eye*, 1 Aug. 1980, EMN 4/26.
25. Minutes, WWF Intl., Executive Committee, 12 Sept. 1980, WWF Intl.
26. AGN/GM [WWF-UK], [draft for letter to supporter], 1 Aug. 1980, EMN 4/26.
27. Anon. [WWF-UK], Comments on 'Private Eye Article', [Aug. 1980]; AGN/GM [WWF-UK], [draft for letter to supporter], 1 Aug. 1980, EMN 4/26. On WWF's cooperation with other environmentalist organisations, see Huxley, *Peter Scott*, pp. 280–93.
28. Anon. [WWF-UK], Comments on 'Private Eye Article', [Aug. 1980], EMN 4/26.
29. Minutes, WWF Intl., Executive Committee, 24 March 1982, WWF Intl.
30. For a scientific overview of the effects of the disaster provided by Hoffmann-La Roche, see E. Homberger et al., 'The Seveso accident. Its nature, extent and consequences', *The Annals of Occupational Hygiene*, vol. 22, 1979, pp. 327–68. For a fictionalised account of the Seveso disaster by one of the authors of the 1979 study, see Jörg Sambeth, *Zwischenfall in Seveso. Ein Tatsachenroman*, Unionsverlag, Zurich, 2004, a book which was turned into a documentary film: Sabine Gisiger, *Gambit*, 107 mins, Switzerland, 2005.
31. See Minutes, WWF Intl., Executive Council, 1 May 1977, WWF Intl.
32. See 'Seveso und die Entschädigungsfrage', *Neue Zürcher Zeitung*, 26 Aug. 1976.
33. 'Pour ma part, je me suis demandé si je ne devrais pas m'en aller malgré la décision du comité', 'volontairement déformé la vérité', 'difficile au public italien de se faire une idée objective', 'intensifier les attaques contre l'organisation', 'Si l'on ne se sent pas coupable, il vaut mieux ne pas s'affoler et laisser passer la tempête.' Luc Hoffmann to Fulco Pratesi, 23 May 1977, Archive Charles de Haes, Winchester.
34. On the Lockheed scandal, see John T. Noonan, *Bribes*, Macmillan, London, 1984, pp. 652–80.
35. Rapport van de Commissie Van Drie. Onderzoek naar de juistheid van verklaringen over betalingen door een Amerikaanse vliegtuigfabriek, Staatsuitgeverij, 's-Gravenhage, 1976.
36. See, for example, 'Ämterverzicht Prinz Bernhards', *Neue Zürcher Zeitung*, 27 Aug. 1976.
37. Emphasis in the original. Peter Scott to Prince Bernhard, 11 Sept. 1976, EPS M.2942.
38. Niels Halbertsma to Alexis Schwarzenbach, 11 Feb. 2010.
39. Peter Scott to Prince Bernhard, 11 Sept. 1976, EPS M.2942.

40. Niels Halbertsma to Alexis Schwarzenbach, 11 Feb. 2010. For Bernhard's involvement with WWF-Netherlands, see Willem Vermeulen and Niels Halbertsma (eds), *Operatie Natuur. Het natuurbeschermingsleven van Zijne Koninklijke Hoogheid Prins Bernhard*, Wereld Natuur Fonds, Zeist, 2006.

41. On the historical significance of modern honours systems, see Arno Mayer, *The Persistence of the Old Regime. Europe to the Great War*, Croom Helm, London, 1981, pp. 79–127; Catherine Brice, *La Monarchie et la construction de l'identité nationale italienne. 1861 à 1911*, Thèse d'Etat, Institut d'Etudes Politiques, Paris, 2004, pp. 206–35.

42. See Minutes, WWF Intl., Executive Council, 3 Oct. 1973, WWF Intl.

43. See Proceedings, Second Meeting of the WWF International (Advisory) Council, 21/22 May 1984, WWF Intl. [AS file 20/5].

44. WWF Intl. (ed.), WWF Yearbook 1970/71, Morges, 1971, p. 273.

45. 'tot onderscheiding van hen die zich bijzondere verdiensten hebben verworven voor het behoud van flora en fauna op aarde' Orde van de Gouden Ark, 10 July 1971, PB DKH. See also WWF Intl. (ed.), World Wildlife Yearbook 1973–74, Morges, 1974, p. 16.

46. Peter Scott, The Order of the Golden Ark, 8 Nov. 1970, PB DKH.

47. See WWF Intl. (ed.), World Wildlife Yearbook 1973–74, Morges, 1974, p. 17.

48. WWF Intl. (ed), Yearbook 1970–71, Morges, 1971, plate XXIX.

49. See Scott, *Launching of a New Ark*, p. 10.

50. A. Löhr/WWF-Deutschland to Trustees of WWF International, 20 Sept. 1976, PB DKH.

51. John Loudon, Address, in WWF Intl. (ed.), Celebration […] for WWF's 20th Anniversary, 27 May 1981, EMN 4/19/1, 2.

52. John Loudon to EXCO, 29 April 1980, BP, WWF Box 1/A2.

53. Minutes, Joint WWF International Board/National Organisations Meeting, 26–28 May 1981, WWF Intl.

54. See Minutes, 22nd meeting of WWF Intl. Board of Trustees, 24 Oct. 1975, WWF Intl.

55. See Luc Hoffmann to WWF Honorary Officers, 14 Aug. 1975, EMN 4/26, and interview Luc Hoffmann, 17 Dec. 2009.

56. See interview, Charles de Haes, 11 Dec. 2009.

57. Luc Hoffmann to WWF Honorary Officers, 14 Aug. 1975, EMN 4/26.

58. 'Von Anfang an musste klar sein, dass die Schaffung einer solchen Doppelspitze in der operativen Leitung des WWF jeglichen Prinzipien der Organisationslehre und der Führungshandbücher widersprach und früher oder später zum Scheitern verurteilt war.' [second quote is in English in the original] Fritz Vollmar to Alexis Schwarzenbach, 9 Dec. 2009.

59. '[A]n die 200 Dank- und Anerkennungsschreiben aus aller Welt, und insbesondere auch von allen WWF National Appeals.' Fritz Vollmar to Alexis Schwarzenbach, 9 Dec. 2009.

60. Charles de Haes, Strategic Considerations for Management Plan, 1 Sept. 1977, appendix to Minutes, WWF Intl., Executive Council, 6 Sept. 1977, WWF Intl.

61. Minutes, WWF Intl., Executive Council, 6 Sept. 1977, WWF Intl.

62. Charles de Haes, Strategic Considerations for Management Plan, 1 Sept. 1977, appendix to Minutes, WWF Intl., Executive Council, 6 Sept. 1977, WWF Intl.

63. Ibid.

64. See Bernt Engelmann and Günter Wallraff, *Ihr da oben – Wir da unten*, Kiepenheuer & Witsch, Cologne, 1973.

65. ['sich der Schweiz dankbar zeigen'] Interview, Luc Hoffmann, 17 Dec. 2009, and cf. Minutes, WWF Intl., Executive Council, 14/15 Oct. 1970, WWF Intl.

66. See Fritz Vollmar to Alexis Schwarzenbach, 9 Dec. 2009; Minutes, WWF Intl., Executive Council, 16 Jan. 1972, WWF Intl.

67. Interview, Hans Hüssy, 9 June 2009, and cf. Minutes, WWF Intl., Executive Committee, 13 Nov. 1986 [sic], WWF Intl., which contains a summary of the events.

68. Charles de Haes to Prince Philip, 26 March 1979, BP, WWF Box 11/B2.

69. Prince Philip to Charles de Haes, 29 March 1979, BP, WWF Box 11/B2.

70. Prince Philip to Charles de Haes, 3 May 1979, BP, WWF Box 11/B2.

Broadening the scope

1. Nancy Nash, 1979, quoted in George Schaller, *The Last Panda*, University of Chicago Press, Chicago, 1993, p. 11.

2. See Huxley, *Peter Scott*. pp. 319–20.

3. Memo to EXCO from Chairman [Peter Scott], attachment to Minutes, WWF Intl., Executive Council, 24 June 1980, WWF Intl.

4. Niels Halbertsma to Alexis Schwarzenbach, 9 Feb. 2010.

5. See Minutes, WWF Intl., Executive Council, 24 June 1980, WWF Intl.; Huxley, *Peter Scott*, pp. 319–20.

6. Memo to EXCO from Chairman [Peter Scott], attachment to Minutes, WWF Intl., Executive Council, 24 June 1980, WWF Intl.

7. Minutes, WWF Intl., Executive Committee, 24 March 1982, WWF Intl.

8. See WWF Intl. (ed.), WWF Yearbook 1983–84, Gland, 1984, p. 351; Minutes, WWF Intl., Executive Committee, 24 March 1983, WWF Intl.

9. Minutes, WWF Intl., Executive Council, 18 Feb. 1972, WWF Intl.

10. On the difficult start of the panda breeding programme see Schaller, *The Last Panda*, pp. 218–34, and Nicholls, *The Way of the Panda*, pp. 204–30.

11. Max Nicholson, The First World Conservation Lecture, 12 March 1981, WWF-UK, HIS 410.50.

12. Minutes, 31st meeting of WWF Intl. Board of Trustees, 26 May 1981, WWF Intl. A copy of Nicholson's lecture given on 12 March 1981 is located at WWF-UK, HIS 410.50.

13. Minutes, WWF Intl., Executive Committee, 20 Nov. 1981, WWF Intl.

14. See Minutes, WWF Intl., Executive Committee, 24 March 1982, WWF Intl.

15. Ibid.

16. Ibid.

17. See Huxley, *Peter Scott*, p. 285.

18. See Minutes, WWF Intl., Executive Council, 12 Dec. 1980, WWF Intl.

19. Minutes, WWF Intl., Executive Committee, 20 Nov. 1981, WWF Intl.

20. See Sonja Bata to Hans Hüssy, 11 Jan. 1982, EMN 7/3/1.

21. Minutes, 41st meeting of WWF Intl. Board of Trustees, 28 Sept. 1986, WWF Intl.

22. Minutes, 46th meeting of WWF Intl. Board of Trustees, 13 June 1989, WWF Intl.

23. 'Wir haben dort beschlossen, dass es eine Revolution geben muss.' Interview, Hans Hüssy, 9 June 2009. The date of the meeting, which none of the participants could remember, could be traced to 'early January' [1982] in a letter by Hans Hüssy to the Board of Trustees and management of WWF International, 29 Jan. 1982, EMN 7/3/1.

24. Niels Halbertsma to Alexis Schwarzenbach, 11 Feb. 2010.

25. Arthur Norman to Alexis Schwarzenbach, 25 Nov. 2009.

26. Claude Martin to Alexis Schwarzenbach, 26 Dec. 2009; see Niels Halbertsma to Alexis Schwarzenbach, 9 and 11 Feb. 2010.

27. George Medley to Arthur Norman, 21 Nov. 2009.

28. Niels Halbertsma to Alexis Schwarzenbach, 9 Feb. 2010.

29. See interview, Hans Hüssy, 9 June 2009. He had created Pro Natura Helvetica in June 1979.

30. Inverted commas in the original quote. Claude Martin to Alexis Schwarzenbach, 26 Dec. 2009.

31. Arthur Norman to Alexis Schwarzenbach, 25 Nov. 2009.

32. Peter Scott to Anton Rupert, 10 April 1979, BP, WWF Box 1/A2; see Prince Philip to John Loudon, 9 May 1980, and John Loudon to Prince Philip, 1 June 1980, BP, WWF Box 1/A2.

33. The issue is first discussed in Minutes, WWF Intl., Executive Committee, 28 Sept. 1989, WWF Intl. The quote appears in both Prince Philip to Charles de Haes, 12 Feb. 1990, BP, WWF Box 12/B2, and Minutes, 48th meeting of WWF Intl. Board of Trustees, 3 July 1990, WWF Intl.

34. Minutes, WWF Intl., Executive Committee, 24 March 1982, WWF Intl.

35. Prince Philip, President's message, in WWF Intl. (ed.), World Wildlife Fund Twentieth Anniversary Review, Gland, 1981, p. 3.

36. Charles de Haes, Strategic Considerations for Management Plan, 1 Sept. 1977, appendix to Minutes, WWF Intl., Executive Council, 6 Sept. 1977, WWF Intl.

37. Richard Davies to Rupert Nevill [Private Secretary of Prince Philip], 29 Jan. 1981, BP, WWF Box 1/A2. A copy of the Private Eye of 1 Aug. 1980 is located in EMN 4/26.

38. Luc Hoffmann to Prince Philip, 15 March 1982, BP, WWF Box 2/A3.

39. Prince Philip to John Loudon, 9 May 1980, BP, WWF Box 1/A2.

40. Minutes, WWF Intl., Executive Committee, 20 Nov. 1981, WWF Intl.

41. Prince Philip to John Loudon, 21 April 1981, BP, WWF Box 2/A3.

42. Dame Anne Griffiths, Librarian and Archivist to HRH The Duke of Edinburgh, to Alexis Schwarzenbach, 24 Nov. 2010.

43. See Minutes, WWF Intl., Executive Committee, 1982–1992, WWF Intl.

44. Interview, Charles de Haes, 11 Dec. 2009.

45. On the historical relevance of the paper, see John McCormick, 'The origins of the world conservation strategy', Environmental Review, 10(3), 1986, pp. 177-87.

46. See Holdgate, The Green Web, p. 190.

47. See Minutes, Joint WWF International Board/National Organisations Meeting, 26-28 May 1981, WWF Intl.

48. Minutes, WWF Intl., Executive Committee, 1 March 1985, WWF Intl.; see also interview, Charles de Haes, 11 Dec. 2009.

49. For details, see Holdgate, The Green Web, pp. 162-7, 170-72, 189-92.

50. Ibid., p. 194.

51. Minutes, 40th meeting of WWF Intl. Board of Trustees, 29 April 1986, WWF Intl.

52. Holdgate, The Green Web, p. 217.

53. Minutes, WWF Intl., Executive Council, 8 Nov. 1979, WWF Intl.

54. Minutes, 3rd meeting of WWF Intl. Board of Trustees, 27-29 Nov. 1962, WWF Intl.

55. The question 'whether we should now have a trade mark showing the Panda symbol, which would protect our interests and prevent others from using commercially our own symbol', was first discussed in 1963. See Minutes, 4th meeting of WWF Intl. Board of Trustees, 14/15 May 1963, WWF Intl. For reports on the slow and complicated registration process, see Minutes, 6th meeting of WWF Intl. Board of Trustees, 29 June–1 July 1964, WWF Intl.; Minutes, 7th meeting of WWF

Intl. Board of Trustees, 29 Nov.–1 Dec. 1964, WWF Intl.

56. Minutes, 33rd meeting of WWF Intl. Board of Trustees, 22 Nov. 1982, WWF Intl.

57. Charles de Haes, Strategic Considerations for Management Plan, 1 Sept. 1977, appendix to Minutes, WWF Intl., Executive Council, 6 Sept. 1977, WWF Intl.

58. The streamlined version is first used in the Yearbook 1979–1980, and for the first time appears with the ® sign indicating its registration as a trademark. See WWF Intl. (ed.), Yearbook 1979–80, Gland, 1980, back cover.

59. For a reference to the Danish double panda, see Minutes, Joint WWF International Board/National Organisations Meeting, 24/25 June 1980, WWF Intl. For samples of logo variations, see Landor Associates, WWF-Panda Design Project, [1986], BP, WWF Box 7/A14.

60. See Minutes, 33rd meeting of WWF Intl. Board of Trustees, 22 Nov. 1982, WWF Intl.

61. Minutes, 40th meeting of WWF Intl. Board of Trustees, 29 April 1986, WWF Intl.

62. Landor Associates, WWF-Panda Design Project, [1986], BP, WWF Box 7/A14.

63. Ibid.

64. See Schaller, The Last Panda, p. 245.

65. Underlining in original. Landor Associates, WWF-Panda Design Project, [1986], BP, WWF Box 7/A14.

66. See Minutes, 40th meeting of WWF Intl. Board of Trustees, 29 April 1986, WWF Intl.

67. Minutes, 38th meeting of WWF Intl. Board of Trustees, 17-20 May 1985, WWF Intl.

68. http://www.arcworld.org/about_ARC. htm, last consultation 3 Dec. 2010.

69. Minutes, 7th meeting of WWF Intl. Board of Trustees, 29 Nov.–1 Dec. 1964, WWF Intl.

70. Minutes, 39th meeting of WWF Intl. Board of Trustees, 19 Nov. 1985, WWF Intl.; for the Afrikaans name of WWF-South Africa, see WWF Intl. (ed.), Yearbook 1968, Morges, 1969, p. 298.

71. See Extracts from Proceedings of the Third Meeting of the WWF International (Advisory) Council […], 19/20 May 1985, EMN 5/1.

72. Charles de Haes to Ad Personam Council Members, Possible change in name and symbol, 24 Oct. 1985, EMN 5/1.

73. Minutes, 39th meeting of WWF Intl. Board of Trustees, 19 Nov. 1985, WWF Intl.

74. Bill Reilly to Alexis Schwarzenbach, 3 Nov. 2009.

75. Minutes, WWF Intl., Executive Committee, 5 Oct. 1987, WWF Intl.

A family row

1. Charles Lindbergh to Peter Scott, 28 Aug. 1966, EPS C.338.

2. Russell E. Train, Politics, Pollution and Pandas. An environmental memoir, Island Press, Washington, DC, 2003, p. 32.

3. Apart from his autobiography, see J. Brooks Flippen, Conservative Conservationist. Russell E. Train and the Emergence of American Environmentalism, Louisiana State University Press, Baton Rouge, 2006.

4. Russell Train to Alexis Schwarzenbach, 9 Dec. 2009.

5. Ibid.

6. Minutes, WWF Intl., Executive Committee, 20 Nov. 1981, WWF Intl.

7. See WWF-US, Annual Reports 1985 and 1990, WWF-US, IRC.

8. Russel Train to Alexis Schwarzenbach, 9 Dec. 2009.

9. See Charles Lindbergh to Peter Scott, 28 Aug. 1966, EPS C.338.

10. Bill Reilly in The Conservation Foundation, A Report on the Year 1985. On the history of CF see also the twelve-page untitled speech manuscript by Russell Train, no date [1993], WWF-US, IRC.

11. The photographs were mostly provided by CF's founding trustee, David Hunter McAlpin. See Annual Report of The Conservation Foundation, 1978–1984, WWF-US, IRC.

12. See Bill Reilly in The Conservation Foundation, A Report on the Year 1985.

13. Russell Train to Alexis Schwarzenbach, 9 Dec. 2009.

14. Revenue: WWF-US: 43'857'330, CF: 5'456'747; assets: WWF-US: $ 34'302'542, CF: 6'991'439. See WWF-US, Annual Report 1990, WWF-US, IRC

15. Minutes, WWF Intl., Executive Committee, 14 Feb. 1986, WWF Intl.

16. On the refusal of WWF-US to transfer the income of The 1001, see Minutes, 42nd meeting of WWF Intl. Board of Trustees, 5 May 1987, WWF Intl.

17. Bill Reilly to Alexis Schwarzenbach, 3 Nov. 2009.

18. Dame Anne Griffiths, Librarian and Archivist to HRH The Duke of Edinburgh, to Alexis Schwarzenbach, 24 Nov. 2010.

19. See Manhattan Agreement, no date [1982], Tab C of Abraham D. Sofaer, Memorandum Concerning the Relationship Between – World Wide Fund for Nature and World Wildlife Fund, Inc., 6 March 1991, EMN 5/1.

20. Russell Train to Alexis Schwarzenbach, 9 Dec. 2009.

21. Bill Reilly to Alexis Schwarzenbach, 3 Nov. 2009.

22. Dame Anne Griffiths, Librarian and Archivist to HRH The Duke of Edinburgh, to Alexis Schwarzenbach, 24 Nov. 2010.

23. Abraham D. Sofaer, Memorandum Concerning the Relationship Between –

World Wide Fund for Nature and World
Wildlife Fund, Inc., 6 March 1991, EMN
5/1.
24. Prince Philip to Russell Train, 4 March
1991, EMN 5/1.
25. Bill Reilly to Alexis Schwarzenbach, 3
Nov. 2009.
26. Minutes, WWF Intl., Executive
Committee, 5 Oct. 1987, WWF Intl.
27. Minutes, WWF Intl., Executive
Committee, 27 Nov. 1989, WWF Intl.
28. Interview, Kathryn Fuller, 30 Oct. 2009.
29. Russell Train to Alexis Schwarzenbach,
9 Dec. 2009.
30. Minutes, WWF Intl., Executive
Committee, 9 April 1990, WWF Intl.
31. Minutes, WWF Intl., Executive
Committee, 13 Oct. 1990, WWF Intl.
32. Russell Train to Alexis Schwarzenbach,
9 Dec. 2009; interview, Kathryn Fuller,
30 Oct. 2009.
33. Prince Philip to Russell Train, 4 March
1991, EMN 5/1.
34. Interview, Kathryn Fuller, 30 Oct. 2009;
see Minutes, 51st meeting of WWF Intl.
Board of Trustees, 6 Dec. 1991, WWF
Intl.
35. Claude Martin to Alexis
Schwarzenbach, 31 Dec. 2009.
36. Jim Leape to Alexis Schwarzenbach, 6
April 2010.
37. See Memorandum of Understanding
between WWF – World Wide Fund for
Nature and World Wildlife Fund, Inc.,
3–9 April 1992, WWF Intl.
38. Kathryn Fuller to Charles de Haes,
21 June 1991, quoted in Minutes,
50th meeting of WWF Intl. Board of
Trustees, 25 June 1991, WWF Intl.
39. Interview, Kathryn Fuller, 30 Oct. 2009.
40. Minutes, 50th meeting of WWF Intl.
Board of Trustees, 25 June 1991, WWF
Intl.
41. Ibid.
42. See Minutes, 51st meeting of WWF Intl.
Board of Trustees, 6 Dec. 1991, WWF
Intl.
43. Minutes, WWF Intl., Executive
Committee, 26 April 1992, WWF Intl.
44. See Russell Train and Kathryn Fuller to
Prince Philip, 3 Jan. 1993, BP, WWF Box
8/A16.
45. Prince Philip to Claude Martin, 10 Jan.
1992, BP, WWF Box 8/A16.
46. Hans Hüssy to Prince Philip, 10 Jan.
1992, BP, WWF Box 8/A16.
47. '[P]articulièrement compétentes dans
les domaines utiles aux buts de la
Fondation.' Statuts du WWF – World
Wide Fund for Nature, 3 Nov. 1993,
in Dossier WWF, Canton de Vaud,
Registre du commerce, Moudon.
48. Telephone conversation with Hans
Hüssy, 12 April 2010.
49. Russell Train and Kathryn Fuller to
Prince Philip, 3 Jan. 1993, BP, WWF Box
8/A16.
50. Minutes, 52nd meeting of WWF Intl.
Board of Trustees, 2 July 1992, WWF
Intl.

51. Telephone conversation with Hans
Hüssy, 12 April 2010.
52. Russell Train, quoted in Minutes,
53rd meeting of WWF Intl. Board of
Trustees, 20 Nov. 1992, WWF Intl. The
original letter could not be located in
the WWF archives.
53. Interview, Kathryn Fuller, 30 Oct. 2009.
54. See Interview, Hans Hüssy, 4 June
2009; Niels Halbertsma to Alexis
Schwarzenbach, 11 Feb. 2010; George
Medley to Arthur Norman, 21 Nov.
2009.
55. See Minutes, 53rd meeting of WWF Intl.
Board of Trustees, 20 Nov. 1992, WWF
Intl. On the debates in Buenos Aires,
see George Medley to Arthur Norman,
21 Nov. 2009, Claude Martin to Alexis
Schwarzenbach, 25 March 2010.
56. See Minutes, 53rd meeting of WWF Intl.
Board of Trustees, 20 Nov. 1992, WWF
Intl.; Prince Philip to Charles de Haes,
23 Nov. 1992, BP, WWF Box 3/A5; Prince
Philip to Charles de Haes, 17 Dec. 1992,
file CdH/BA RET, Archive Charles
de Haes, Winchester; Russell Train to
Alexis Schwarzenbach, 9 Dec. 2009.
57. See Babar Ali to McLain Stewart, 29
Nov. 1992; Babar Ali to Charles de
Haes, 16 Dec. 1992, file CdH/BA RET,
Archive Charles de Haes, Winchester.
58. Prince Philip to Charles de Haes, 17
Dec. 1992, file CdH/BA RET, Archive
Charles de Haes, Winchester.
59. Russell Train to Prince Philip, 22 Jan.
1993, BP, WWF Box 4/A7.

Operation Lock

1. Minutes, 42nd meeting of WWF Intl.
Board of Trustees, 5 May 1987, WWF
Intl.
2. WWF Intl. (ed.), WWF Conservation
Yearbook 1987/88, Gland, 1988, p. 137.
3. See Eric Dinerstein, The Return of
the Unicorns. The Natural History and
Conservation of the Greater One-Horned
Rhinoceros, Columbia University Press,
New York, 2003, pp. 29–33.
4. Minutes, 42nd meeting of WWF Intl.
Board of Trustees, 5 May 1987, WWF
Intl.
5. Judge Abraham Sofaer, Operation
Lock – Chronology, 17 June 1993, entry
22 July 1987, BP. This document, to
which Prince Philip has kindly given me
access, will forthwith be referred to as
Sofaer Chronology 1993.
6. On Stirling, see Alan Hoe, David
Stirling. The Authorised Biography of
the Founder of the SAS, Little, Brown,
London, 1992.
7. Sofaer Chronology 1993, entry 13 Nov.
1987.
8. See Minutes, WWF Intl., Executive
Committee, 24 May 1993, WWF Intl.
9. Justice M. E. Kumleben, Report,
Commission of Inquiry into the alleged
smuggling of and illegal trade in ivory
and rhinoceros horn in South Africa,
Durban, January 1996, WWF Intl. This

document will forthwith be referred to
as Kumleben Report 1996.
10. Ibid., pp. 137–8.
11. John Hanks, quoted in ibid., p. 138.
12. Ibid., p. 138.
13. See Sofaer Chronology 1993, entry 13
Nov. 1987.
14. Kumleben Report 1996, p. 139.
15. John Hanks, 'The Need for a
Continental Strategy for the
Conservation of Rhino in Africa', Oct.
1987, quoted in Sofaer Chronology 1993,
entry Oct. 1987.
16. Minutes, 3 Nov. 1987, quoted in Sofaer
Chronology 1993, entry 3 Nov. 1987.
17. John Hanks, 'Continental Strategy for
the Conservation of Rhino in Africa,
Revised edition for consideration by
WWF's Conservation Committee', Dec.
1987, quoted in Kumleben Report 1996,
p. 142.
18. John Hanks, quoted in Kumleben
Report 1996, p. 144.
19. John Hanks, 'Continental Strategy for
the Conservation of Rhino in Africa',
quoted in Kumleben Report 1996, p.
142.
20. Sofaer Chronology 1993, entry Dec. 1987.
21. John Hanks, quoted in Kumleben
Report 1996, p. 144.
22. Kumleben Report 1996, p. 147.
23. John Hanks, quoted in ibid., p. 145.
24. On the ESPU, see ibid., pp. 161–71.
25. Details on the training of the anti-
poaching units in Namibia were
revealed in the Independent, 'WWF
bankrolled rhino mercenaries', 17 Nov.
1991. The Sofaer Chronology contains
a reference to the funding of '2 KAS
employees' based in the Namibian town
of Outjo in the course of Operation
Lock, entry 25 April 1989.
26. Ian Crooke to John Hanks, 21 Oct. 1988,
quoted in Sofaer Chronology 1993, entry
21 Oct. 1988.
27. Ian Crooke, 'Operation Lock
(A Report on the Findings and
Recommendations)', 19 Oct. 1988,
quoted in Sofaer Chronology 1993, entry
21 Oct. 1988.
28. Ibid.
29. [Operation Lock], Terms of Reference,
17 Nov. 1988, quoted in Sofaer
Chronology 1993, entry 2 Dec. 1988.
30. Ian Crooke, 'Operation Lock
(A Report on the Findings and
Recommendations)', 19 Oct. 1988,
quoted in Sofaer Chronology 1993, entry
21 Oct. 1988.
31. Sofaer Chronology 1993, entry 13 Nov.
1987.
32. See ibid., entry 25 Aug. 1989.
33. See ibid., entries 10 Aug. 1988; 24 Jan.
1989; 25 April 1989.
34. Ibid., entry 25 April 1989.
35. Ibid., entry Oct. 1989.
36. Kumleben Report 1996, p. 140.
37. Ibid., pp. 139, 12.
38. For a summary, see Stephen Ellis, 'Of
elephants and men: politics and nature
conservation in South Africa', Journal of

Southern African Studies, 20(1), 1994, pp. 53–69.

39. See Kumleben Report 1996, pp. 34–73, 161–71, 176–87.
40. See ibid., pp. 74–135.
41. Ibid., pp. 131, 130.
42. Colonel Jan Breytenbach, quoted in ibid., p. 26.
43. Kumleben Report 1996, p. 150.
44. Colonel Pieter Lategan, quoted in ibid., p. 150.
45. Kumleben Report 1996, p. 150.
46. Colonel Pieter Lategan, quoted in ibid., p. 150.
47. Ibid., p. 151.
48. See Kumleben Report 1996, p. 151.
49. Ibid., pp. 157–8.
50. Ibid., pp. 158, 157.
51. [Mike Richards aka Harry Stevens], Document Q, [c. 1989], quoted in ibid., p. 155.
52. Ibid.
53. Kumleben Report 1996, pp. 153–4.
54. Ibid., pp. 158–9.
55. Dame Anne Griffiths, Librarian and Archivist to HRH The Duke of Edinburgh, to Alexis Schwarzenbach, 10 Nov. 2009.
56. Kumleben Report 1996, p. 159.
57. See Sotheby's (ed.), *Auctions for the Benefit of WWF International*, London & Geneva, 1988/89, pp. 22–4.
58. Sofaer Chronology 1993, entry 7 Dec. 1988.
59. Tatiana Gortchacow to Charles de Haes, 12 Jan. 1989, file January 1991 to December 1992, Archive Charles de Haes, Winchester.
60. Charles de Haes to Prince Bernhard, 16 Jan. 1989, quoted in Sofaer Chronology 1993, entry 16 Jan. 1989.
61. Sofaer Chronology 1993, entry 21 Jan. 1989.
62. Minutes, WWF Intl., Executive Committee, 13 Oct. 1990, WWF Intl.
63. See R. M. Smits, Treasurer of Her Royal Highness Princess Juliana of the Netherlands, to Henner Ehringhaus, WWF Intl., 13 June 1989, file January 1991 to December 1992, Archive Charles de Haes, Winchester; on 3 Aug. 1989 the Sofaer Chronology notes: 'Proceeds of Sotheby's painting sale remitted by Sotheby's to the account of Princess Juliana.'
64. Charles de Haes, quoted in Dr Heydorn to Frans Stroebel, 28 April 1990, Sofaer Chronology 1993, entry 28 April 1990.
65. Sofaer Chronology, entry 3 July 1989; additional information provided by Charles de Haes by telephone, 24 Aug. 2010.
66. Sofaer Chronology, entry 1 June 1990.
67. Ibid., entry 28 April 1990.
68. Ibid., entry 27 June 1990.
69. Ibid., entry 2 July 1990. See also Minutes, WWF Intl., Executive Committee, 2 July 1990, WWF Intl.
70. Minutes, WWF Intl., Executive Committee, 13 Oct. 1990, WWF Intl.
71. Sofaer Chronology, entry 23 Aug. 1990.

72. Ibid., entry Sept. 1990.
73. Ibid., entry 13 Oct. 1990.
74. Minutes, WWF Intl., Executive Committee, 24 May 1993, WWF Intl.
75. Sofaer Chronology, entry 8 Jan. 1991.
76. Stephen Ellis, 'Prince paid thousands into wildlife sting', *Independent*, 8 Jan. 1991.
77. Sofaer Chronology, entry 6 Jan. 1991.
78. Ibid., entry 8 Jan. 1991.
79. Prince Philip to Gavin Relly, 6 Feb. 1991, quoted in ibid., entry 6 Feb. 1991.
80. Gavin Relly to Prince Philip, 6 Feb. 1991, quoted in ibid., entry 6 Feb. 1991.
81. Paul Brown, 'Web of African intrigue foils ivory plot', *Guardian*, 2 March 1992. The Sofaer Chronology refers to another article published on 6 March 1992 in an unidentified paper entitled 'WWF served interests of South Africa'.
82. Charles de Haes to Prince Philip, 22 May 1992, BP, WWF Box 13/B2.
83. George Medley, WWF-UK, to Trustees WWF-UK, 20 May 1993, EMN 7/1/3.
84. Bonner's statements include: '[I]mpoverished Africans should be allowed to utilize wildlife, including elephants for their ivory'; Raymond Bonner, *At the Hand of Man*, Knopf, New York, 1993, p. 99. A discussion of the long-term merits of the ivory ban, which is still in place, would go far beyond the scope of this book.
85. See Bonner, *At the Hand of Man*, pp. 53–60, 87–113.
86. Ibid., p. 78.
87. Ibid., pp. 70–71.
88. Ibid., p. 74.
89. See George Medley to Trustees of WWF-UK, 28 April 1993, EMN 7/1/3.
90. Minutes, WWF Intl., Executive Committee, 24 May 1993, WWF Intl.
91. Ibid.
92. Minutes, WWF Intl., Executive Committee, 7 Oct. 1993, WWF Intl. The memorandum dated 12 July 1993 could not be located in the course of this research but is referred to in the EXCO minutes.
93. Ibid.
94. Claude Martin to Alexis Schwarzenbach, 31 Dec. 2009.
95. Bonner, *At the Hand of Man*, p. 78. Stephen Ellis summed up his views on Charles de Haes in 'Of elephants and men', pp. 53–69.
96. Bonner, *At the Hand of Man*, p. 69.
97. Ellis, 'Of elephants and men', p. 62; Bonner, *At the Hand of Man*, p. 69; for a recent reference to The 1001 as a 'platform for South African businessmen', see Marja Spierenburg and Harry Wels, 'Conservative philanthropists. Royalty and business elites in nature conservation in southern Africa', *Antipode, a Radical Journal of Geography*, 42(3), 2010, pp. 647–70.
98. 'Lowlife fund (2)', *Private Eye*, 13 Aug. 1980, EMN 4/26.
99. On the Broederbond, whose power and influence during the apartheid era have

often been exaggerated, see Hermann Giliomee, *The Afrikaners. Biography of a People*, Hurst, London, 2003, who concludes on pp. 420–21: 'Historians, journalists and political opponents of the Broederbond have attributed an importance to the organization that is out of all proportion.' See also Annette Knecht, 'Ein Geheimbund als Akteur des Wandels. Der Afrikaner Broederbond und seine Rolle im Transformationsprozess Südafrikas', PhD thesis, University of Mannheim, 2006, Lang, Frankfurt am Main, 2007.
100. See above, Chapter 5.

Implementing a new mission

1. See Minutes, 56th meeting of WWF Intl. Board of Trustees, 29 Oct. 1993, WWF Intl.
2. Claude Martin to Alexis Schwarzenbach, 26 Dec. 2009; and see Claude Martin, 'Status and ecology of the Barasingha (*Cervus duvauceli branderi*) in Kanha National Park (India)', PhD thesis, University of Zurich, 1975.
3. 'Ask Claude Martin', Nov. 2005, http://wwf.panda.org/who_we_are/organization/dg_bios/claude_martin. cfm, last consultation 13 Oct. 2010, and see Claude Martin, *The Rainforests of West Africa: Ecology – Threats – Conservation*, Birkhäuser, Basle, 1991.
4. See above, Chapter 7.
5. Charles de Haes, quoted in Minutes, 50th meeting of WWF Intl. Board of Trustees, 25 June 1991, WWF Intl.
6. Claude Martin to Alexis Schwarzenbach, 31 Dec. 2009.
7. Interview, Kathryn Fuller, Washington, DC, 30 Oct. 2009.
8. Prince Philip to Claude Martin, 1 Nov. 1993, BP, WWF Box 4/A7; and see Minutes, 56th meeting of WWF Intl. Board of Trustees, 29 Oct. 1993, WWF Intl.
9. See Minutes, WWF Intl., Executive Committee, 20 Nov. 1991, WWF Intl.; Minutes, WWF Intl., Executive Committee, 16 Oct. 1992, WWF Intl.
10. Minutes, 58th meeting of WWF Intl. Board of Trustees, 18 Nov. 1994, WWF Intl.; see Minutes, 60th meeting of WWF Intl. Board of Trustees, 27 Oct. 1995, WWF Intl.
11. The Peace Park Foundation's major donors include the Rupert Family Foundation, Cartier, Richemont and Remgro, the holding created out of the Rembrandt Group in 2000; see Peace Parks Foundation (ed.), Review 1997–2006, Stellenbosch, 2006.
12. On Anton Rupert and the Peace Parks Foundation, see Dommisse, *Anton Rupert*, pp. 377–90. For a critical if somewhat superficial assessment, see Malcolm Draper, Marja Spierenburg

and Harry Wels, 'African dreams of cohesion: elite pacting and community development in transfrontier conservation areas in southern Africa', *Culture and Organization*, 10(4), 2004, pp. 341–53.

13. Minutes, WWF Intl., Executive Committee, 22 May 2000, WWF Intl.
14. Claude Martin to Alexis Schwarzenbach, 31 Dec. 2009.
15. Ibid.
16. See Minutes, WWF Intl., Executive Committee, 13 Oct. 1997, WWF Intl.
17. Claude Martin to Alexis Schwarzenbach, 31 Dec. 2009.
18. John Phillipson, Evaluation of the Effectiveness of WWF Projects, Executive Summary, Sept. 1989, BP, WWF Box 12/B2.
19. Charles de Haes to Prince Philip, 5 Oct. 1989, BP, WWF Box 12/B2.
20. John Phillipson, Evaluation of the Effectiveness of WWF Projects, Executive Summary, Sept. 1989, BP, WWF Box 12/B2.
21. '[I]ntransparente Praktik', Claude Martin to Alexis Schwarzenbach, 4 Oct. 2010.
22. 'Hier anerkannte man […], dass wir eine Organisation sein wollten, die nicht einfach ein paar punktuelle Projekte hat, sondern in einer umfassenden Art und Weise die Grundursachen der Umweltzerstörung angehen wollte.' Interview, Claude Martin, 23 Nov. 2009.
23. Interview, Kathryn Fuller, 30 Oct. 2010.
24. 'Daraus entstand dann das Mission Statement, das brauchte also manch eine Sitzung, und manche Diskussion und Papers, obwohl es nachher nur eine Seite lang war.' Interview, Claude Martin, 23 Nov. 2009.
25. WWF Intl. (ed.), Mission for the 1990s, Gland, 1990, p. 1.
26. For the current, slightly adapted version which still contains the core passage – 'To stop the degradation of the planet's natural environment and to build a future in which humans live in harmony with nature' - see www.panda.org/who_we_are/, last consultation 5 Oct. 2010.
27. Minutes, 46th meeting of WWF Intl. Board of Trustees, 13 June 1989, WWF Intl.
28. Claude Martin to Alexis Schwarzenbach, 26 Dec. 2009.
29. Chris Hails, 'The evolution of approaches to conserving the world's natural heritage: the experiences of WWF', *International Journal of Heritage Studies*, 13(4/5), 2007, p. 370.
30. Norman Myers, Russell A. Mittermeier, Cristina G. Mittermeier, Gustavo A. B. da Fonseca and Jennifer Kent, 'Biodiversity hotspots for conservation priorities', *Nature*, 403, 2000, pp. 853–8.
31. Hails, 'The evolution of approaches …', p. 370.
32. D. M. Olson and Eric Dinerstein, 'The Global 200: a representation

approach to conserving the Earth's most biologically valuable ecoregions', *Conservation Biology*, 12, 1998, pp. 502–15.
33. Hails, 'The evolution of approaches', p. 370.
34. Ibid., pp. 370–71; and see Chris Hails to Alexis Schwarzenbach, 10 Oct. 2010.
35. Chris Hails to Alexis Schwarzenbach, 10 Oct. 2010.
36. Siegfried Woldhek, quoted in Art Kleiner, 'Zealot profile: Siegfried Woldhek', *strategy + business*, 1 April 2001.
37. See Minutes, 70th meeting of WWF Intl. Board of Trustees, 13 Nov. 2000, WWF Intl.
38. Chris Hails to Alexis Schwarzenbach, 14 Nov. 2010.
39. See Minutes, WWF Intl., Executive Committee, 9 April 1990, WWF Intl.
40. Claude Martin to Alexis Schwarzenbach, 31 Dec. 2009.
41. Ibid.; and see Minutes, WWF Intl., Executive Committee, 7 Jan. 1997, WWF Intl.
42. Hails, 'The evolution of approaches', p. 370.
43. Claude Martin to Alexis Schwarzenbach, 31 Dec. 2009.
44. Minutes, 58th meeting of WWF Intl. Board of Trustees, 18 Nov. 1994, WWF Intl.
45. Minutes, 6th meeting of WWF Intl. Board of Trustees, 29 June–1 July 1964, WWF Intl.
46. See Jane Carruthers, 'Designing a wilderness for wildlife: the case of Pilanesberg, South Africa', Paper presented at the conference Designing Wildlife Habitats, Dumbarton Oaks, Washington, DC, 14/15 May 2010.
47. Prince Philip to Charles de Haes, 25 Oct. 1991, BP, WWF Box 13/B2.
48. Claude Martin to Alexis Schwarzenbach, 31 Dec. 2009.
49. Mac Chapin, 'A challenge to conservationists', *World Watch*, 6, Nov./Dec. 2004, p. 17.
50. Minutes, WWF Intl., Executive Committee, 10 Nov. 2004, WWF Intl.
51. Carter Roberts and Chris Hails, 'From the World Wildlife Fund (WWF)', *World Watch*, Jan./Feb. 2005, pp. 6–7.
52. Jenny Springer and Janis Alcorn, *Strengthening WWF Partnerships with Indigenous Peoples and Local Communities: Key Findings and Recommendations*, WWF, Gland and Washington, DC, 2007.
53. Chris Hails to Alexis Schwarzenbach, 19 Oct. 2010; and see 'Enron pipeline leaves scar on South America', *Washington Post*, 6 May 2002.
54. Maria Boulos, Director, Corporate Relations at WWF International, to Alexis Schwarzenbach, 21 July 2010.
55. On the ecological footprint, see http://www.footprintnetwork.org, last consulted 4 Dec. 2010.
56. WWF & Lafarge joint press release, 'WWF – Lafarge, a worldwide partnership for environmental

protection', 16 Dec. 2003, available online at users.skynet.be/idd/documents/energie/se3d2.pdf, last consultation 4 Dec. 2010.
57. Speech by Prime Minister Mahathir, United Nations Conference on Environment and Development, Rio de Janeiro, 13 June 1992, www.pmo.gov.my/ucapan/?m=p&p=mahathir&id=1631, last consulted 9 Oct. 2010.
58. 'Das fuhr ein wie ein Blitz.' Interview, Claude Martin, 23 Nov. 2009.
59. See Minutes, 70th meeting of WWF Intl. Board of Trustees, 13 Nov. 2000, WWF Intl.
60. Minutes, 56th meeting of WWF Intl. Board of Trustees, 29 Oct. 1993, WWF Intl.
61. For an overview, see WWF Center for Conservation Finance, WWF Commercial Debt-for-Nature Swaps 1988 to present, 1 Sept. 2003, http://www.cbd.int/financial/debt.shtml, last consulted 10 Oct. 2010.
62. Minutes, 64th meeting of WWF Intl. Board of Trustees, 31 Oct. 1997, WWF Intl.
63. Minutes, 60th meeting of WWF Intl. Board of Trustees, 27 Oct. 1995, WWF Intl.
64. http://go.worldbank.org/CNBMVNCCC0, last consulted 10 Oct. 2010.
65. See WWF-US (ed.), World Bank/WWF Alliance for Forest Conservation & Sustainable Use, [2005], http://www.worldwildlife.org/what/globalmarkets/forests/worldbankalliance.html, last consulted 15 Oct. 2010.
66. Minutes, WWF Intl., Executive Committee, 22 May 2001, WWF Intl.
67. See Minutes, WWF Intl., Executive Committee, 26 June 1995, WWF Intl.
68. See Minutes, 68th meeting of WWF Intl. Board of Trustees, 19 Nov. 1999 , WWF Intl.
69. See Minutes, WWF Intl., Executive Committee, 12 Nov. 2000, WWF Intl.
70. Minutes, 72nd meeting of WWF Intl. Board of Trustees, 12 Nov. 2001, WWF Intl.
71. Ibid.
72. Claude Martin to Alexis Schwarzenbach, 31 Dec. 2009.
73. Minutes, WWF Intl., Executive Committee, 5 March 2002, WWF Intl.
74. Minutes, 71st meeting of WWF Intl. Board of Trustees, 15 June 2001, WWF Intl.
75. Claude Martin to Alexis Schwarzenbach, 31 Dec. 2009.
76. Claude Martin to Alexis Schwarzenbach, 26 Dec. 2009, including clippings of articles he published in the *International Herald Tribune*, 5 Aug. 1999; 24 July 2002.
77. Minutes, 54th meeting of WWF Intl. Board of Trustees, 25 Jan. 1993, WWF Intl.

Saving the World's Wildlife

78. Minutes, WWF Intl., Executive Committee, 5 March 2002, WWF Intl.
79. See Medienmitteilung WWF-Schweiz, 'Dramatische Entwicklung an der Spitze des WWF-Schweiz', 30 Oct. 2001, WWF-CH.
80. See Esther Banz, 'Tri-Tra-Trallala – der WWF ist da', *Wochenzeitung*, 11 October 2001.
81. See Medienmitteilung WWF-Schweiz, 'Neubeginn beim WWF-Schweiz', 24 Nov. 2001, WWF-CH.
82. Minutes, 73rd meeting of WWF Intl. Board of Trustees, 14 June 2002, WWF Intl.; and see Minutes, WWF Intl., Executive Committee, 6 May 2002, WWF Intl.
83. Minutes, 73rd meeting of WWF Intl. Board of Trustees, 14 June 2002, WWF Intl.
84. See Medienmitteilung WWF-Schweiz, 'Neuer CEO beim WWF-Schweiz', 30 June 2003, WWF-CH.
85. Claude Martin to Alexis Schwarzenbach, 11 Oct. 2010.
86. See WWF Intl. (ed.), Annual Review 2005, Gland, 2005, WWF Intl.; for estimates of global supporters: Minutes, 77th meeting of WWF Intl. Board of Trustees, 7 June 2004, WWF Intl.
87. WWF Intl. (ed.), Annual Review 2005, Gland, 2005, WWF Intl.
88. Minutes, 78th meeting of WWF Intl. Board of Trustees, 6 Dec. 2004, WWF Intl.
89. See Press Release, WWF Intl, 'Royal Elephants Auctioned for Conservation', 2 Oct. 2005, http://wwf.panda.org/what_we_do/where_we_work/borneo_forests/news/?23617/Royal-elephants-auctioned-for-conservation, last consulted 15 Oct. 2010.

WWF – the first 50 years

1. Rob Soutter, WWF International, to WWF Conservation Committee, 6 Sept. 2010, WWF Intl.
2. http://wwf.panda.org/what_we_do/where_we_work/coraltriangle/, last consultation 15 Nov. 2010.
3. http://wwf.panda.org/what_we_do/endangered_species/tigers/tiger_initiative/political_process/, last consultation 14 Dec. 2010.
4. See Valmik Thapar, 'The tragedy of the Indian tiger: starting from scratch', in John Seidensticker, Sarah Christie and Peter Jackson (eds), *Riding the Tiger. Tiger Conservation in Human-dominated Landscapes*, Cambridge University Press, Cambridge, 1999, pp. 296–306.
5. Guy Mountfort, 'The WWF, Present and Future', no date [April 1993], EMN 7/1/3; and see Robin Pellew, WWF-UK, to Claude Martin, 12 July 1995, BP, WWF Box 15/B2.
6. Claude Martin to Robin Pellew, 14 July 1995, BP, WWF Box 15/B2. For a comprehensive overview of recent approaches to tiger conservation see Seidensticker et al., *Riding the Tiger.*
7. WWF Intl. (ed.), Tiger Fact Sheet, May 2010, WWF Intl.
8. Max Nicholson to Fritz Vollmar, 22 Dec. 1977, WWF Intl., file 'WWF History', no. 8/2
9. See Jean-Benoît Falisse, 'Entrepreneurs humanitaires. Médecins sans frontières belgique, genèse d'une ONG atypique, 1980–1987', *Cahiers d'Histoire du Temps Présent*, 21, 2009, pp. 11–54.
10. See Frank Zelko, 'Greenpeace and the development of international environmental activism in the 1970s', in Ursula Lehmkuhl and Hermann Wellenreuther (eds), *Historians and Nature. Comparative Approaches to Environmental History*, Berg, Oxford, 2007, pp. 296–318.
11. Jim Leape to Alexis Schwarzenbach, 6 April 2010.
12. Max Nicholson, 'How to save the world's wildlife', 6 April 1961, WWF Intl., file 'WWF History', no. 1/1.
13. 'Es war hart, die Marken an die Leute zu bringen. Naturschutz war noch nicht in aller Munde. Aber der Name der Aktion hat mich fasziniert: Nakuru.' Peter Weber to Alexis Schwarzenbach, 7 Nov. 2010.
14. 'Die Lithografie von Fritz Hug hängt heute noch in meinem Wohnzimmer. Ich war als Kind wirklich stolz darauf, ein Bild zu besitzen, mit meinem Namen darunter! Und irgendwie blieb eine spezielle Beziehung zu Flamingovögeln zurück. Ich habe immer Freude, wenn ich einen sehe, auf Fotos oder im Zoo.' Magdalena Hilfiker to Alexis Schwarzenbach, 30 Oct. 2010.
15. 'Ich habe sie dann halt auf die Briefe an meine Brieffreundinnnen und Brieffreunde geklebt, um ein bisschen Werbung zu machen für "meinen" WWF! Und trotz meines persönlichen kurzzeitigen "Ruins" bin ich dem WWF bis heute treu geblieben. Und dies wohl mit Recht, gehört der WWF doch zu einer der besten Organisationen der Welt.' Cornelia Urscheler to Alexis Schwarzenbach, 28 Nov. 2010.

Sources and acknowledgements

1. For an example of an academic text focusing on WWF's policy rather than on those responsible for it, see Paul Wapner, *Environmental Activism and World Civic Politics*, State University of New York Press, Albany, 1996, pp. 72–116.
2. Frank Zelko, 'Greenpeace and the development of international environmental activism in the 1970s', in Ursula Lehmkuhl and Hermann Wellenreuther (eds), *Historians and Nature. Comparative Approaches to Environmental History*, Berg, Oxford, 2007, p. 296.
3. The only missing document is the minutes of a board meeting held on 22 June 1979.
4. Minutes, 2nd meeting of WWF Intl. Board of Trustees, 18–20 May 1962, WWF Intl.

BIBLIOGRAPHY

Print

Kaj Arhem, *Pastoral Man in the Garden of Eden. The Maasai of the Ngorongoro Conservation Area, Tanzania*, Uppsala: Uppsala University, Department of Cultural Anthropology, 1985

Mark Barrow, *Nature's Ghosts. Confronting Extinction from the Age of Jefferson to the Age of Ecology*, Chicago: University of Chicago Press, 2009

Raymond Bonner, *At the Hand of Man. Peril and Hope for Africa's Wildlife*, New York, NY: Knopf, 1993

Daniel Branch, *Defeating Mau Mau. Creating Kenya Counterinsurgency, Civil War, and Decolonization*, Cambridge: Cambridge University Press, 2009

Catherine Brice, 'La Monarchie et la construction de l'identité nationale italienne. 1861 à 1911', dissertation, Institut d'Études Politiques, Paris, 2004

Rachel Carson, *Silent Spring*, Boston: Houghton Mifflin, 1962

Jane Carruthers, *The Kruger National Park. A Social and Political History*, Pietermaritzburg: University of Natal Press, 1995

Jane Carruthers, 'Designing a wilderness for wildlife: the case of Pilanesberg, South Africa', paper presented at conference, 'Designing Wildlife Habitats', Dumbarton Oaks, Washington, DC, 14–15 May 2010

Mac Chapin, 'A challenge to conservationists', *World Watch*, No. 6, Nov–Dec 2004

Winston Churchill, *My African Journey*, London: Hodder & Stoughton, 1908

Ronald W. Clark, *The Huxleys*, London: Heinemann, 1968

Conseil International de la Chasse (ed.), CIC Newsletter, 3–4 (2008), special edition. '80 years of conservation through sustainable hunting, 1928–2008'

John Darwin, *The Empire Project. The Rise and Fall of the British World-System, 1830–1970*, Cambridge: Cambridge University Press, 2009

Eric Dinerstein, *The Return of the Unicorns the Natural History and Conservation of the Greater One-Horned Rhinoceros*, New York: Columbia University Press, 2003

Ebbe Dommisse, *Anton Rupert. A Biography*, Cape Town: Tafelberg, 2005

Malcolm Draper, Marja Spierenburg, Harry Wels, 'African dreams of cohesion: elite pacting and community development in transfrontier conservation areas in southern Africa', *Culture and Organization*, 10 (4), 2004, pp. 341–53

Nigel Leader-Williams and Holly T. Dublin, 'Charismatic megafauna as "flagship species" ', in Abigail Entwistle and Nigel Dubstone (eds), 2000

Stephen Ellis, 'Of elephants and men: politics and nature conservation in South Africa', *Journal of Southern African Studies*, 20(1), 1994, pp. 53–69

Bernt Engelmann and Günter Wallraff, *Ihr da oben – Wir da unten*, Cologne: Kiepenheuer & Witsch, 1973

Abigail Entwistle and Nigel Dubstone (eds.), *Priorities for the Conservation of Mammalian Diversity. Has the Panda Had Its Day?*, Cambridge: Cambridge University Press, 2000

Edward Fairholme, *A Century of Work for Animals. The History of the RSPCA, 1824–1924*, John Murray: London, 1924

Jean-Benoît Falisse, 'Entrepreneurs humanitaires. Médecins sans Frontières Belgique, Genèse d'une ONG atypique, 1980–1987', *Cahiers d'Histoire du Temps Présent*, 21, 2009, pp. 11–54

Richard Fitter and Peter Scott, *The Penitent Butchers: The Fauna Preservation Society 1903–1978*, London: Collins, 1978

J. Brooks Flippen, *Conservative Conservationist. Russell E. Train and the Emergence of American Environmentalism*, Baton Rouge, LA: Louisiana State University Press, 2006

Prosser Gifford and William Roger Louis (eds), *The Transfer of Power in Africa. Decolonization, 1940–1960*, New Haven, CT: Yale University Press, 1982

Hermann Giliomee, *The Afrikaners. Biography of a People*, London: Hurst, 2003

Alison Goddard, *The Unsung Ornithologist. A Biography of Luc Hoffmann*, Oxford: Oxford University Press, forthcoming

Chris Hails, 'The Evolution of Approaches to Conserving the World's Natural Heritage: The Experiences of WWF', *International Journal of Heritage Studies*, 13(4–5), 2007, pp. 365–79

Catherine M. C. Haines and Helen M. Stevens, *International Women in Science. A biographical dictionary to 1950*, Santa Barbara, CA: ABC-Clio, 2001

Alan Hoe and David Stirling, *The Authorised Biography of the Founder of the SAS*, London: Little, Brown & Co., 1992

Martin Holdgate, *The Green Web. A Union for World Conservation*, London: Earthscan, 1999

E. Homberger et al., 'The Seveso accident. its nature, extent and consequences', *The Annals of Occupational Hygiene*, 22, 1979, pp. 327–70

Stephen Howarth and Joost Jonker, *A History of Royal Dutch Shell, Band 2: Powering the Hydrocarbon Revolution, 1939–1973*, Oxford: Oxford University Press, 2007

Elspeth Huxley, *Peter Scott. Painter and Naturalist*, London: Faber and Faber, 1993

Garry Jenkins, *A Home of Their Own. 150 Years of Battersea Dogs & Cats Home*, London: Bantam, 2010

Art Kleiner, 'Zealot profile: Siegfried Woldhek' in *strategy + business*, 1 April 2001

Saving the World's Wildlife

Annette Knecht, 'Ein Geheimbund als Akteur des Wandels. der Afrikaner Broederbond und seine Rolle im Transformationsprozess Südafrikas', PhD thesis, University of Mannheim, 2006, Lang: Frankfurt am Main, 2007

Patrick Kupper, *Atomenergie und Gespaltene Gesellschaft. Die Geschichte des Gescheiterten Projektes Kernkraftwerk Kaiseraugst*, Zürich: Chronos, 2003

Robert Lamb, *Promising the Earth*, London: Routledge, 1996

E. H. Lamont, *Wild Life among the Pacific Islanders*, London: Hurst and Blackett, 1867

Marc Languy and Emmanuel de Merode (eds), *Virunga. The Survival of Africa's First National Park*, Tielt: Lannoo, 2009

Ursula Lehmkuhl and Hermann Wellenreuther (eds), *Historians and Nature. Comparative Approaches to Environmental History*, Oxford: Berg, 2007

Bernhard Graf zur Lippe, *In den Jagdgründen Deutsch-Ostafrikas*, Berlin: Reimer, 1904

Susan Lumpkin and John Seidensticker, *Smithsonian Book of Giant Pandas*, Washington, DC: Smithsonian Institution Press, 2002

Claude Martin, 'Status and ecology of the Barasingha (Cervus duvauceli branderi) in Kanha National Park (India)', PhD thesis, University of Zurich, 1975

Claude Martin, *The Rainforests of West Africa: Ecology – Threats – Conservation*, Basel: Birkhäuser, 1991

Arno Mayer, *The Persistence of the Old Regime. Europe to the Great War*, London: Croom Helm, 1981

John McCormick, 'The origins of the world conservation strategy', in *Environmental Review*, 1986, 10(3), pp. 177–87

John McCormick, *Reclaiming Paradise, The Global Environmental Movement*, Bloomington: Indiana University Press, 1989

Robert McNeill, *Something New under the Sun. An Environmental History of the Twentieth-century World*, New York: Norton, 2000

Guy Mountfort, *Memories of Three Lives*, Braunton: Merlin Ltd. 1991

Guy Mountfort, *Saving the Tiger*, London: Michael Joseph, 1981

Norman Myers et al., 'Biodiversity hotspots for conservation priorities', in *Nature*, 2000, 403, pp. 853–8

Henry Nicholls, *The Way of the Panda. The Curious History of China's Political Animal*, London: Profile Books, 2010

John T. Noonan, *Bribes*, London: Macmillan, 1984

Paul Nugent, *Africa Since Independence. A Comparative History*, Basingstoke: Palgrave Macmillan, 2004

D. M. Olson and Eric Dinerstein, 'The Global 200: a representation approach to conserving the earth's most biologically valuable ecoregions', in *Conservation Biology*, 1998, 12, pp. 502–15

Dan O'Meara, *Forty Lost Years. The Apartheid State and the Politics of the National Party 1948–1994*, Randburg: Ravan Press, 1996

C. T. Onions, *The Shorter Oxford English Dictionary on Historical Principles*, Oxford: Clarendon Press, 1988 [1973]

Fairfield Osborn, *Our Plundered Planet*, Boston: Little Brown, 1948

Peace Parks Foundation (ed.), 'Review 1997–2006', Stellenbosch, 2006

Roger Tory Peterson, Philip Arthur Dominic Hollom and Guy Mountfort, *A Field Guide to the Birds of Britain and Europe*, London: Collins, 1954

Christian Pfister (ed.), *Das 1950er Syndrom. Der Weg in die Konsumgesellschaft*, Bern: Haupt, 1995

Pro Natura (ed.), *Die Stimme der Natur. 100 Jahre Pro Natura*, Zurich: Kontrast, 2009

Frank Prochaska, *Royal Bounty. The Making of a Welfare Monarchy*, New Haven, CT: Yale University Press, 1995

Carter Roberts and Chris Hails, 'From the WWF (WWF)', in *World Watch*, 2005, 1–2, pp. 6–7

Theodore Roosevelt, *African Game Trails. An Account of the African Wanderings of an American Hunter-naturalist*, New York: Scribner, 1910

Anton Rupert, *Priorities of Coexistence*, Cape Town: Tafelberg, 1982

Jörg Sambeth, *Zwischenfall in Seveso. Ein Tatsachenroman*, Zurich: Unionsverlag, 2004

George B. Schaller, *The Last Panda*, Chicago, IL: University of Chicago Press, 1993

Emil Schulthess, *Afrika: Vom Mittelmeer zum Äquator* (Vol. 1) and *Vom Äquator zum Kap der guten Hoffnung* (Vol. 2), Zurich: Manesse, 1958–9

Emil Schulthess and Ernst Lang, *Wildtiere im Kongo*, Zurich: Silva, 1957

Peter Scott, *The Eye of the Wind*, London: Hodder & Stoughton, 1961

Peter Scott, *Launching of a New Ark. First Report of the President and Trustees of the WWF*, Collins: London, 1965

John Seidensticker, Sarah Christie and Peter Jackson (eds), *Riding the Tiger. Tiger Conservation in Human-Dominated Landscapes*, Cambridge: Cambridge University Press, 1999

Richard Sellars, *Preserving Nature in the National Parks. A History*, New Haven: Yale University Press, 1997

Claudia Sewig, *Bernhard Grzimek, Der Mann, der die Tiere liebte*, Bergisch Gladbach: Lübbe, 2009

Jan Bender Shetler, *Imagining Serengeti. A History of Landscape Memory in Tanzania From Earliest Times to the Present*, Athens: Ohio University Press, 2007

J. A. Simpson and E. S. C. Weiner (eds), *The Oxford English Dictionary*, Vol. XX, Oxford: Clarendon Press, 1989

Sotheby's (ed.), *Auctions for the Benefit of WWF Iinternational*, London and Geneva 1988–9, pp. 22–4

Marja Spierenburg and Harry Wels, 'Conservative philanthropists, Royalty and business elites in nature conservation in southern Africa' in *Antipode. A Radical Journal of Geography*, 42(3), 2010, pp. 647–70

Walther Stötzner, *Ins unerforschte Tibet. Tagebuch der deutschen Expedition Stötzner 1914*, Leipzig: Koehler, 1924

Valmik Thapar, 'The tragedy of the Indian tiger: starting from scratch', in John Seidensticker, Sarah Christie and Peter Jackson (eds), 1999
Martin Thomas, Bob Moore and L. J. Butler (eds), *Crises of Empire. Decolonization and Europe's Imperial States, 1918–1975*, London: Hodder, 2008
Russell Train, *Politics, Pollution and Pandas. An Environmental Memoir*, Washington, DC, Island Press, 2003
Willem Vermeulen and Niels Halbertsma (eds), *Operatie Natuur. Het natuurbeschermingsleven van Zijne Koninklijke Hoogheid Prins Bernhard*, Zeist: Wereld Natuur Fonds, 2006
François Walter, *Bedrohliche und bedrohte Natur. Umweltgeschichte der Schweiz seit 1800*, Zürich: Chronos, 1996
Paul Wapner, *Environmental Activism and World Civic Politics*, Albany State University of New York Press, 1996
Ludo de Witte, *L'assassinat de Lumumba*, Paris: Karthala, 2000
Francis M. Wyndham, *Wild Life on the Fjelds of Norway*, London: Longman, 1861
Frank Zelko, 'Greenpeace and the development of international environmental activism in the 1970s', in Ursula Lehmkuhl and Hermann Wellenreuther (eds), Berg, 2007

Digital

Speech by Prime Minister Mahathir, United Nations Conference on Environment and Development, Rio de Janeiro, 13 June 1992: www.pmo.gov.my/ucapan/?m=p&p=mahathir&id=1631, last consulted 9 October 2010
'Ask Claude Martin': November 2005, http://wwf.panda.org/who_we_are/organization/dg_bios/claude_martin.cfm, last consulted 13 October 2010
Club 1001: membership list: http://www.scribd.com/doc/25693537/1978-1001-Club-Confidential-Membership-List, last consulted 15 December 2010
Fundraising Principles: Greenpeace, http://www.greenpeace.org/international/about/our-core-values/fundraising-principles/, last consulted 8 November 2010
IUCN: www.iucn.org, last consulted 11 February 2010
Max Nicholson memorial page: www.maxnicholson.com, last consulted 15 December 2010
World Bank: http://go.worldbank.org/CNBMVNCCC0, last consulted 10 October 2010, WWF I: History, People, Operations, wwf.panda.org/who_we_are/, last consulted 5 October 2010
WWF Center for Conservation Finance, WWF Commercial Debt-for-Nature Swaps 1988 to present, 1 September 2003, http://www.cbd.int/financial/debt.shtml, last consulted 10 October 2010

Other media

Kein Platz für wilde Tiere, Bernhard Grzimek and Michael Grzimek (director), Germany, 1956, 81 mins
Serengeti darf nicht sterben, Bernhard Grzimek (director), Germany, 1959, 85 mins
Gambit, Sabine Gisiger (director), Switzerland, 2005, 107 mins

WWF publications

Jenny Springer and Janis Alcorn, 'Strengthening WWF partnerships with indigenous peoples and local communities: key fundings and recommendations', Gland and Washington, DC: WWF, 2007
Charles Vaucher, 'Nakuru. See der Flamingos', Zurich: WWF, 1972
WWF International (ed.), 'Mission for the 1990s', Gland, 1990
WWF International, 'Yearbooks', each published in Morges and later in Gland
WWF International, press release, 'Royal elephants auctioned for conservation', 2 October 2005, http://wwf.panda.org/what_we_do/where_we_work/borneo_forests/news/?23617/Royal-elephants-auctioned-for-conservation, last consulted 15 October 2010
WWF International (ed.), *WWF Twentieth Anniversary Review*, Gland, 1981
WWF-Switzerland, media release, 'Dramatic developments at the top in WWF-Switzerland', 30 October 2001, WWF-Switzerland
WWF-Switzerland, media release, 'New CEO for WWF-Switzerland', 30 June 2003
WWF-Switzerland (ed.), *Jenseits der Sachzwänge. Ein Beitrag der Umweltorganisationen zur schweizerischen Gesamtenergiekonzeption*, Zürich: Ropress 1978
WWF-USA (ed.), 'World Bank/WWF Alliance for Forest Conservation & Sustainable use, [2005]', http://www.worldwildlife.org/what/globalmarkets/forests/worldbankalliance.html, last consulted 15 October 2010

Saving the World's Wildlife

Contributions of WWF national appeals to WWF International, 1961–73

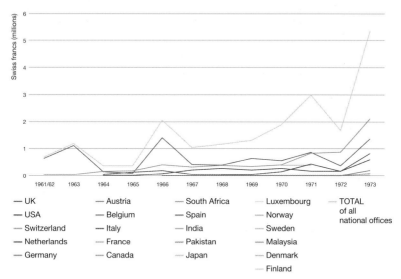

UK — USA — Switzerland — Netherlands — Germany — Austria — Belgium — Italy — France — Canada — South Africa — Spain — India — Pakistan — Japan — Luxembourg — Norway — Sweden — Malaysia — Denmark — Finland — TOTAL of all national offices

Contributions of WWF national appeals to WWF International plus direct payments to projects approved by the fund, 1961–73

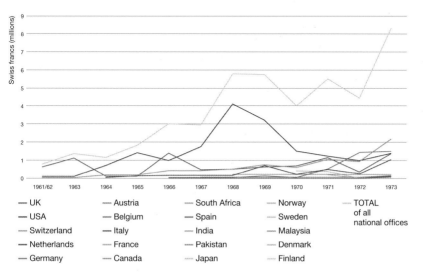

UK — USA — Switzerland — Netherlands — Germany — Austria — Belgium — Italy — France — Canada — South Africa — Spain — India — Pakistan — Japan — Norway — Sweden — Malaysia — Denmark — Finland — TOTAL of all national offices

WWF International

Index

(Page references in *italics* are to captions)

Saving the World's Wildlife

Fritz Vollmar, elephant (*Loxodonta africana*), Amboseli
Park, Kenya, 1956

Saving the World's Wildlife

Photograph credits

Overleaf: Polar bears (*Ursus maritimus*), Kaktovik, Alaska, 2010

SCHWEIZERISCHES NATIONAL
MUSEUM. MUSÉE NATIONAL
SUISSE. MUSEO NAZIONALE
SVIZZERO. MUSEUM NAZIUNAL
SVIZZER.

This book is based on research by the Swiss National Museum. It is
published on the occasion of the exhibition 'WWF. A Biography'.

MIX
Paper from
responsible sources
FSC® C013736

First published in Great Britain in 2011 by
Profile Books Ltd
3a Exmouth House
Pine Street
London EC1R 0JH
www.profilebooks.com

Originally published © 2011 by Collection Rolf Heyne GmbH & Co. KG, München

Text © 2011 by Alexis Schwarzenbach

'WWF – five decades of conservation milestones' © by WWF International, Gland

A CIP catalogue record for this book is available from the British Library.

Lithography: Lorenz & Zeller, Inning am Ammersee
Printer: Kösel, Altusried-Krugzell

Printed in Germany

ISBN 978 1 84668 530 9